THE PSYCHOLOGY OF PROPERTY LAW

PSYCHOLOGY AND THE LAW
General Editor: Linda J. Demaine

The Psychology of Property Law

Stephanie M. Stern and Daphna Lewinsohn-Zamir

With a Preface by Linda J. Demaine

NEW YORK UNIVERSITY PRESS
New York

NEW YORK UNIVERSITY PRESS
New York
www.nyupress.org

References to Internet websites (URLs) were accurate at the time of writing. Neither the author nor New York University Press is responsible for URLs that may have expired or changed since the manuscript was prepared.

Library of Congress Cataloging-in-Publication Data
Names: Stern, Stephanie M., author. | Lewinsohn-Zamir, Daphna.
Title: The psychology of property law / Stephanie M. Stern and Daphna Lewinsohn-Zamir.
Description: New York : New York University Press, 2020. | Series: Psychology and the law |
Includes bibliographical references and index.
Identifiers: LCCN 2019009446| ISBN 9781479835683 (cl : alk. paper) |
ISBN 9781479878895 (pb : alk. paper)
Subjects: LCSH: Property. | Right of property. | Acquisition of property. |
Property—Psychological aspects. | Possessiveness.
Classification: LCC K720 .S74 2020 | DDC 346.0401/9—dc23
LC record available at https://lccn.loc.gov/2019009446

New York University Press books are printed on acid-free paper, and their binding materials are chosen for strength and durability. We strive to use environmentally responsible suppliers and materials to the greatest extent possible in publishing our books.

Manufactured in the United States of America

10 9 8 7 6 5 4 3 2 1

Also available as an ebook

To Eyal, Abigail, and Yaara
D. L. Z.

To Josh, Gabe, Clara, and Wren
With thanks, S. M. S.

CONTENTS

PREFACE

LINDA J. DEMAINE

The NYU Press Psychology and the Law book series addresses an intriguing state of affairs in legal scholarship. Although law and legal process are inherently psychological in nature, traditionally, relatively few law professors, judges, or legal practitioners have drawn on empirical psychological research to inform their perspectives and decisions. In recent years, the legal community has increasingly recognized that both substantive law and legal procedure rest on a multitude of testable assumptions about human behavior that can be informed by psychological research. Without formal training in psychology, however, it can be challenging for legal experts to identify relevant and informative psychological research, evaluate its methodological rigor, and interpret the empirical results. Consequently, in the absence of trusted resources to translate findings from psychological studies and apply them to core legal issues, psychology's potential to inform legal doctrine and practice will remain unfulfilled. Lawyers, in particular, will lack the tools that would enable them to better understand the law's effects on human behavior and how the law might be better constructed to achieve its goals.

Three important exceptions to psychology's peripheral status in legal scholarship are eyewitness testimony, false confessions, and jury decision making. In each of these realms, insights from psychological research have entered legal discussions and debates, resulting in marked improvements in the legal system's functioning. These exceptions, which developed precisely because lawyers communicated the fundamental legal issues to psychologists, and psychologists introduced lawyers to informative research findings, demonstrate the potential of psychology to inform the law.

The Psychology and the Law series is intended to help make the exceptions into the rule by expanding and strengthening the intersection of law and psychology. To achieve this goal, the series applies psychology to subjects covered in the core law school curriculum. The books are designed to facilitate exchanges between lawyers and psychologists about these fundamental legal issues by introducing lawyers to the most pertinent research methods and findings and introducing psychologists to the central and generally complex legal issues. The books are valuable assets for law professors who desire to incorporate psychological science into their classes. To facilitate their adoption in law classrooms, the books map on to popular casebooks and are relatively brief and practical. The books are also prime resources for participants in psychology-law graduate programs, professors who teach undergraduate law and psychology courses, and mainstream psychologists who study legal issues. The books' expansive coverage of psychological research on core legal topics and their identification of areas in need of further research will provide these audiences with current knowledge and a road map to inspire empirical study. Finally, the books will be useful to legal practitioners whose work in particular areas of law can benefit from an understanding of psychology. All volumes are authored by eminent scholars who are conversant in both psychology and the law and possess the expertise necessary to identify and articulate legal issues of import, apply psychological theory and research findings to them, and identify areas of future research for psychologists.

In *The Psychology of Property Law*, Stern and Lewinsohn-Zamir examine several core psychological dimensions of owning and possessing property. As in other areas of law, many facets of property doctrine are inherently psychological in nature yet have developed largely in the absence of psychological theory and research. Legal practitioners and policy makers have instead employed their intuitions and personal assessments regarding what elements constitute a fair property law regime, with mixed success. Stern and Lewinsohn-Zamir examine the alignments and disjunctions between property law policy goals and psychological empirical results. Further, they draw upon psychological research to improve property law doctrine and process.

Stern and Lewinsohn-Zamir begin by discussing the legal nature of property rights; the reasons societies recognize property rights; and the ubiquity of property ownership, transfers, and disputes. From this foundation, they consider several cross-cutting psychological dimensions of property law, including the distinction between psychological ownership and legally recognized property rights; the degree to which the rational actor assumption undergirding traditional economics fails to describe property-related decisions; how property allocation and protection affects people's well-being; the role of property law in furthering or challenging bias and discrimination; and the importance of legal process in the property law regime.

Stern and Lewinsohn-Zamir apply these psychological dimensions to central topics of property law. They first address the psychology of state-recognized rights in property; conflicts between owners and possessors of property; and the differential value states place on different types of property, with correspondingly different legal protections against dispossession. They then examine government takings and redistribution of property, including procedure and compensation. Third, they discuss real estate transactions, including seller disclosure of conditions and defects and buyer characteristics such as attention limitations, commitment, sunk costs, and anchoring; conflicts of interest; and the legal and psychological (social norm) regulation of discrimination in this realm. The authors close by discussing the psychology of remedies for injury to property, focusing on the differential psychological underpinnings of property rules versus liability rules and in-kind versus monetary remedies.

Taken as a whole, *The Psychology of Property Law* illustrates the varied and complex nature of human claims regarding real and personal property. It underscores the centrality of property rights to understanding individuals and society by showing that our claims to property reflect as well as shape core aspects of ourselves, including the innermost sense of personal and group identity.

Introduction

Property law presents an expansive canvas filled with colorful conflicts between neighbors, sobering tones of exclusion and discrimination, standardized and customized real estate transactions, and evocative rights of ownership and possession. Psychological perceptions, behavior, and in some cases foibles are integral to this canvas, guiding certain aspects of property law and suggesting reforms for others. Property may be particularly psychologically resonant, as the English jurist William Blackstone suggested: "There is nothing which so generally strikes the imagination, and engages the affections of mankind, as the right of property" (1893, *393). Since Blackstone, a growing body of research on human mental processes and behavior has illuminated the psychological components of ownership, dispossession, and other aspects of property law.

Property rules and doctrines aim to increase people's welfare, create socially desirable distributions of property rights, and shift property to high-value uses. In seeking to accomplish these objectives, the law of property is concerned with human behavior driven by psychological traits and states. How do we allocate property rights, both initially and over time, and what factors determine the perceived fairness of those distributions? How do owners and courts determine and compare property values? What social and psychological forces underlie determinations by courts or property owners and users that certain uses of property are reasonable? What remedies do property owners prefer and find most psychologically satisfying? Property law, with its focus on the distribution of gains and losses, fairness and spillover effects, and social context, calls for illumination provided by psychological research.

In this book, we examine property rules and long-standing theoretical debates through the lens of psychology. Psychology research enables us to compare the assumptions about human behavior that underlie laws against the empirical data and to suggest ways to improve property law. For some property rules, the empirical research points to ways that their underlying goals could be achieved more successfully with a different rule or no rule at all. Psychology also suggests new perspectives and justifications for theories of private property rights and the goals of property law.

Not only does psychology offer insights into property law, but property law in turn affords psychology ways to apply, and refine, its insights outside of the lab. As one example, while psychology experiments often fail to differentiate between ownership and possession, law is highly attentive to this distinction. As this book will show, there are substantial opportunities for applied psychology research in numerous aspects of property law such as conflicts over possession and ownership, appropriation of property by the state or loss of property to creditors, housing transactions, and remedies.

The Nature and Function of Property Rights

The right to property is fundamental. Property law governs the acquisition, use, possession, ownership, leasing, and transfer of land, buildings and fixtures, chattel, and other resources.[1] Property law resolves competing claims to property; provides legal rules for transactions; reconciles different, and sometimes conflicting, land uses; and determines remedies. In addition, property law addresses the protection of private property rights from interference or appropriation by the state. In these functions, the law of property structures legal relationships between people with regard to valuable resources (Hohfeld 1913; Singer 2017, 2). Property can be held by individuals, groups, entities, or the state. This book focuses primarily on private property, which is the dominant property system in most countries.

Unlike contractual rights, which generally pertain only to the contracting parties, property rights are in rem. This means that one's rights in private property are "good against the world" (or, more precisely, they bind an unidentified set of people). Property right holders can enforce their rights against nonconsenting third parties. For example, if person A has ownership rights over a parcel of land, then others generally cannot use A's land without her consent. Any person who comes onto the land without permission has violated A's property rights, which the law typically recognizes in an action for trespass.

Property rights, including ownership, are not absolute. At times, individual property rights cede to social goals and the needs of others. For example, rights to exclude others from one's land or other property are subject to a variety of limitations, including statutes and constitutional laws prohibiting discrimination. The common law doctrine of necessity makes it lawful for a person to pass through another's property when required to prevent greater harm to the trespasser, his property, or the community (e.g., due to storms, flooding, or other conditions) (Epstein 1990).[2] Property rights are also routinely limited by environmental laws that restrict use and development and the constitutional power of governments to appropriate property for public use with just compensation.

While people intuitively think of property as "ownership of a thing," many judges and legal scholars conceive of property as a "bundle of rights" representing distinct interests in and rights to property (Corbin 1922; Honoré 1961; J. R. Nash and Stern 2010; for critiques of the "bundle of rights" conception of property, see Penner 1996, 723; Merrill and Smith 2011, S82). The "sticks" in the bundle of rights include the right to possess the property, to control its use, to convey all or part of the property, to mortgage it, to exclude others from the property, and, in many circumstances, to destroy it. An interest in property may not include all of the sticks in the bundle of rights. Renting, termed a "leasehold estate" in property law, grants tenants possessory rights while landlords maintain residual ownership and the ability to convey the property (with the lease carrying over to the new owner). In other cases, a person may hold a property interest but not the right to use or possess the property until a future point in time. For example, in US law, the "remainderman" to a life tenancy lacks current possessory rights and instead holds a future interest. The life tenant has the right to use and profit from the property during her lifetime but not the right to sell or mortgage it. When the life tenant dies, the property will pass to a third party specified in the grant (the remainderman) or, if there is no remainderman, will revert to the original grantor (Thompson and Goldstein 2014, 527–28).

An important function of property law is to resolve competing claims to property. Property rules determine how claimants establish possession and ownership of property in the first instance and how subsequent conflicts over property rights are to be resolved. For example, laws governing the capture of wild animals and acquisition of natural resources and water rights determine how people gain, and lose, property rights in these resources. Another example is the doctrine of adverse possession, which allows a trespasser, under certain conditions and with the passage of time, to gain rights over the land or property of another. Property law also determines whether one party may injure the property rights of another. The law of nuisance offers a classic example. If a landowner builds a polluting factory or noxious-smelling hog pen that significantly affects neighboring owners' enjoyment of their property, she has possibly impaired her neighbors' rights, and they can sue for an injunction to make her stop or to provide damages to compensate for the harm. To minimize such conflicts, local governments regulate the location of various types of property uses (e.g., residential, commercial, industrial); the size, spacing, and structure of buildings; and noise, pollution, and other disturbances.

Property law offers both ex ante protections and remedies ex post for injury to property rights. In some instances, such as government appropriation or some property and bankruptcy laws, the legal system extends heightened protection against dispossession to certain types of property. For example, while government entities have the constitutional right to take private property for public use with just compensation, some American states have adopted laws that forbid government appropriation of residential homes unless the home is blighted (i.e., unsafe and substantially deteriorated). Legal protections also take the form of remedies that seek to make the injured party whole with respect to his or her property rights. Remedies include injunctions, which are court orders compelling parties to take or refrain from taking specified actions, and monetary damages to compensate the wronged party or punish the wrongdoer.

At the level of markets, property law governs transactions and promotes trade. A key role of property law is to create configurations of rights (e.g., "ownership" or "rental") that facilitate buying and selling property. Property law creates a degree of standardization that lowers the costs of transacting property (Merrill and Smith 2000). Property laws also reduce the costs and risks of transactions by creating land registration systems to record sales and different forms of deeds that provide varying levels of assurance of the seller's good and marketable title. For residential real estate transactions, statutory law and common law offer a number of protections to buyers. Many of these laws aim to ameliorate information asymmetries by providing information to buyers about the property's condition or mortgage products. Other property laws, such as the Fair Housing Act (FHA) in the United States, seek to ensure fair and open property markets by prohibiting discrimination in real estate sales, leasing, and lending.[3]

While property systems allocate property rights, they often fail to define prospectively what resources constitute property. Throughout history, there has been controversy about what is included in the set of items defined as legal "property." For example, courts and policy makers have debated whether to extend property rights to government entitlements (e.g., government-funded income and benefits, subsidies, licenses, franchises), gene sequences, and domesticated pets (see, e.g., Reich 1964; Barrad 1993; Root 2002). Because property serves human ends, its definition cannot cohere in a unitary theory or remain static across time and context. Social and economic forces drive the creation of novel forms of property and reshape property rights over time (Banner 2011, 175, 238–48). Throughout this book, we consider the interrelations between legal conceptions of what constitutes property and psychological research on what people perceive as property.

Justifications for Private Property

The theoretical justifications for private property depict property's critical role in furthering autonomy, liberty and freedom, self-development, social welfare, and efficiency. These theories differ in content but converge to support private property rights. For the purposes of this overview, these theories can be loosely divided into two groups: one focusing on individual rights and the other based on efficiency and aggregate welfare.

First, a number of theories of private property justify property rights based on individual rights to the fruits of one's labor, autonomy and liberty, and personhood development. John Locke argued that each individual has the right to one's own person and the fruits of one's labors; as a result, when people "mix" their labor with unowned property, they acquire property rights under natural law, which is antecedent and superior to government-made law ([1690] 1967, 305–06). Locke qualified his labor theory based on distribution: labor creates ownership "at least where there is enough, and as good left in common for others" (306). Other theorists have focused on property's role as a boundary that safeguards individual liberty and creates a zone of freedom from interference from the state (see, e.g., Ely 1992; Buchanan 1993). Jennifer Nedelsky (1990) has critiqued this conception of autonomy as individualistic and proposed a legal model of autonomy based on human relations and their role in self-constitution.

Some theories of property's importance to individuals' rights make distinctly psychological claims about property's role in self-development and well-being. In the early nineteenth century, Hegel ([1821] 1967) developed a theory of property's necessity to develop personality. In order to develop freedom, which Hegel describes as personal agency and free will, people must impose their will on the external world. Property is the "embodiment of personality" and enables people to move from a subjective sense of free will to objectively acting upon their will through the appropriation and control of their property (51). These actions vis-à-vis property make one's self concrete so that the property holder can perceive her personality and communicate it to others (for further discussion, see Waldron 1988, 353). Building on Hegel's philosophy, Margaret Radin (1982) contends that property law should secure owners' ongoing rights to certain forms of property that are integral to personhood. Other theorists have described a role for property in well-being and flourishing. Amartya Sen has articulated a philosophy of capabilities where certain property, such as shelter, is necessary for citizens to have freedom to achieve their capabilities to live a life they have reason to value (A. Sen 1984; Nussbaum and Sen 1993, 40–42). Martha Nussbaum's interpretation of capabilities theory specifically cites the ability to hold property and for those property rights to be on an equal basis with others (2011, 307–24).

Second, a constellation of theoretical work justifies private property rights on the basis of efficiency and creating value in society. Stable private property rights create incentives for people to invest in and improve property (Demsetz 1967; cf. S. M. Stern 2017). Without such rights, people cannot reap the fruits of their labors and investments, leading to the dissipation of value (e.g., A. Bell and Parchomovsky 2005). Private property rights allow people to realize the rewards of beneficial actions and require them to bear the costs of harmful behavior (Demsetz 1967,

347–50). For example, Harold Demsetz (1967) described how the advent of the European fur trade led to the emergence of private hunting grounds and property rights in certain Native American communities in order to capture gains from trade not possible under the tribe's traditional open-access hunting commons. Private property rights created incentives for owners to maintain and increase hunting stock by rotating hunting grounds, retaliating against trespassers, and negotiating with neighboring owners whose actions threatened hunting stock (351–58).

Another efficiency justification for property law is its potential to move property to its highest value use, either through a system of market transfer or through legal rules that seek to approximate this efficiency function.[4] As the Coase (1960) theorem famously observed, in a world where there is no cost or effort to bargaining, voluntary negotiation among private parties to resolve property disputes (i.e., without the intervention of courts or law) leads to the most efficient outcomes for society. Efficiency means that resources and goods are held by the users who value them the most. Yet, as Coase cautioned, such a low-transaction-cost world does not exist. When transaction costs are high, it is desirable to have legal rules that reduce them or, failing that, initial allocations that mirror the likely outcome had bargaining been able to occur (Cooter and Ulen 2012, 93). Secure property rights reduce transaction costs and facilitate private bargaining (Coase 1960). Property law also enhances transactional efficiency by lowering the costs of delineating, and deciphering, property rights (Merrill and Smith 2000).

Real-World Impacts of Property Law

Among legal disciplines, no area of law has more widespread impact on our daily lives than property law. The vast majority of us own some form of property, ranging from valuable real estate to prosaic items such as the clothes on our backs. In the United States, the homeownership rate is 64 percent, and the rate in other developed countries commonly ranges from 30 to 65 percent (with some, such as Bulgaria, as high as 90 percent) (US Census Bureau 2018; Laurie Goodman and Mayer 2018).[5] In 2017, more than 6 million homes were sold in the United States (National Association of Realtors 2018). Commercial real estate is also a major market sector, with $490 billion in deal activity in 2017 alone.[6] And, of course, all manner of personal property from manufactured goods to livestock is bought, owned, sold, or disposed of every day.

Not surprisingly in light of the ubiquity of property rights and volume of property transactions, property disputes generate substantial litigation. Looking at the United States, in the twelve-month period ending in September 2016, more than 10,000 cases concerning real property and housing civil rights actions commenced in US federal district courts, with the highest number of federal actions concerning lenders foreclosing on property as a result of unpaid debts (US Courts 2016). The actual number is likely higher, since many cases involving property, such as commercial real estate cases, are brought as breach of contract claims. In a study sampling state courts, the National Center for State Courts (2015) found that cases involving real and personal property are common categories of civil litigation, with the most frequent categories of claims overall including debt collection, landlord-tenant claims, and foreclosure, as well as tort and small claims cases. Landlord-tenant cases are the most common state court case, representing 29 percent of all state court civil cases (19).

Many property cases are not high-dollar claims. Seventy-five percent of real property awards in US state courts total less than $106,000 (most of these judgments occurred following lower-cost administrative court proceedings or settlements in the early stages of litigation) (24, 27). In both small claims courts and state trial and appellate courts, the majority of litigants in property cases represent themselves (32). This reflects the fact that more sophisticated and well-resourced litigants, in both the United States and other countries, have turned to private forums, such as alternative dispute resolution and arbitration. The propensity of litigants to bring claims pro se, meaning without legal counsel, underscores the importance of layperson perceptions and attitudes in property disputes and in shaping property law. Absent knowledge of property law or recourse to lawyers, people's intuitive or instinctive perceptions of property rights and obligations can fuel disputes and litigation.

The Psychology of Property Law

A number of areas of psychological research are highly relevant to property law and will be featured throughout this book.

Psychological Ownership versus Formal Property Rights

Amitai Etzioni describes property as existing at two levels, first as an "attribute of the mind" derived from perceptions, attitudes, and culture; and, second, at the concrete level, as a real object or resource owned by a person, entity, or group (1991, 465–66). Psychologists describe the former as psychological ownership and have studied it in the context of feelings toward possessions, as well as the psychological commitment employees feel toward their work, the products of their labor, or the organizations they work for. According to Pierce, Kostova, and Dirks, psychological ownership is "the feeling of possessiveness and of being psychologically tied to an object" (2001, 299). In some cases, a possession becomes an important component of an individual's identity (Belk 1988; Dittmar 1992). There are different theories of how psychological ownership develops. Using the property or controlling its use, forming an association that over time leads the person to know the item well or intimately, and creating or constructing the possession all appear to increase psychological ownership (Rudmin and Berry 1987; Beggan and Brown 1994; Csikszentmihalyi and Rochberg-Halton 1981).[7]

Research on psychological ownership suggests new ways to think about theories of private property and laws protecting property from appropriations by the state and from dispossession by private parties. For example, as discussed earlier, John Locke famously argued that "mixing one's labor" with property should give rise to ownership of unowned property. Psychology research suggests more specifically that creating or constructing, not merely laboring, may produce the strongest attachments and subjective feelings of ownership (Levene, Starmans, and Friedman 2015; Norton, Mochon, and Ariely 2012; Sarstedt, Neubert, and Barth 2016). Other applications come from the common law of property. For example, common law doctrines base possessory rights and acquisition of unowned property on touchstones such as physical contact or, in the case of certain natural resources (e.g., wild animals) attaining "certain control." Yet, psychology research shows that people can develop feelings of ownership or attachment from mere proximity, purchase of a good (prior to delivery), and imagining contact with an object.

Evidence about how people view their property and rights enables us to align property doctrines with commonly held perceptions when such alignment is desirable for policy making. Our claim is not that psychological ownership and perceptions alone should determine property law, but rather that they are important factors that policy makers should consider in the design of legal rules. Reducing the friction between law and public perceptions can enhance efficiency, the perceived legitimacy of property law, and compliance. For example, research suggests that on the basis of psychological harm the law may overprotect residential property and underprotect other kinds of property, such as commercial real estate, unrealized development rights, or personal possessions. Psychology also offers an explanation for why people sometimes react quite negatively to regulations that burden their property rights, despite the fact that such regulations usually do not rise to the level of a regulatory taking under US federal constitutional law. Attentiveness to how people view and value their property rights in the design of property laws can lessen public disapproval or backlash against those laws.

Property laws that are out of sync with citizens' perceptions, preferences, or psychological ownership can threaten the operation of property law systems. For example, a study in Korea of squatter eviction found that 37 percent of city officials and police charged with evictions and 43 percent of members of the general public believed, contrary to the law, that owners should evict only if they need to use the land or after they have tried to pay the squatter to leave (Hahm 1963, 66, 69). The divergence between Korea's European-derived system of eviction law and the perceptions of Koreans resulted in lower use of the eviction process by owners and more friction and unrest when owners did resort to formal ouster (64–65). Laws that do not reflect commonly held perceptions about property rights may also be more vulnerable to gradual undermining or nullification by common law judges, who interpret and fill gaps in statutes. The legal realism movement has shown how judges and other lawmakers can stray over time from the law on the books to reflect their perceptions and "inarticulate and unconscious judgment" (Holmes [1897] 1997, 998). For example, while some state legal doctrines maintain that state of mind and intent are irrelevant to an adverse possessor's claim of title, courts in those jurisdictions frequently impose a good faith requirement on adverse possessors (Helmholz 1983). Requiring that adverse possessors believe that they own the property they have possessed reflects norms against taking property from others and strategic behavior or land-grabbing.

Bounds on Rationality

While property law often assumes rational and comprehensive information processing, people exhibit systematic limitations on their ability to gather, process, and remember information (Jolls, Sunstein, and Thaler 1998, 1477–79). People hold persistent biases, including the tendency to be averse to losses; exhibit undue optimism about outcomes; and overweigh recent, publicized, or otherwise salient, but not determinative, information (Kahneman, Knetsch, and Thaler 1990; Sharot 2011; Tversky and Kahneman 1974). For example, in real estate transactions sellers tend to overvalue their property, and all parties may struggle to understand information about property condition or financing and update property valuation accordingly.

The psychological research on bounded rationality indicates that sometimes people will not intuit or understand property law or relevant information sufficiently to achieve the underlying aims of the laws in question. Bounded rationality also suggests that people experience information-processing barriers or emotional sticking points that impede bargaining to efficient outcomes over property rights. For example, it may be efficient and socially desirable for a property owner to negotiate with a neighbor who has built a high and unsightly fence, rather than utilizing complex zoning laws, local enforcement, and court process. However, strong emotions, conflicting intuitions about the neighbors' respective property rights, and difficulties valuing the fence's impact on property value and enjoyment may stymie efforts to resolve the conflict privately.

Property law might respond to or "debias" bounds on rationality in three different ways. First, legal reforms can minimize information-processing shortfalls and biases by reducing cognitive load and other circumstances likely to create or exacerbate biases. In an attempt to do just this, the US Consumer Finance Protection Bureau recently created a standardized and greatly simplified mortgage disclosure form that lenders must provide to residential borrowers.[8] Second, property law can exploit existing biases to achieve desired ends or correct one psychological bias by activating another (S. M. Stern 2016, 49–51; Pi, Parisi, and Luppi 2004). For example, local officials might seek to counteract residents' oversized risk aversion to the possibility of increased traffic following city approval of the construction of a "big-box" retail store. The city could do this by informing citizens that without taxes and impact fees from the big-box store, residents will face an average $200 in increased property taxes. Because people tend to overvalue losses, they are likely to be more receptive to avoiding the certain loss from paying additional taxes by accepting the uncertain impacts of the new development (Kahneman and Tversky 1979). Discomfort with the state manipulating people's psychological tendencies makes this form of debiasing controversial, perhaps particularly so in the domain of property, which many equate with autonomy and liberty (see, e.g., R. A. Posner 2009; S. M. Stern 2016, 68–72). Third, property law might remove the opportunity for bias—and for choice—through regulation that prohibits transactions with high risks of consumer confusion and harm. For example, as we will see, there has been significant debate about whether states should prohibit brokers from simultaneously representing residential buyers and sellers in the same transaction. It is exceedingly difficult to debias real estate brokers from conflicts of interest—a fact that buyers often fail to grasp when they receive disclosures about the conflict of interest.

The Science of Well-Being

One goal of legal systems, including property law systems, should be to increase human welfare. In the past, the most common proxy was preference satisfaction, a measure that focuses on whether one fulfills specific, ex ante desires. Yet, psychology research suggests that often we lack well-delineated, ex ante preferences. Instead, preferences are often unstable and context dependent and change with task, choice-environment, and in response to shifting personal goals (Kahneman and Tverskey 1982; Slovic 1995; for a review, see Warren, McGraw, and Van Boven 2011). Moreover, preference satisfaction does not inevitably increase welfare in an objective sense. According to an objective approach to welfare, certain things—such as knowledge of ourselves and the world around us, accomplishment of worthwhile goals, and attainment of meaningful relationships—have intrinsic value, independent of whether individuals desire them (for an objective-welfare theory of property law, see Lewinsohn-Zamir 2003).

A rapidly growing body of research on well-being, referred to as "positive psychology," has begun to clarify how life circumstances, experiences, relationships, health, wealth, homeownership, and personal possessions affect happiness. Psychologists measure well-being in a variety of ways, including surveys asking people to describe how they feel about their lives, measures of positive or negative affect (emotion), and experience sampling where participants report their level of happiness at multiple, random points throughout the day (Diener 2000, 34–35). The psychology research shows that without intervention, people frequently misestimate the circumstances and actions that are likely to improve their well-being (Wilson and Gilbert 2005).

Happiness and well-being data can offer an approximate measure of social welfare, an outcome that economics and law have long sought to increase but struggled to define. Policy makers and governments have taken note of well-being research. The United Nations annual World Happiness Report now measures well-being in 156 countries, the former French president Nicolas Sarkozy proposed making a happiness index the key economic indicator for France, and the constitution of the country of Bhutan states that the government should "strive to promote those conditions that will enable the pursuit of Gross National Happiness."[9] Yet there is division about whether well-being itself should be the end goal or whether government should seek to provide citizens with the liberties and resources necessary for them to pursue well-being.

The research on happiness has a variety of applications for property rules and institutions. Happiness metrics can inform the degree of protection we accord owners against dispossession of their property by government, creditors, or private parties, the tax and legal incentives we provide for homeownership versus renting, the monetary compensation required to "make someone whole" following property loss or infringement, and the type and magnitude of government-mediated property redistribution between private citizens. We can use happiness to measure the value of public goods, such as public parks and clean water, and to improve cost-benefit analysis (Bronsteen, Buccasfusco, and Masur

2014; Stutzer and Frey 2012). Correlating citizens' reported well-being with public goods (and bads) has provided valuations for the harms caused by airport noise, air pollution, and flood hazards (see Stutzer and Frey 2012, 664–65).

Well-being research has other implications for land use regulation and planning. For example, if commuting decreases well-being, as some research has found, then "smart growth" land use policies that favor higher-density development proximate to work centers and transportation networks should increase objective well-being (though not necessarily subjective preferences for lower-density residential living) (Fagundes 2017, 1920–22; Stutzer and Frey 2008; Roberts, Hodgson, and Dolan 2011; but see Dickerson, Hole, and Munford 2014). In the legal scholarship, Dave Fagundes (2018) has proposed reforms to support the "sharing economy" (e.g., person-to-person short-term rentals via Airbnb or ride sharing through Uber) and enable zoning and construction of more affordable apartments and homes with very low square footage (micro-housing). He bases these proposals on psychology research showing that sharing property and devoting more time and attention to social relationships increases happiness, not accumulating property. Abundant psychology research on the harms to well-being from social isolation may also cause us to rethink aspects of housing policy (Baumeister and Leary 1995; Myers 2000). For example, the growing numbers of elderly and disabled citizens may benefit from "accessory dwelling units" attached to or on the lots of primary dwellings (e.g., coach houses, in-law apartments) that enable them to reside with family or remain in their community. Currently, local ordinances typically prohibit or restrict accessory dwelling units.

In-Groups, Bias, and Discrimination

Property law, as we have noted, structures legal relationships among people with respect to property. Social psychology is similarly concerned with understanding a person's relationships with other individuals, including the impact of group membership. The research in psychology on the power and influence of one's identification with a group provides a new vantage point from which to consider property law. Property law, in its conceptualization and its rules, at times has neglected the legal relationships among *groups* with respect to property in favor of a more atomistic focus on individuals.

Social psychologists have found that bias against members of groups other than one's own and tendencies to stereotype (i.e., develop beliefs about an individual based on generalizations about that person's group) are ubiquitous features of social life (see, e.g., Brewer and Brown, 1998; Dovidio 2002). When intergroup bias and stereotyping translate into discriminatory behaviors, this creates a range of harms and lost opportunities that property law often seeks to address. In particular, psychology research points to ways to improve fair housing law and local land use laws to reduce discrimination and promote residential integration. For example, nondiscriminatory social norms can be a powerful deterrent to discrimination—perhaps even more so than "command and control" regulations that explicitly prohibit and penalize discrimination. When people learn that members of a group who they identify with hold or do not hold negative beliefs about another group (e.g., African American students) their attitudes shift in the direction of the group to which they belong (Sechrist and Stangor 2001; Stangor, Sechrist, and Jost 2001; Haslam et al. 1996; Wittenbrink and Henly 1996). This research suggests underappreciated importance to provisions of the FHA that promote nondiscriminatory norms, such as the act's prohibition on making discriminatory housing statements or publishing discriminatory housing advertisements.

Psychology also suggests limitations to law for addressing bias. For example, psychologists have found that bias is often unconscious (i.e., people are not aware they are biased), that victims of bias face harsh social judgment for reporting discrimination, and that negative bias often increases as a result of antibias mandates or forced inclusion (Gaertner and Dovidio 2005; Kaiser and Miller 2001, 2003; Dobbin and Kalev 2016). All of these factors represent challenges for fair housing law and suggest the need to expand the legal and nonlegal tools that governments employ to combat housing discrimination.

Process, Meaning, and Outcomes

The characteristics of legal process and the social meaning of legal rules matter to people as much as, and sometimes more than, outcomes.

Property law, and law and economics, focus heavily on outcomes, such as the magnitude of compensation or property redistribution. Yet, people often care greatly how outcomes are achieved and whether the outcome is associated with success or failure (Tyler 2006; Lewinsohn-Zamir 2006, 385–89). One example of this is the research on source dependence, which shows that the source of an object affects how people value that object and their willingness to part with it. A number of experiments have found that when people are told that an object they were given, such as a mug, is an award or recognition for their performance, they value it more highly than those who are given the identical object randomly (Loewenstein and Issacharoff 1994; Bühren and Plessner 2014). Property and, as we will suggest, property rules that are associated with success, talent, intelligence, or other socially desirable characteristics confer heightened value to recipients.

In some cases, it may be possible to deliver greater gains to social welfare through careful design of the processes and social meaning of legal rules and remedies. For example, people may derive greater utility from redistribution through property, such as adequate housing, rather than an equivalent amount of cash, because of the stigma and loss of esteem associated with welfare payments. Similarly, with respect to remedies, people are not always indifferent between remedies of equal monetary value. For example, in some circumstances they may prefer in-kind remedies to monetary ones or favor an injunction halting the injury rather than a remedy that provides monetary compensation but allows the injury to continue. Other examples come from the rich literature on procedural justice in law and psychology. People want legal systems to hear their voices, treat them respectfully, and employ neutral rules and impartial decision makers (Tyler and Jackson 2013, 78–79). This research highlights costs to laws that truncate legal process, such as state "quick-take" statutes for government appropriation of property or mandated fair housing settlement procedures.[10]

The Limits of Psychology for Property Law

In this book, we delve deeply into psychology research and theory to offer new perspectives on property law. We examine the psychology evidence and consider ways in which this research can improve the design of property rules and institutions. Our goal is to provide an empirically based account of the psychological forces affecting property law. Judges, legislators, lawyers, law students, and citizens can benefit from appreciating how human psychology affects the property rules, transactions, and remedies that they encounter in their work or in everyday life. Understanding psychology's relevance to property law is essential to optimizing the development of property rules, articulation of rationales, and distribution of property rights in complex property systems.

While psychology research offers valuable insights for property law, there are important caveats as well. First, psychological forces are not the only factor that is relevant to the design of property law systems. At times, efficiency, administrability, political sentiments, social needs, and a variety of other context-specific factors may demand a different property rule or outcome than what psychological considerations would suggest. Appreciating the psychological costs and benefits of different property law rules enables citizens and other decision makers to weigh psychological considerations against social, economic, and administrative factors in order to design effective property law systems.

Second, as with any method of inquiry, empirical research has both inherent strengths and limitations. The rigors of the scientific method, data collection and analysis, and peer review increase the quality of empirical psychology work and complement theoretical work in law and other fields. However, it is possible that an empirical study will produce anomalous findings or that psychological effects will not generalize from the laboratory to real-world settings. To reduce these risks, empirical researchers often replicate findings, both in the same context as the original experiment and in other settings and with participants of different backgrounds. In view of the importance of reliability and validity, this book focuses on well-established psychological findings.

Scope of the Book

The ways that psychology can inform property law are numerous. In this book, we have selected eight important topics from property law to which psychology has a great deal to contribute. The following chapters examine how psychology research may cause us to rethink legal rules for rights in property, state interference with property, real estate transactions, and remedies. Throughout the book, we draw from diverse fields of psychology, including social, cognitive, personality, and moral psychology. The book addresses the implications of psychology for real property (i.e., land and immovable fixtures attached to land) and personal or "chattel" property (movable property, including manufactured goods, animals, and other possessions). We do not consider intellectual property, not due to any inapplicability of psychology to intellectual property, but in order to focus on the substantial topics of real and personal property. In addition, although we focus more strongly in this book on formal property law, we recognize that most property disputes are resolved informally (or do not occur in the first place because people follow social norms regarding possession, trespass, infringement, and other aspects of property) (Ellickson 1994). The psychological research we apply to formal law in this book also matters greatly in the domain of social norms, or, as Robert Ellickson has described it, order without law.

PART I

Rights in Property

1

Ownership and Possession

Ownership is the greatest possible interest in an asset that the law recognizes; it typically consists of several rights, including the rights to possess, use, manage, exclude others from, transfer, and destroy the asset (Honoré 1961, 108–24). Possession is commonly said to consist of two elements: control over an asset and an intention to exercise such control. The possessor of a thing may be its owner or some other person (Lawson and Rudden 1982, 41–44), and the latter may possess the asset either legally (e.g., as a tenant or a bailee) or illegally (e.g., as a trespasser).

In this chapter, we offer a behavioral analysis of certain key aspects of ownership and possession. Furthermore, we highlight the existing gaps in the psychological and legal literatures on ownership and possession and the ways in which they may be filled. In doing so, we demonstrate the potential for mutual enrichment between the fields of law and psychology. The chapter opens with a general discussion of the psychological significance of ownership and possession. Following that, it explores people's perceptions of ownership and possession. Among other things, we show how people's notion of possession is not necessarily "physical" but may extend to intangible entitlements and expectations as well. This state of affairs may justify a broadening of the law's understanding of possession. We also analyze the relative strength of ownership and possession, which is highly relevant to legal conflicts between owners and possessors of property. Finally, the chapter addresses various rights that property owners enjoy, and their limitations. Specifically, we suggest psychological justifications for seemingly paradoxical legal rules, according to which owners have more freedom to use their property intensively than to refrain from using it at all, more freedom to restrict the transfer of property totally than to subject it to conditions, and more freedom to destroy the property fully than to modify or change it.

The Significance of Ownership and Possession

Why do people place high value on the property they own and/or possess? Psychological studies offer various explanations, which are not mutually exclusive. Here, we focus on the two most influential accounts.

The first account is commonly connected to the "endowment effect" (EE), which is one of the best-known and robust phenomena found by behavioral studies. Numerous experiments in a wide variety of settings have shown that people value an entitlement or object they already have much more than an identical entitlement or object they have an opportunity to acquire. Specifically, individuals demand a significantly higher price to give up an existing asset—such as a coffee mug—than they are willing to pay in order to purchase it in the first place. The divergence between the former price, often referred to as "willingness to accept," and the latter, commonly called "willingness to pay," may reach up to many times the lower value (Camerer 1995, 665–70; Kahneman, Knetsch, and Thaler 1990, 2008; Knetsch and Sinden 1984; for surveys of the literature on the EE and various explanations for this phenomenon, see Marzilli-Ericson and Fuster 2014; Morewedge and Giblin 2015; Zamir 2015, 21–28).[1]

A major explanation for the EE is loss aversion. Parting with an entitlement is perceived as a loss, whereas acquiring the same entitlement is viewed as a gain. The loss in utility from giving up an entitlement is larger than the gain in utility from receiving the same entitlement. Since losses loom larger than gains, people's selling price is significantly higher than their purchase price (Kahneman 1992; Korobkin 2003, 1250–55; Marzilli-Ericson and Fuster 2014, 560–61, 574; Zamir 2012, 835–40).[2] According to this account, the EE does not result from the enhanced attractiveness of an asset that one owns; rather, it represents the pain of giving it up. This explanation was supported, for example, in an experiment by Kahneman (1992). Half of the participants were given attractive pens, while the others were given a token, redeemable later for one of several gifts (including a pen and a Swiss chocolate bar). All participants were asked to rank the relative attractiveness of these gifts. After completing the ratings, all participants were asked to choose between receiving (or keeping) a pen and two chocolate bars. Fifty-six percent of participants in the group endowed with pens at the outset preferred

OWNERSHIP AND POSSESSION | 23

a pen, while only 24 percent of the other group members chose pens. Notably, the attractiveness ratings revealed that the former group did not rate pens as more attractive than the latter group.

The second central explanation for people's high valuation of their property was coined the "mere ownership" effect (Beggan 1992). Beggan discovered that individuals are biased in favor of an object and rate it as more valuable just because they own it (and regardless of whether they are about to part with it). He argued that people seek to maintain a positive self-image, and given the psychological association between possessions and the self, they overvalue the objects they own (Beggan 1992, 235; see also Gawronski, Bodenhausen, and Becker 2007; and Ye and Gawronski 2016, who emphasize the connection between positive self-perception and valuation of one's chosen—rather than randomly received—objects). This desire to enhance one's positive image is intensified when the image is threatened, such as by experiment participants' failure in an assigned task or remembrance of a failed social relationship. Thus, a decrement in self-image increases the magnitude of the mere ownership effect (see, respectively, Beggan 1992, 233–34; Dommer and Swaminathan 2013). In addition, self-enhancement through the valuation of one's assets extends to interpersonal relations: individuals not only enhance themselves when comparing themselves with others but also enhance their possessions when comparing them with other people's possessions; they associate more positive traits with their own possessions than with others' possessions (Nesselroade, Beggan, and Allison 1999).[3]

Importantly, the "mere ownership effect" appears to be a general phenomenon; it is not limited to certain types of assets but has been observed even with respect to trivial and mundane objects, such as a cold drink insulator.[4] Furthermore, the emergence of this effect does not necessarily depend on lengthy exposure to the asset (LeBarr and Shedden 2017) or familiarization with its characteristics. For instance, De Dreu and van Knippenberg (2005) found a mere ownership effect with regard to an intangible asset—arguments to be used in a debate—not only when participants saw these arguments beforehand but also when they did not know the content of the arguments and were just informed that they "owned" a certain set of arguments (which they could then decide to sell) (see De Dreu and van Knippenberg 2005, 347, 355–56). These findings suggest that the increased value attributed to one's possessions is not only due to perceptions about their substantive features.

Likewise, Belk (1987, 1988) and Dittmar (1992) offered extensive evidence to support the claim that people often regard their possessions as part of their identity or extended self. The perception of possessions as part of one's self is not limited to objectively unique assets but extends to fungibles (including money) and to everyday items—such as electronic and sporting goods, grooming products, clothing, books, furniture, and vehicles (Belk 1987, 156–59; Ahuvia 2005; Dittmar 1992, 129–54; for a distinction between the private and public meanings of possessions, see Richins 1994).[5] This phenomenon is created in various ways, such as through controlling, creating, or knowing an asset (Belk 1988, 150–51, 155). Thus, a regular bicycle may invoke pleasant memories, a standard chair may be associated with a loved person who sat in it, and ordinary athletic equipment may symbolize skills and talents.[6] Belk (1988, 142–43) explained that involuntary loss of such possessions—for example, by theft, natural disaster, or forced disposition due to economic necessity—causes trauma and loss of self; voluntary disposition, in contrast, does not produce this effect.[7] Csikszentmihalyi and Rochberg-Halton (1981) also established the connection between commonplace assets and the development of the self. As they explain, objects affect what a person can do, and since what a person does broadly represents who he or she is, objects have a determining effect on self-development. Thus, for instance, a person's professional trade tools help define who that person is as an individual (Csikszentmihalyi and Rochberg-Halton 1981, 53, 92).[8]

Given the psychological significance of ownership and possession, let us take a closer look at people's perceptions of these two basic concepts.

Physical and Nonphysical Possession

Within the legal arena, "possession" is typically perceived as tangible, and individuals often receive greater protection against interference with their physical possession than against interference lacking any physical attribute. Take, for instance, the compensation rules that apply to the expropriation of land by the state for public use. Some American states require compensation surpassing market value for physical expropriation of homes. Thus, for example, condemnors in the state of Indiana are required to pay 150 percent of fair market value for occupied residences (Ind. Code § 32-24-4.5-8(2)(A); for further discussion of compensation for takings of property, see chapter 3). Psychological studies, however, indicate that people's notion of "possession" is not always physical, but may extend to intangible entitlements and expectations. If, indeed, the impact of nonphysical injuries is not necessarily qualitatively different from that of physical ones, the law should consider updating its understanding of possession.

Legal Possession and Psychological Possession

One example of the centrality of tangibility in legal possession extends back to the famous case of *Pierson v. Post*,[9] which involved a dispute between two hunters over a fox. Post was pursuing the wild animal across a deserted beach, when Pierson rode up and physically caught it. Post demanded that Pierson hand over the fox, based on the doctrine of first possession. According to this doctrine, the first person to gain possession of a previously unowned object, with the intent of becoming its owner, acquires ownership rights (Epstein 1998, 63). In principle, wild animals are considered to be ownerless until they are captured. Thus, Post claimed that his hot pursuit of the animal counts as "possession" and hence that he was already the fox's owner at the time that Pierson seized it. The majority ruled in favor of Pierson, holding that possession requires strong tangible manifestations: if not actual bodily capture, then at least mortal wounding or securing in a trap. Through the present, the definition of possession includes a significant physical element: taking in hand, occupying, or some other sort of physical control (Epstein 1998, 63).

Some evidence exists that both children and adults tend to infer that the first person known to physically possess an object is its owner (O. Friedman 2008; O. Friedman and Neary 2008; O. Friedman et al. 2011), even in the presence of other possible cues for ownership, such as sex stereotypes (toys associated with either girls or boys), or duration of possession (which was longer for the subsequent possessor) (O. Friedman 2008; for additional studies on the development of ownership notions in children, see Blake and Harris 2011; Hood et al. 2016; Rossano, Rakoczy, and Tomasello 2011; Shaw, Li, and Olson 2012; for a useful summary, see Nancekivell, Van de Vondervoort, and Friedman 2013).

Psychological findings, however, challenge this overly rigid perception of possession. Take, for instance, studies of the aforementioned endowment effect. Although many of these experiments involved physical possession of tangible goods, such as coffee mugs and pens, some have explored the possibility that an EE can also exist in relation to intangible goods, or without physical possession of the relevant good. Thus, for example, an EE was found with respect to intangible entitlements like hunting rights (Hammack and Brown 1974), working hours (Ortona and Scacciati 1992), promotional coupons for restaurants (S. Sen and Johnson 1997), academic chores (Galin et al. 2006), arguments in a debate (De Dreu and van Knippenberg 2005), and default rules (Korobkin 1998; Sunstein 2002). Furthermore, experimental studies have shown that the mere expectation of receiving a tangible or intangible resource can create an EE. Feldman, Schurr, and Teichman (2013) have demonstrated that the future gains a party expects to realize from a contract produce an EE; hence, the disutility associated with not realizing those gains is similar to that of losing goods already in possession. For example, promisors who viewed unrealized expectations as a loss were more likely to interpret their contractual obligation in a self-serving manner. In a similar fashion, Marzilli-Ericson and Fuster (2011) found that expectations determined by the probability of receiving a mug created an EE: subjects who had a high (80 percent) chance of obtaining a mug valued it 20 to 30 percent higher than subjects who had only a low (10 percent) chance of obtaining the asset (for additional studies of expectations as reference points for evaluating gains and losses, see Camerer et al. 1997; Abeler et al. 2011).

Experiments with online auctions are also informative. Various studies (Ariely and Simonson 2003; Heyman, Orhun, and Ariely 2004) have shown that participants who were the highest bidders for a certain period of time developed an EE with respect to the auctioned item, even before they became its actual owners or physical possessors. They perceived the possibility of being outbid by others as a loss, which in turn increased their valuation of the item. Moreover, the "opponent effect" (i.e., a competitive impulse to win the auction) was ruled out in explaining this higher valuation.

Another relevant line of research concerns consumers' behavior in online and offline purchases. Byun and Sternquist (2008, 2012) examined the effect of product-marketing techniques that induce perceptions of limited availability (by using phrases such as "limited time only," "while stocks last," and so forth). They found that consumers perceive not buying as the loss of an opportunity that they currently have. Consumers react to this feeling of loss by hoarding numerous items in their shopping cart, which eventually leads to excessive purchases. In other words, aversion to losing an intangible opportunity increases instances of physical possession and ultimately ownership.

In a similar vein, Tom, Lopez, and Demir (2006) observed an EE in both retail purchases (where the product usually is delivered on the spot) and direct marketing purchases (where the product is bought online or through a catalog). In the latter case, an EE was found even though the product was purchased remotely and physical possession was obtained only after a period of time. Brasel and Gips (2014) investigated the significance of the *type* of interface used in online purchasing. They discovered that touch screen devices like tablets lead to higher product valuations in comparison to indirect-touch devices, such as a computer mouse or a touch pad. It appears that enhancing the perception of "virtual touch" affects consumers' sense of endowment and their valuation of an asset that they have not actually touched.[10]

Finally, Peck and Shu (2009) and Peck, Barger, and Webb (2013) discovered that asking nonowners to *imagine* touching an object can produce an EE. It appears that even imagination can sometimes substitute for actual ownership or physical possession.[11]

These diverse experimental data support the claim that people's notion of "possession" is not confined to physical occupation, touch, or control of tangible assets. Rather, feelings of possession may relate to intangible assets, entitlements, and expectations;[12] in addition, they may exist in the absence of any physical proximity to a tangible asset.[13] These findings bear potential legal implications, as explained in the following.

Expanding the Legal Concept of Possession

In his seminal article "The New Property," Charles Reich (1964) argued that government largesse in the form of welfare benefits, licenses, franchises, subsidies, and the like should be regarded as "property." The main motivation for including intangible, government-created entitlements in the institution of property was to improve their protection against injurious state interference. Reich claimed that increased protection is necessary in light of the fact that an ever-increasing portion of individuals' wealth consists of government largesse—such as Social Security benefits, a license to practice medicine, or a taxi medallion—rather than traditional types of property. In a somewhat analogous fashion, perhaps we should consider "The New Possession." If perceptions, preferences, and reactions conventionally associated with physical possession are also manifested without physical control and with respect to intangible entitlements and expectations, then we may need to broaden our definition of legal possession. In the following, we demonstrate the fruitfulness of the psychological insights with two potential applications: compensation for takings of property and the doctrine of first possession.

First Application: Takings Compensation

Recognizing a broader, more flexible notion of possession may have implications for various legal debates—including, for example, the takings issue. Law in the United States (and elsewhere) sharply distinguishes between physical and nonphysical injuries to land. Landowners are afforded much broader protection against physical injuries (such as the taking of physical possession of their land) than against nonphysical injuries (such as restricting development rights on land that remains with its owners). Whereas in the former case even a small injury requires full compensation, in the latter case enormous reductions in the land's value are legitimized without compensation (Lewinsohn-Zamir 1996, 114–19).

Some scholars have justified these rules by relying on the EE phenomenon. Ellickson, for example, rationalized that a physical injury to land would ordinarily be viewed as a loss. In contrast, a nonphysical injury is likely to be perceived as an unattained gain. Since people experience more disutility from a loss than from an unrealized profit of the same magnitude, the former type of injury is worthier of legal protection than the latter (Ellickson 1989, 35–38). This argument is based on the crucial assumption that, usually, nonphysical injuries are perceived as foregone gains. However, the preceding experimental evidence regarding intangible possession indicates that this may not necessarily be the case. Why wouldn't landowners experience restrictions on permissible construction on their land as a loss of formerly "held" development rights? This presumption seems especially plausible if the land's purchase price reflected the value of the development rights. Absent direct testing of the matter, one cannot presume one way or the other.

Moreover, even if restriction of development rights is viewed as an unattained gain—and thus the injury to the landowner is lesser than if such restriction were regarded as a loss—the injury may still be substantial enough to warrant compensation. If perceptions of nonphysical possession affect the magnitude of the injury and cause a considerable harm, those suffering such injury may be entitled to state compensation (for detailed discussion of the takings issue, see chapter 3).

Second Application: First Possession

Another possible application of the psychological findings relates to the previously mentioned doctrine of first possession. Acknowledging the possibility of intangible possession suggests that the majority view in *Pierson v. Post*—which conditioned the doctrine of first possession on there being a near certainty of attaining physical possession—is too stringent. The minority view, which sufficed with a reasonable likelihood of physical capture, may better accord with people's perception of possession. Interestingly, the minority judge explicitly used the language of expectations when he conditioned the first hunter's ownership on his having "a reasonable prospect" of capturing the fox. Epstein (1979, 1230–31) noted that the custom of hunters in the region to regard "hot pursuit as giving rights to take an unimpeded first possession" might justify the reversal of the court's decision. In this context, he described a universal maritime custom that assigned an escaped whale to the fishing crew that first stuck a harpoon into it, rather than to the crew that first physically captured it.[14] This latter understanding of possession may also be characterized as sufficing with a certain degree of physical proximity to the asset or some weak form of physical contact.

A broader definition of possession may possibly support the claim that the similar, modern-day dispute involving a million-dollar home-run-record-breaking baseball should have been resolved in favor of the first person who stopped the flight of the ball with his glove but was thrown to the ground by other spectators before he could physically secure it in his hand.[15] However, in the *Popov v. Hayashi* case, the court held that the ball should be sold and its proceeds divided equally between the above individual and the person who eventually picked it up, and who did not take part in the scuffle over the ball.[16] Still, and importantly for our purposes, the court did recognize the legitimate claim of an individual who did not attain physical control of the ball.

To sum up, behavioral studies cast doubt on the assumption that "possession" necessarily requires a significant physical component. Such an understanding of possession may sometimes be overly rigid, since people may perceive themselves as possessors of intangible entitlements and expectations, as well as nonphysical possessors of tangible assets.

Two important caveats are in order. First, we do not claim that notions of intangible possession always exist, or that they invariably are equal in strength to those of physical possession. Further experimentation is necessary to map out the circumstances that give rise to nonphysical perceptions of possession and to assess their relative intensity in comparison to physical possession. For example, it may transpire that nonphysical notions of possession occur when a person has high expectations of receiving (but has not yet received) physical possession, or when the object of possession itself is intangible. In contrast, we may discover that such notions do not arise when the owner of a tangible asset voluntarily decides to part with its physical possession, as is the case when a landlord leases her property to a tenant. Furthermore, while notions of possession may indeed exist without physical contact with an asset, it may be the case that such contact increases the effect of possession.

Second, even when perceptions of intangible possession exist, it does not automatically follow that they should have normative implications. The legal system may have good reason not to acknowledge these perceptions, and countervailing considerations—varying according to the specific issue at stake—may eventually prevail. For instance, in the context of first possession, one might argue that possession must be such to provide a clear and acceptable signal to others that the possessor intends to control the asset and claim it as her property (Rose 2015; Singer 2017, 821). In some cases, at least, nonphysical possession may not satisfy this requirement. In addition, the unwillingness to encourage object fetishism, or the high administrative costs of identifying and catering to nonphysical possession, may limit the law's consideration of this phenomenon.

However, if one holds that enhancing human welfare is a central goal of legal policy making, and if one espouses a theory of welfare that is concerned with the fulfillment of people's preferences, then awareness of the potential flaws of an overly physical definition of possession is crucial. This is particularly true for efficiency analysis, which aims to maximize people's welfare as measured by the extent to which their preferences are satisfied (S. Shapiro and McClennen 1998). It also holds for objective theories of well-being, which accept that fulfilling people's wishes is one element of human welfare (Lewinsohn-Zamir 2003). Furthermore, to the extent that the magnitude of an individual's losses is relevant to the pertinent legal rule, and to the extent that the law's protection of possession assumes that possessors feel more strongly about assets than do nonpossessors,[17] we should take into account that such reactions may be present even without tangible possession.

Possession, Legal Ownership, and Psychological Ownership

Ownership and possession are basic building blocks of property law and can certainly vest in the same person. Such is the case of a car owner who drives her own car, or an apartment owner who resides in her apartment. Legal scholars, however, are well aware of the important distinction between ownership and possession, and of the fact that the two may diverge. In addition, jurists acknowledge the significance of distinguishing between lawful and unlawful possession, as well as between actual and prospective possession. Thus, for example, a case of adverse possession usually involves an owner who does not occupy some parcel of land and a trespasser who unlawfully possesses it. In a similar vein, a dispute between a landlord and a tenant is typically one between a nonpossessing owner and a lawful possessor of the tenement. Indeed, conflicts between owners and possessors—both lawful and unlawful— are not uncommon. The legal treatment of such situations could benefit from behavioral research. Moreover, the relevance of psychological data extends beyond disputes between owners and possessors. In crafting legal rules, it would be helpful to know, for instance, whether the attitudes and reactions of tenants (both short- and long-term) to property resemble or markedly differ from those of owners. Next, we examine behavioral studies that are relevant for these issues and show that such studies often do not differentiate between ownership and possession. A major manifestation of this phenomenon is found in experimental studies of the aforementioned endowment effect.

The Endowment Effect and the Doctrine of Adverse Possession

In the typical EE experiment, participants are informed that they are owners of some object (such as a mug, a pen, or a chocolate bar), which they also physically possess. The value of the endowed object is elicited and often compared to the value of some alternative object, which participants neither own nor possess (Kahneman, Knetsch, and Thaler 1990, 1991; Kahneman 1992; Knetsch and Sinden 1984; Morewedge et al. 2009; van Dijk and van Knippenberg 1996, 1998). Terms pertaining to ownership and possession are often used interchangeably throughout the studies, and the potential differences between lawful and unlawful possession are not investigated. Put differently, most psychological studies do not test what happens when ownership and possession diverge.

These shortcomings of current behavioral research should have limited their application to law-related issues; yet, legal studies do apply such general data to owner-possessor disputes. A prominent example is the discussion of adverse possession. According to this doctrine, a trespasser may gain title to the land or immunity from an ejection suit if her possession is adverse to the owner's interest (i.e., without the owner's permission) and is actual, open and notorious, exclusive, and continuous for the statutory period of limitation. Cohen and Knetsch (1992, 751–52), Ellickson (1989, 38–39), and Stake (2001, 2423–32) rely on the EE and loss aversion to justify adverse possession. The longtime possessor, so the argument goes, would perceive giving up the land as a loss, whereas the owner would view not receiving it back as a foregone gain. Since losses loom larger than gains, incurring the second cost—rather than the first—maximizes the parties' joint welfare. Stake (2001, 2459–64) addresses the possibility that the nonpossessing owner may perceive the rejection of her suit as a loss (rather than an unattained gain), but believes that this loss would be smaller than the corresponding loss to the possessor, for the latter's loss of a tangible object would be greater than the former's loss of what she probably sees as only an intangible financial asset.

These claims may be plausible, yet without direct behavioral research it is difficult to know whether an owner would view herself as being in the domain of gains or in the domain of losses (Korobkin 2003, 1259–62; Rose 2000, 489), or if she would perceive her land as merely a financial resource. Arguably, a registered landowner who loses her title or the ability to ever use the land may perceive this outcome as the loss of a nonfungible asset. Moreover, regardless of whether the situation is framed as an unattained gain or as a loss, a crucial factor is the magnitude of these gains and losses.[18] In real life, the owner may have purchased the land in the past for its market price and therefore will be deprived of this value, whereas the possessor may have knowingly trespassed on unpaid-for land. The value of the foregone gains or losses to the owner may surpass the value of the losses to the possessor. In sum, one should be cautious in applying behavioral findings to legal issues, absent a good "fit" between the two.

Note that even after these issues are resolved, the case for adverse possession would not be settled automatically one way or the other. The possible asymmetry in the subjective costs to each party—highlighted by behavioral studies—is but one relevant consideration among many. For example, it is particularly difficult to adjudicate old cases: relevant documents may have been lost, important witnesses might have died or moved elsewhere, and so forth. Thus, the high costs of adjudication to all parties involved—plaintiffs, defendants, and courts—support a statute of limitation (for discussion of the traditional justifications for adverse possession, see Merrill 1985, 1128–33).

Although most behavioral studies have not tested the relative strength of possession vis-à-vis ownership directly—by pitting owners against possessors—a small number of experiments lend support to the possibility that sometimes possession may be the more crucial factor psychologically. We examine these studies next.

Ownership Effect versus Possession Effect

A few studies have demonstrated the effect of mere possession. Knetsch and Wong (2009) found an EE when participants were offered a choice between an object (a mug or a pen) that they possessed but were expressly told that they did not own, and an alternative object (a pen or a mug, respectively) that they neither possessed nor owned yet. Participants strongly preferred to become owners of the object that they possessed: only 14 percent of the initial pen holders traded the pen for a mug, and only 33 percent of the initial mug possessors traded the mug for a pen (Knetsch and Wong 2009, 411–12). Likewise, experiments have shown that touch increases the valuation of objects for both owners and nonowners. Peck and Shu (2009) examined, inter alia, the effect of touching a mug on its valuation by potential buyers. Participants who had a mug placed in front of them but did not touch it offered lower prices for the mug than did participants who touched it before indicating the price they were willing to pay. Similarly, touch increased owners' valuation of the pen they owned, making them more reluctant to trade it, in comparison to owners who did not touch the owned object.[19] In this context, studies on the behavior of territorial animals may also be of relevance. These studies have found that defenders of a territory invariably overcome intruders of the same species who try to take over their territory (Alcock 2009, 278–84; Bradbury and Vehrencamp 1998, 711–30). Since animals have no notions of legal ownership, these studies also attest to the strong instinctive protection of possession.

Another behavioral study demonstrated the effect of length of physical contact with an unowned object. Wolf, Arkes, and Muhanna (2008) varied the amount of time during which participants could examine an item before bidding for it in an online auction. Half of the participants inspected the coffee mug for ten seconds and the other half for thirty seconds. This small difference in the duration of time spent touching the object was found to increase significantly nonowners' valuation of the mug and their bid amounts.[20]

The study that came closest to testing the relative significance of possession and ownership is that of Reb and Connolly (2007). The authors elicited the monetary valuations of chocolate bars in four groups of subjects: the first group had both ownership and possession of the object; the second group owned the object but did not possess it; the third group owned the object but did not possess it; the third group possessed the object but did not own it; and the fourth group neither possessed nor owned the object. The results revealed a significant main effect for possession. That is to say, participants gave the chocolate bar a higher monetary value when they possessed it than when they did not possess it. Ownership, in itself, did not produce a similar significant effect. These results were replicated with coffee mugs (Reb and Connolly 2007, 109, 111). Although Reb and Connolly's study is unique in its attempt to disentangle the effects of ownership and possession, it did not directly test competition or conflict between the two. Owners and possessors did not interact with each other (e.g., in order to negotiate a sale or an exchange). Thus, we still lack data regarding direct competition between owners and possessors.

In sum, the available findings indicate that mere possession may suffice for creating an EE, even when people are aware that they are not the owners of the asset they possess. Furthermore, it appears that the duration of possession intensifies this effect, even after a very short period of time. Researchers have not yet tested scenarios in which ownership and possession are pitted against each other, although one study lends initial support to the possibility that the possession effect may sometimes be stronger than the ownership effect.

Pierce, Kostova, and Dirks (2003, 87–93) theorized that feelings of ownership ("psychological ownership")—without formal legal ownership—are induced by controlling an asset, becoming familiar with it (through actual or imagined use), and/or immersing oneself in it. Psychological ownership may occur, for example, through labor—by creating an object, or even just investing time, effort, and care in it (on the role of creation, labor, and value enhancement in establishing perceptions of ownership, see Beggan and Brown 1994; Kanngiesser, Gjersoe, and Hood 2010; Kanngiesser and Hood 2014; Levene, Starmans, and Friedman 2015). While legal ownership can materialize immediately, once the formal rights are acquired, the emergence of psychological ownership is a more gradual process, since it requires sufficient control over, intimate knowledge of, and self-investment in an asset (Pierce, Kostova, and Dirks 2003, 96). To the extent that this theory is true, it can explain why nonowning possessors (including consciously unlawful possessors) may develop strong attachments to the property, whereas nonpossessing legal owners might not always experience similar feelings of psychological ownership.

The state of the available data on this issue requires caution when one moves from laboratory results to real-world applications. Nevertheless, we proceed to offer some tentative observations regarding two legal issues: the self-help remedy with respect to property and the rights of long-term tenants.

First Application: Self-Help Measures to Protect Property

The apparent strength of possession per se justifies most of the prevailing legal rules regarding self-help measures to recover possession. Ordinarily, a person whose proprietary rights have been violated must turn to state judicial and enforcement mechanisms. Thus, for instance, a buyer who is entitled to specific performance of a contract cannot obtain the promised asset from the seller by herself but must go to court. In the transition from a "state of nature" to a state, individuals surrendered their power to take their due by force and delegated this authority to the state. This rule is perfectly justifiable, as it prevents breaches of the peace, which might result in grave consequences for many.

Nevertheless, the law sometimes allows individuals to forcefully reclaim their property. This privilege of self-help often operates as a defense against what would otherwise be a tort of assault or battery (Keeton et al. 1984, 131).[21] Self-help is limited to reasonable force and can be exercised only as an immediate response to an attempted—or very recent—invasion of property rights. The main prerequisite is that the force user be the lawful and actual possessor of the property (Restatement (Second) of Torts §§ 77, 81, 91, 94, 103, 106; Keeton et al. 1984, 131, 137–40). Mere ownership or right to receive possession does not suffice (Dobbs, Hayden, and Bublick 2011, §§ 90–91). Consequently, an owner of a vacant parcel of land cannot forcibly expel a wrongful possessor (Weisman 1995, 254), and a landlord usually cannot evict defaulting tenants by herself (M. R. Friedman 1997, 1246–47).

The psychological data support this distinction between possessors and nonpossessors. Although all owners (and persons entitled to possession) may prefer quick self-recovery of assets from wrongdoers to a lengthier judicial process, the preferences of the freshly dispossessed for a self-help remedy are likely to be stronger. Society most probably cannot expect individuals to successfully curb their spontaneous, powerful inclination to prevent dispossession by force. As Justice Holmes famously stated:

> Law, being a practical thing, must found itself on actual forces. It is quite enough, therefore, for the law, that man, by an instinct which he shares with the domestic dog . . . will not allow himself to be dispossessed . . . of what he holds, without trying to get it back again. Philosophy may find a hundred reasons to justify the instinct, but it would be totally immaterial if it should condemn it and bid us surrender without a murmur. As long as the instinct remains, it will be more comfortable for the law to satisfy it in an orderly manner, than to leave people to themselves. If it should do otherwise, it would become a matter for pedagogues, wholly devoid of reality.[22]

Assuming that nonpossessors, in contrast, typically have significantly weaker preferences to obtain immediate possession, educating them to control their urge to seize their property by force is much more likely to be successful. Therefore, the general advantages of preventing violence override nonpossessors' desire to regain their property, and the usual rule that aggrieved parties must go to court is appropriate.

While justifying the general prerequisite that only possessors can employ self-help, the behavioral findings may also support two changes to current legal rules. First, to the extent that possession—rather than ownership—is the main driving force of the EE and of people's inclination to gain possession by force, we may want to consider expanding self-help to *unlawful* possessors as well, at least vis-à-vis subsequent trespassers (if not also against the true owner of the property). This recommendation is in harmony with the common law rule that does not allow defendant-wrongdoers to raise a *ius tertii* claim against plaintiff-possessors. Thus, for instance, a person who trespasses on land held by another cannot defeat the possessor's suit by claiming that she has no right to possess the land either. As long as the land's owner is not present (or is not interested in suing the trespasser herself), wrongdoers must treat possessors as if they are the rightful owners (Epstein 1998, 65; Weisman 1995, 254). Like the latter rule, awarding self-help to unlawful possessors would reduce the incidence of public disorder from successive attempts to dispossess current possessors. Second, assuming that the welfare loss of nonpossessing owners due to the absence of a self-help remedy is relatively small in comparison to that of possessing owners, it may be justifiable to hold that defaulting tenants' right to a judicial eviction proceeding cannot be waived in the tenancy agreement. Such a proceeding enables the tenant to contest the landlord's claim or find an alternative residence (Singer 2017, 461–63). Currently, some American states permit such contractual waivers, which allow the landlord to use self-help to regain possession of the tenement (M. R. Friedman 1997, 1248–49; Schoshinski 1980 § 6:6).

Second Application: The Rights of Long-Term Tenants

A different potential implication of the preliminary data on possession is that the law should examine whether certain rights and protections currently afforded to owners should also be given to tenants, particularly to long-term ones (see also Barros 2006, 300–05). This, to a large extent, is the practice in Israel, where most lands are held in public ownership and individuals usually receive only long-term leases (for discussion of reasons to adopt long-term leases as an alternative to ownership, see Weisman 1997, 105–14). Israeli law often extends the rules applying to ownership—such as those pertaining to statutory rights of first refusal—to leases for a term that exceeds twenty-five years. According to these rules, for example, when spouses are either co-owners or cotenants of their joint place of residence, jointly operated business, or jointly tended farm, each of them has a right to purchase the other's share in the property when it is about to be sold.[23] Moreover, long-term tenants in Israel most probably regard themselves as "owners," and it would be politically unfeasible to require them to vacate the land at the end of the lease or else pay the full market value of a new lease (Weisman 1997, 115–17). Recognition of these facts has led the state to gradually transfer ownership in developed urban lands to the long-term tenants, rather than perpetually renew the lease without requiring payment from the tenants.

After this discussion of people's perceptions of ownership and possession, as well as conflicts involving owners and possessors, we now turn to specific rights enjoyed by property owners, and their limitation.

The Rights of Property Owners

As mentioned, ownership of an asset typically entails a wide array of rights, such as to possess, use, transfer, and destroy it. Intuitively, one would think that the ability to carry out an extreme measure with respect to property encompasses also the power to take a more moderate measure. Thus, if an owner may freely destroy, consume, or sell an asset before her death, thereby completely denying it to her descendants, then she can also bequeath the asset subject to restrictions (Epstein 1986, 705; Shavell 2004, 68–69). Similarly, since an owner is ordinarily entitled to entirely exclude others from entering her property, she may also allow only partial or conditional entrance or simply regulate the property's disposition and use (Epstein 1992, 1109). The force of this reasoning rests on the underlying assumption that the owner's employing of greater power would be worse for the affected individuals than her exercising a lesser power.

Legal rules, however, frequently reject this reasoning. Often, in practice, the law is *less* tolerant of moderate measures by property owners than it is of extreme ones. For instance, total inalienability of the property may be respected, whereas restrictions on alienability are struck down; intensive use of the property may be permitted, but nonuse leads to its loss; destruction of property may be allowed, while its modification is forbidden. Next, we provide some examples of such rules and show how psychological insights lend them support. In certain situations, by granting greater deference to extreme measures, the law can reduce instances of mistakes and cognitive biases.[24]

Some Puzzling Legal Rules

Nontransfer versus Conditioned Transfer. Under American law, an owner is under no obligation to bestow her property as a gift during her lifetime or to bequeath it to a particular person upon death. Thus, property owners have considerable freedom to disinherit their close relatives.[25] At the same time, owners' freedom to transfer property subject to restrictions is curtailed. For example, courts have struck down conditions in a will or a gift that required the recipients to sever relationships with certain people or to adopt or abandon a religious faith, as well as restrictions that limited the recipients' career choices. Such rules apply equally to long-term and short-term restrictions and thus cannot be explained simply by the existence of transaction costs or changed circumstances (Lewinsohn-Zamir 2008, 644–47).

A similar phenomenon may be found with respect to landlord-tenant agreements, for example, with contractual clauses that restrict the tenant's right to assign the lease or sublet the apartment. Restrictions that absolutely prohibit any alienation by the tenant are generally enforceable under American law. Accordingly, the landlord enjoys complete discretion, and her reasons for prohibiting alienation are not examined. In contrast, if the contract permits alienation provided the landlord grants her consent, the latter's subsequent refusal may be examined and overruled by the court if deemed to be unreasonable (M. R. Friedman 1997, 321, 325).

Use versus Nonuse. Although the right *not* to use one's property is assumed to be a natural corollary of the—more burdensome to others— right to *use* property, sometimes owners cannot choose the more moderate measure. This is because nonuse of the property right may lead to its loss. Two examples are servitudes and water rights.[26] Servitudes are nonpossessory property rights in land, providing their holders with a variety of possible enjoyments, such as a right of way through another person's land, a right to sever and remove minerals, or a right to prevent construction that would block a pleasing view (Stoebuck and Whitman 2000, § 8.1). Servitudes bind not only the original servient landowners but also their successors in title, and may be of unlimited duration. However, nonuse of a servitude may result in its loss (Bruce and Ely 2007, §§ 10:18–10:20; Yiannopoulos 1982, 1291).

The rules governing water rights often apply a similar principle. According to the "prior appropriation" system (adopted in American western states),[27] the first person to use the water beneficially acquires a property right in the water, which grants her the right to divert a specified quantity of the flow of the water source, in priority over others.

However, failure to exercise the water right without sufficient cause results in its forfeiture (Tarlock 2017, §§ 5:90–5:93).

Destruction versus Modification. Arguably, the most extreme measure that an owner can take with respect to her property is to destroy it. Although the right to destroy is not absolute,[28] no general prohibition exists against destroying valuable assets (Lawson and Rudden 1982, 116). Moreover, the law may sometimes allow total destruction, while more moderate measures such as modification are restricted. A good example relates to authors' moral rights. Accordingly, authors are entitled to have their work attributed to them, and they have the right to prevent modifications of the work that are prejudicial to their honor or reputation. For instance, the owner of a painting or a sculpture cannot alter it in a way that is detrimental to the artist's honor or reputation (Ricketson and Ginsburg 2006, 585–87, 602–10). While all legal systems that recognize moral rights protect creators against injurious changes of their work, international and most national legislation does not refer specifically to the case of destruction, and courts and commentators are reluctant to extend moral rights to encompass a right not to have one's work destroyed (Lewinsohn-Zamir 2008, 662–63; Ricketson and Ginsburg 2006, 605; Rigamonti 2006, 371). American legislation is an exception in this regard, as it explicitly protects a work of visual art not only from alteration but also from destruction. However, the protection against destruction is much narrower than that against alteration, since it is limited to works of "recognized stature." Furthermore, property owners have considerable freedom to destroy a work of art (such as a mural) that otherwise cannot be removed from the premises (Nimmer and Nimmer 2017, § 8D.06[C]; Sherman 1995, 418–22).

To sum up, legal rules in a wide variety of contexts afford property owners more freedom to pursue extreme measures with respect to their property than to engage in more moderate measures. There may be various justifications for this phenomenon, but we focus here on behavioral insights supporting such rules.

Psychological Explanations

Protecting Property Recipients. A major reason for intervening where property owners take moderate measures is the protection of the potential property transferees. The law may wish to prevent significant harm to the latter's welfare and to avoid confusion and mistakes. Take, for instance, a will conditioning a bequest of property on the beneficiary's marrying a person who meets some restrictive criteria, or adopting a certain religious faith. Imposing such conditions is an attempt to exert power and control a person's most significant and intimate life choices and express disrespect for the transferee as an autonomous individual. Fulfillment of the conditions by recipients who are tempted by the prospect of owning the property might gravely injure their autonomy and opportunity for self-development and self-realization. In contrast, when property is not transferred at all, these injuries do not occur; no insulting message is conveyed along with the property, and no harmful consequences from satisfying offensive conditions transpire.

Moreover, when conditions attached to the transferred property are not easily met, an additional reason emerges for preferring extreme measures to moderate ones. Take the previously mentioned example of landlords' restrictions on alienation by tenants. The law enforces absolute prohibitions on transferring the lease even if they are arbitrary or capricious, but it intervenes in transfers conditioned upon the landlord's consent, if the landlord has no objectively reasonable ground for withholding her consent. Imagine an opposite rule granting landlords absolute discretion also under a conditioned-transfer clause. Although both types of clauses would now give landlords similar, complete control over the transfer of the lease, tenants are likely to perceive them differently. Whereas an absolute prohibition clause is clear and unequivocal, the conditioned-transfer clause is more ambiguous and open to misunderstanding. When the lease indicates that alienation is a viable option, tenants may mistakenly believe that they are entitled to transfer their right (as long as they find a suitable candidate) and that the landlords would not unreasonably withhold their consent. Therefore, a rule subjecting a conditioned-transfer clause to a reasonableness test protects tenants from confusion by giving landlords an incentive to state in unequivocal terms their preference for total control over the choice of prospective tenants.

Behavioral studies confirm the likelihood of such mistakes on the part of tenants. First, there is a well-documented cognitive bias toward overoptimism (Jolls 1998, 1659–61; Sunstein 2000b, 4). Thus, for instance, notwithstanding correct information about the chances of being involved in an automobile accident, suffering a heart attack, or divorcing from one's spouse, most individuals overconfidently believe that they are much less likely than the average person to experience these events (Baker and Emery 1993; DeJoy 1989; Weinstein 1980, 1987). Overoptimism is especially prevalent with respect to occurrences people perceive to be (at least somewhat) under their control (S. E. Taylor 1989, 36–39).[29] Second, people tend to think that others will treat them fairly and decently. Thus, for example, although respondents in a study of perceptions of divorce estimated that only 40 percent of spouses who have been awarded alimony or child support actually receive these payments, they confidently predicted that their own spouse would fully comply with the court's decision (Baker and Emery 1993, 443). Therefore, it is highly likely that a tenant signing a conditioned-transfer lease would believe she stood a good chance of persuading the landlord to grant permission and would discount the possibility that the latter would arbitrarily withhold consent.

Overconfidence in this regard may be reinforced by another well-known behavioral phenomenon: the "framing effect." Cognitive studies have observed that people's evaluation of a situation depends on the way in which the relevant data are presented to them. In particular, an individual's evaluation is made in relation to a certain reference point or status quo, which, in turn, determines whether a scenario is framed as one that involves gain or loss (Tversky and Kahneman 1986). As Amos Tversky and Daniel Kahneman's prospect theory famously demonstrated, an inflicted loss "hurts" much more than an unobtained gain of the same magnitude (Kahneman and Tversky 1979; Kahneman, Knetsch, and Thaler 1991). In the context of restrictions on transferring the lease, a clause unequivocally prohibiting alienation conveys the message that no right to transfer exists. Although a tenant may try at some point in the future to convince the landlord to allow a transfer, her reference point is that she is not entitled to transfer the lease. Therefore, the tenant would likely consider renegotiation of this issue as involving the possibility of obtaining a gain. Consequently, failure on her part would be more readily accepted, and its adverse impact on her mitigated. By contrast, a tenant reasonably might regard a conditioned-transfer clause as creating a right to alienate, albeit a qualified one. As a result, the landlord's subsequent refusal would be viewed as inflicting a loss that, in turn, would intensify the negative impact on the tenant and her frustration from not being able to exercise what she perceives as her right.[30]

Viewed from this perspective, legal rules that interfere more with moderate-phrased measures than with extreme-phrased ones can be understood as debiasing devices. By encouraging property owners intending to grant a certain right to frame it in unconditioned and unambiguous terms—rather than in a moderate, conditioned manner that might be misleading—these rules reduce cognitive biases.

Promoting Efficient Use of Property. A different reason for greater intervention with moderate measures relating to property than with extreme ones is that the former are more prone to inefficiencies. Once again, behavioral insights support this assumption. Recall the issue of use versus nonuse of property, where intensive use (that burdens others) is permitted, yet nonuse (imposing fewer burdens on others) leads to loss of the right. A possible justification for this outcome is that the value of property may be intimately connected with its actual use. Take, for instance, a right of way through another person's land. The servitude's sole goal is to enable passage. If its owner neither uses the servitude for a lengthy period nor attempts to transfer it or negotiate a change in its scope, one can reasonably infer that the servitude has little (or no) value to her.

Why, then, does she not expressly relinquish the right? A possible explanation is that the owner of the servitude simply has not bothered to do so. The acquisition of the right is typically a sunk cost, whereas affirmatively relinquishing a right and communicating this fact to the relevant parties entail new costs in terms of thought, time, and money. Usually, in addition to the servient landowner, the land registry would also have to be informed of the need to erase the servitude from its records. Hence, it may be cheaper or easier to do nothing at all. Furthermore, psychological studies have demonstrated that people seek to avoid regret, and that regret looms larger for commissions than for omissions (Samuelson and Zeckhauser 1988, 38). An economic loss from an action generates stronger feelings of regret than a loss of similar magnitude resulting from inaction (Baron and Ritov 1994; Ritov and Baron 1992). Thus, for example, one study has shown that monetary loss from a decision to move stock from one investment to another is perceived to cause more regret than an equivalent loss from failing to switch one's stock to an alternative investment (Kahneman and Tversky 1982). Likewise, researchers found that people are reluctant to vaccinate a child, even when the risk of death from the disease is significantly higher than the risk of death from vaccinating against it (Ritov and Baron 1990). These phenomena support the contention that people may be overly reluctant to part with low-valued property rights. Such parting requires a commission, which is particularly prone to the regret avoidance bias. In contrast, holding on to the property right involves an omission, which engenders lower regret costs. Consequently, in order to minimize future regret, individuals will unnecessarily hold on to unused property.

In this context, the comparison between nonuse and destruction of property is illuminating. Destruction is usually not susceptible to these problems that may lead to inefficient choices regarding property. A decision to destroy cannot be the product of neglect, inertia, or lack of thought. One main reason is that there is no way back from it. A decision to destroy, once carried out, is irreversible. The finality of the act naturally draws the owner's attention to other possible courses of action and compels her to examine them carefully. Excluding relatively rare cases such as owner insanity and accidental destruction, if an owner prefers destruction even over abandonment of her property, this indicates the high value of destruction for her.[31] The fact that, in practice, owners usually do not destroy valuable assets (Honoré 1961, 118) strengthens—rather than weakens—this argument. In those special cases where owners intentionally opt for destruction of their property notwithstanding its market value, there is a strong prima facie case that this extreme measure was taken for good reason and that it is the efficient course of action.[32]

Moreover, the cognitive biases described earlier strengthen the argument regarding the differences between nonuse of property and its destruction. The choice to hold on to unused property (which may result from neglect, lack of knowledge and thought, or transaction costs) is further bolstered by aversion to regret. This aversion, in turn, is reinforced by the omission/commission bias, since holding on to the property constitutes inaction, which engenders lower costs of regret. In contrast, a decision to destroy an asset represents not merely a commission but an irreversible one at that. As a result, it is subject to the highest potential costs of regret. Those committing acts of destruction must first overcome the bias against regret-producing commissions. Consequently, higher nonexistence value and stronger reasons than otherwise are needed to enable owners to prevail over their cognitive bias. The omission/commission bias operating against the destruction of property adds assurance that destruction is the consequence of rational thought. Of course, it is not the case that decisions to destroy can never be mistaken. For example, owners may sometimes be unaware of the existence of an individual whose valuation of the property surpasses their own destruction value.[33] However, there are important differences between nonuse and a decision to destroy property, and as a rule we have greater confidence—albeit not absolute certainty—in the efficiency of the latter.

Since nonuse of property is less likely to be grounded in sound reasons and more prone to cognitive biases, the law aims to counteract these problems by stating that unused rights may be lost. At the same time, to minimize the risk of mistakes, use-it-or-lose-it rules are not applied uniformly to all property rights but are limited to cases where a substantial period of nonuse provides a strong indication of owners' low valuation. For this reason, such rules typically target rights that were created at the outset for a specific, narrow purpose that cannot be unilaterally altered by the right holders—such as servitudes and water rights. In these cases, we can rest assured that nonuse is not motivated by right holders' waiting until the time when their property is ripe for a better use. By extinguishing unused rights of these types, the law reduces instances of low valuation by right holders while saving on the transaction costs, thereby freeing scarce resources for more efficient uses.[34]

In sum, behavioral studies help justify seemingly puzzling rules, according to which the law exhibits greater deference to owners' preferences when they engage in extreme measures regarding their property than when they employ more moderate measures.

Concluding Remarks

In this chapter, we have discussed behavioral literature that is relevant to property ownership and possession. The chapter has underscored the psychological significance of ownership and possession and employed behavioral insights to justify seemingly paradoxical legal rules. The discussion also revealed two phenomena that seem to be partly in tension: people's notion of possession may extend to intangible entitlements and expectations and to assets that they do not physically hold. Concomitantly, preliminary evidence suggests that mere physical possession can have a psychological effect similar to that of ownership, and that the effect of possession may sometimes be stronger than the effect of ownership.

A question that commonly arises regarding experimental findings is whether the law should attempt to "debias" people and steer them in a more rational direction (for general discussions of debiasing through law, see Blumenthal 2007; Jolls and Sunstein 2006). Necessarily, the answer to this question is context dependent. Sometimes, no justification exists for legal intervention. For instance, if people experience feelings of loss not only with respect to tangible goods but also with regard to intangible ones, no compelling reason emerges to try to eliminate the latter type of perceptions as, in principle, there is nothing objectionable or irrational about them. In other cases, an attempt to debias may fail, due to the relative rareness of the type of loss involved in people's lives. Take, for example, ownership of land. If most owners develop their land according to plan and do not experience significant downzoning, it would be hard for the law to educate them that restriction of their development rights constitutes merely unattained gains rather than losses. Similarly, we cannot reasonably expect individuals to curb their powerful instinct to respond to dispossession with force. Therefore, the law cannot avoid acknowledging some forms of self-help behavior.

More generally, the existing body of behavioral research has contributed undoubtedly to our understanding of ownership and possession. At the same time, further work must be undertaken to improve the relevance and fruitfulness of these studies for the law. In particular, a need exists for additional empirical studies that examine directly legal situations involving ownership and possession. For instance, it would be worthwhile to discover the legal contexts giving rise to intangible perceptions of possession and to design scenarios that test the relative strength of physical and nonphysical possession. Such studies would help us understand—and hopefully resolve—the partial tension between some of the phenomena discussed in this chapter. Likewise, researchers should design experiments that expressly employ distinctions between ownership and possession, between lawful and unlawful possession, and between short-term and long-term possession. Of course, laboratory experiments' ability to test the latter distinction is very limited. Empirical studies are likely to give us better knowledge about the effects of long-term possession by nonowners of property.

2

Protecting Homes and Other Types of Property

One function of property law is to calibrate the protection that different kinds of property receive against dispossession or dissipation. Property is an asset that can be voluntarily sold, donated, transferred via a will, or in certain circumstances sold against the owner's wishes to satisfy debts. Both real property (land and affixed buildings) and personal, or "chattel," property (tangible and movable objects) are subject at times to transfer against the wishes of the property owner. Owners may experience a forced transfer of all or part of their property as a result of debts from credit contracts or tort liabilities, expropriation by the state, market forces that make property or its taxes unaffordable, theft or trespass, or conflicts with other property claimants.

A critical tension in property law is whether to treat all property dispassionately and equivalently or to offer enhanced legal protections for certain categories of property (S. M. Stern 2009, 1105–09; Belk 1991; Markell, Tyler, and Brosnan 2012, 221–24). One important rationale for protection against dispossession or dissipation is that loss of the property will cause psychological harm (R. Simon 2008; National Association of Realtors 2012, 12–13).[1] In response to these concerns, property laws sometimes offer compensation, exempt part of the value of the property from a claim, or grant the owner the right to retain the entire property. For example, there is a breadth of special legal protections for owner-occupied residential property in property law, based in part on psychological claims about the importance of maintaining one's home and, in some accounts, one's status as a homeowner (S. M. Stern 2009, 2011; Barros 2006). There are also protections for personal property that are more variable and often less robust than residential protections (Jones 2011a, 123–24). These special protections are carve-outs from the property law system, which generally favors neutral treatment of property and compensation based on objective measures of fair market value.

Research in psychology can inform the use and design of property-protective laws and offer an empirical counterbalance to legal assumptions about the psychological importance of different kinds of property. For more than three decades, social psychologists have investigated people's attachments to their possessions, the relationship between property and identity, and aversions to parting with property. Contrary to the legal notion of dispassionate decision making, people sometimes develop subjective attachments and emotional ties to possessions well above the possession's market value (Beggan 1992; Belk 1988; Tversky and Kahneman 1979). In addition to attachments and subjective value, there is also a great deal of research on the objective effects of property. Psychologists, as well as sociologists, have studied the psychological impacts of relocation and homelessness, how the physical environment shapes personal identity, and the effect on well-being from possessions compared with experiences (Vásquez-Vera et al. 2017; Proshansky, Fabian, and Kaminoff 1983, 61; T. J. Carter and Gilovich 2010).

In this chapter, we explore the following questions: Do certain types of property have special psychological value greater than the social costs of property protection? If so, will enhancing legal protections against dispossession safeguard these attachments and other psychological values? We delve into the empirical evidence for the psychological importance of residential property and personal (chattel) property as well as briefly address protections for leasehold property.

(Over)Protecting Residential Property?

Property law is replete with instances in which residential property receives favorable treatment and special protections. For example, certain forms of property ownership and bankruptcy laws enable owners to shield a portion of their home equity from creditors or to retain their homes (Jacoby 2007, 329–34). When the government expropriates land under the Fifth Amendment takings power, a number of American states require "super-compensation" above market value (for a detailed discussion see chapter 3). Tax laws privileging the home, such as the home mortgage interest deduction in the United States, and foreclosure relief legislation (e.g., government-provided incentives for lenders to refinance loans into lower interest rates, opportunities for underwater owners to refinance into government-backed mortgages, or government subsidized write-downs of principal loan balances) provide additional layers of protection from financial exigency (S. M. Stern 2009).

Does the psychological attachment to one's home or the negative effects on well-being from dispossession support such a high level of protection for residential real estate? While there is significant psychological evidence that people develop emotional attachments to their property, there is much less evidence for the primacy of the home relative to other possessions. As discussed in chapter 1, Beggan (1992) has described a "mere ownership effect" where ownership or possession causes people to prefer certain objects relative to those they do not own or possess. There is evidence that people view their possessions as part of their identity (Prentice 1987; Belk 1987; S. T. Fiske 1998) and in some cases can become strongly emotionally attached (in extreme cases resulting in pathologies such as compulsive hoarding) (Frost and Hartl 1996). Theoretical work in psychology has explored how possessions contribute to self-definition and communicate identity to others (Tajfel and Turner 1986; Wicklund and Gollwitzer 1981). A wealth of experimental evidence also reveals that people are subject to an "endowment effect" and systematically demand more money to sell a good in their possession than they are willing to pay to procure the same good (Tversky and Kahneman 1979; Carmon and Ariely 2000; Kahneman, Knetsch, and Thaler 1990). Yet, as we shall discuss, the psychology studies that have assessed homes relative to other types of possessions paint a more moderate picture of the psychological value of homes to their owners than some property laws have assumed.

Next, we consider debtor protections for residential property, specifically homestead exemptions and tenancy by the entirety. We examine whether the psychological importance of the home warrants the high levels of legal protection found in these laws.

Debtor Protections: Rethinking Homestead Exemptions and Tenancy by the Entirety

Claims by creditors are a common means by which property owners lose title to their property. Creditor claims can arise, for example, from monetary judgments in tort cases or from consensual contracts for credit (such as bank loans, credit card balances, etc.). In either case, property owners who cannot pay their debts are subject to creditor claims and, in some cases, pursue bankruptcy to expunge or partially repay those debts.[2] Through homestead exemptions and tenancy by the entirety, residential property can shield owners from their debts. These laws illustrate a bias in property law, as well as in many states' bankruptcy laws, toward enhanced protection of residential property relative to other forms of property.

State law homestead exemptions protect owner-occupied residential property from claims by creditors by exempting some or all of the equity in a personal residence (Rivera 2004, 77–91). In the United States, the homestead exemption affects debtors in "chapter 7" bankruptcy, which is a form of bankruptcy that enables debtors to liquidate their assets to satisfy creditors, subject to exemptions.[3] In chapter 7 bankruptcy, a homeowner with equity in her home would typically need to pay unsecured creditors (meaning loans where there was no property pledged as collateral) from her assets, including the equity in her home. Exemptions allow debtors to exclude some of their assets from the reach of creditors. In many states, the debtor by law can elect the federal exemption for a homestead, which is currently $47,350 for a married couple, or the state law exemption (some state laws require debtors to utilize state law exemptions).[4] The amount of the homestead exemption and the amount of equity (i.e., the fair market value of the home less the balance of any nonexempt liens or mortgages) the owner has in the home determine whether the homestead exemption affords the homeowner a sum of cash (i.e., the exemption amount) or the ability to retain the house. For example, a homeowner in a state with an unlimited homestead exemption would be able to protect her equity and keep her home. In a state with a partial homestead exemption, the trustee will not sell the debtor's house if the debtor's equity is below the exemption amount (because all of the equity would be exempted) but will sell it if the equity is greater than the statutory exemption amount. In the latter case, the debtor would receive cash equal to the statutory exemption amount, and the trustee would use the remaining equity to satisfy creditor claims.

Several states offer unlimited homestead exemptions, including Florida, Texas, Iowa, Kansas, Oklahoma, the District of Columbia, Arkansas, and South Dakota (both Arkansas and South Dakota have restrictions on the applicability of the unlimited exemption based on acreage).[5] A number of other states offer a very high level of exemption for the home, including $500,000 or more in Rhode Island, Massachusetts, and Nevada, and $250,000 in Montana.[6] These states are more generous than either the federal exemption for homesteads or the remainder of the states, which offer homestead exemptions ranging from approximately $10,000 to $150,000.[7] States and the federal government also offer exemptions for personal property, such as household goods, clothing, jewelry, vehicles, and tools for trade, up to a specified dollar amount per category of personal property or occasionally in toto for low-market-value items such as personal prosthetics or family Bibles. In contrast to the homestead exemption, state exemptions for personal property tend to be less valuable (in one state as low as $500), and no states offer an unlimited exemption for high-value personal property comparable to the unlimited homestead exemption.[8]

A number of states also require that debtors who receive cash proceeds from a homestead exemption reinvest that money in another homestead.[9] For example, Colorado state law maintains the homestead exemption for two years after the sale of the home so long as the money is kept separate. After that, the money is subject to attachment to pay debts unless the money is used to purchase a new homestead, in which case the exemption on that money "carries over" to the new home.[10] These laws effectively privilege the home above other assets by requiring reinvestment in owner-occupied residential property.

In addition to the homestead exemption, married couples can shield property from the creditors of one spouse by holding the property as tenants by the entirety (Orth 1997, 48). Co-owners of property may elect to hold property in one of three different estates in property: tenancy by the entirety (available only in about half of the states), joint tenancy, and tenancy in common. Tenancy by the entirety is the only form exclusively available to property co-owned by spouses. Tenancy by the entirety carries rights of survivorship so that if one spouse dies the other automatically assumes the entire interest in the property. As a rule, one spouse cannot unilaterally terminate or convey the tenancy by the entirety. Most important for our discussion, the property can only be reached by creditors of joint debts of the couple. The creditors of one spouse cannot attach and sell an interest in tenancy by the entirety property (Singer 2017, 361–62).[11] In most states, the creditor can record the lien (i.e., the financial claim against the property), but the lien does not attach or encumber the property except if the spouses divorce or if the nondebtor spouse dies.[12] If the debtor spouse dies, the nondebtor spouse has the right to remain undisturbed in her occupancy. In order to gain the protections of tenancy by the entirety, spouses must either title their property in the tenancy by the entirety form or, in several states, there is a presumption that property held jointly by spouses is tenancy by the entirety property.[13]

Tenancy by the entirety is particularly attentive to protecting the home. In some states, such as Illinois, legislation formally limits tenancy by the entirety property to the family home.[14] In one-third of the states recognizing tenancy by the entirety, the protection applies only to real estate.[15] Commercial real estate can often be held as tenancy by the entirety property, and some states have specifically extended tenancy by the entirety protection to financial instruments and brokerage accounts.[16] In most cases, the home receives the strongest protection de facto as the most valuable real estate asset of most households, and typically the largest household asset of *any* type (Pew Research Center 2011, 24–25). So long as the debt is only of one spouse, tenancy by the entirety creates strong protection for the residence that is similar in some respects to unlimited homestead exemptions. There is one major exception to tenancy by the entirety's protection. In *United States v. Craft*, the Supreme Court held that when the unilateral debt is a federal tax lien, the US government can levy, or collect, on the lien.[17]

High or unlimited homestead exemptions and tenancy by the entirety impose a variety of second-order costs and distributive consequences. Such laws promote overinvestment in protected forms of property, raise the cost of credit, and disproportionately harm lower-income borrowers. Residents of states with unlimited homestead exemptions pay higher interest rates than residents of states with lower exemptions and are at increased risk of credit denial (Gropp, Scholz, and White 1997, 230–31). Poor families are the most severely affected by the increased cost of credit and denial of credit, despite their inability to take advantage of unlimited exemptions (Hynes 2006, 512–15). Special protections also create opportunities for abuse (Zywicki 2005, 1086–88). For example, O. J. Simpson evaded the $33.4 million civil judgment against him for his ex-wife's death by purchasing a multimillion-dollar mansion in Florida, and Ken Lay, Enron's former CEO, diverted his assets to his $7.1 million penthouse in Houston, Texas; both of these states have unlimited homestead exemptions (S. M. Stern 2009, 1104). As a result of such abuses, federal legislation now restricts the use of these exemptions in cases of criminal conduct or intentional tort judgment and requires a lengthy domicile period to prevent debtors from moving states to dodge creditor claims.[18]

The psychological and social benefits of retaining one's home are an important, though not exclusive, justification for the costs imposed by homestead exemptions and tenancy by the entirety. Court cases and legislative history repeatedly reference the home as uniquely important to its owners and deserving of heightened protection. The legislative history of the Texas homestead exemption, for example, describes the home as "sacred" and "the grandest foundation, yet conceived" to promote personal industry and independence.[19] Similarly, in the well-known case of *Sawada v. Endo*, a married couple sought to shield their home from the husband's creditors via tenancy by the entirety.[20] The trial court judge expressed particular concern that the law respect the bond to their home, saying, "That's their residence. . . . No one is going to take that right away" (P. A. Cain 2009, 102).

The view of residential property as psychologically special and personally transformative also features in scholarship on property law. The most influential formulation of this view is Margaret Radin's (1982, 991–1002) theory of property for personhood, which employs homes as the paradigmatic example of property constitutive of personhood. The loss of personhood property "causes pain that cannot be relieved by the object's replacement" (959). Maintaining a secure and ongoing relationship with certain forms of property is vital to being a person and to human flourishing (958–59). Accordingly, personhood property warrants some degree of prima facie protection under the law because its loss impairs personhood (1014). Radin focuses most heavily on homes as property for personhood but also cites body parts such as kidneys, wedding rings, family portraits, clothing, and in some cases cars as property along the personhood end of the continuum (959, 966, 1001, 1005). Fungible property, which is readily interchangeable and held for trade or other instrumental reasons, does not play the same role in personhood and need not receive special protection. For example, Radin describes commercial real estate as fungible and thus deserving lower levels of protection against uncompensated government expropriation of land (i.e., Fifth Amendment takings in US law) and conflicts over free speech rights on commercial premises (1007–11). It is not clear why commercial property that enables one's livelihood, which is often a foremost aspect of personal identity, is not personhood property (S. T. Fiske 1998).

An important task of a property law system is to sift through claims about the personal and psychological importance of property in order to assess, in a rough fashion, the nature and likely degree of harm from loss. There is an incentive for individuals and interest groups to exaggerate their degree of attachment to goods in order to garner valuable protections and benefits. Rent-seeking refers to the practice of seeking to extract benefits or "rents" through the political process (e.g., subsidies or regulations that advantage certain groups at the expense of competitors) (Tullock 1967). In some cases, interest groups seek to mask rent-seeking in claims about the psychological importance of the home and the grave impact of home loss. For example, foreclosure relief legislation and the home mortgage interest deduction have received support from the construction industry and homeowner groups that reference the special importance of the home (S. M. Stern 2009, 1101–03, 1130). State legislatures similarly stress the sentimental and symbolic aspects of home, yet the principal value to states of homestead exemptions and tenancy by the entirety is to attract wealthy residents who boost spending and line tax coffers (Brinig and Buckley 1996, 202–03). Rent-seeking underscores the need for empirical analysis to counterweight politicized claims, but by the same token it illuminates how political interests may impede evidence-based policy making.

There are three principal claims about the psychological primacy of residential property that support stringent debtor protections for the home. First, people form heightened psychological attachment to homes (and their status as homeowners) such that maintaining one's home is important to avoid psychological injury and support personal identity (cf. Radin 1982). Second, maintaining ownership of one's particular home may promote psychological well-being by avoiding the stressors and harms to social ties from relocation. (Barros 2006). Third, debtor protections can increase the likelihood that people have sufficient assets to procure stable shelter following foreclosure. The capability to have some form of shelter is an important aspect of well-being in property, philosophy, and psychology scholarship (Mulvaney and Singer 2018; A. Sen 2005, 158–59; Molnar, Rath, and Klein 1990; Lisa A. Goodman, Saxe, and Harvey 1991). These psychological rationales carry differing implications for debtor protection law. If high levels of injury derive from the social fissures and disruptions of relocation, complete protection against creditors that enables people to stay put in their homes is a rational policy choice. Very strong attachments to one's home may justify "stay put" protection, or, as a second choice, receiving exempted money from home equity as de facto compensation for home loss. Both stay put protection for the home and partial protection of monetary proceeds from the home's sale reduce the risk that debtors will become homeless or insecurely housed.

In the following sections, we consider whether the empirical evidence regarding these three claims about the psychological importance of retaining one's home supports high levels of protection for the residence and state laws incentivizing debtors to reinvest in owner-occupied residential real estate.

Attachments and Identity Functions of Residential Property

If a man owns a little property that property is him, it's part of him and it's like him . . . and in some way he's bigger because he owns it. (Steinbeck [1939] 1992)

The belief in owners' special attachments to their homes and the home's role in identity are important rationales for protections that enable debtors to keep their particular home or exempt high dollar amounts. Yet, the psychology research does not indicate that residential real estate holds a unique or preeminent position in people's self-construct or attachments. Instead, psychology research reveals that personality characteristics, values, social roles, and one's body parts are the conceptual categories most closely linked with self or rated most meaningful. A study of 1,500 American adults asked to tell the experimenters about themselves found that personality characteristics and roles (e.g., mother) accounted for 60 to 72 percent of the responses, with the remainder of responses largely describing activities such as work and hobbies (A. P. Fiske 1998, 927–29). In another study by Russell Belk, participants rated ninety-six cards, each representing a type of physical possession, public place, body organ, person, or personal value, on a four-point scale of "self" and "not self" (1987, 154–56). Relatives, friends, and body organs outranked "own dwelling" in the ratings, as did items such as a favorite vacation place, hair, and the United States. Participants rated "own dwelling" similarly to items such as favorite casual clothes, favorite vehicle now owned, and favorite book. Other research by Deborah Prentice (1987) finds that personal and family memorabilia (e.g., photo albums, diaries) are more strongly linked to self than residential homes. The link between owner-occupied residential property and personhood is also tenuous. A study of 500 households found that homes were rated toward the "necessities" end of a continuum along with money, furniture, and cars and not as symbolic property (Richins 1994). In another study, 55 percent of people asked to describe the feelings associated with their dwelling did not offer responses that included emotions, undermining an account of dwellings as deeply entangled with one's personhood (Csikszentmihalyi and Rochberg-Halton 1981, 126–27).

Only one empirical study has found that homes are more important to identity than other types of possessions (Ball and Tasaki 1992, 166). In this study, participants rated a list of ten personal possessions on a relation-to-self scale. Participants rated the "family home" as most connected to self. However, the evocative phrasing of "family home" and some methodological issues in the way the researchers posed the questions about the various items may have affected the findings. Also, the experiment did not specify whether the home refers solely to the physical housing structure or includes personal possessions and mementos within the home that would inflate its relation to self (see, e.g., Prentice 1987; Richins 1994).

Contrary to law's focus on residential property, an extensive body of research establishes that social relations—not possessions—are the most important contributor to psychological well-being and development (Snyder and Cantor 1998, 654; S. M. Stern 2009; Fagundes 2017). Social interaction is highly correlated with functioning and mental health (Altman and Low 1992, 7), and social relationships are key developers of self and identity (Baumeister 1998, 680). In general, lonely people report higher stress, anxiety, and negative mood; poorer attention; and greater sensitivity to perceived threats or rejection (Cacioppo et al. 2006, 1080–85). Loneliness also has physical effects, with studies showing that it decreases health and longevity in a similar magnitude to smoking, high blood pressure, and obesity (House, Umberson, and Landis 1988, 300–18). The empirical literature does not reveal a comparable magnitude of injurious effect associated with home loss.

In summary, psychology research supports the claim that people have psychological attachments to their possessions, including their homes. However, the evidence does not support the *degree* of protection afforded to the owned home in unlimited or high-value homestead protections and in tenancy by the entirety, as well as in other areas of property law. The psychology evidence also undermines legal theories of residential property as personally transformative or property for personhood. The empirical evidence suggests that one's particular home is less important to self and identity than the legal system has assumed. Conversely, other forms of property, such as real estate for one's small business, tools for one's trade, and even everyday household items, may be more psychologically meaningful than law has allowed (Csikszentmihalyi and Rochberg-Halton 1981, 108–09; Prentice 1987; Richins 1994).

Relocation and the Psychology of Adaptation

Even though homes play only a moderate role in identity and attachments, it is possible that home loss can still wreak serious injury through the stresses of relocation and loss of local social ties. The empirical evidence also sheds light on this claim. The research to date indicates psychological costs to relocation, but these costs are typically neither overwhelming nor long-lasting. The evidence, particularly in the United States, is mixed, with some studies finding no mental health effects from forced relocation (Pollack and Lynch 2009) and others finding harm to mental health from eviction following mortgage or rental arrears (see, e.g., Cagney et al. 2014; Pevalin 2009). It is not clear in what measure the harms reported are due to the financial stress of debt, the prospect of homelessness or insecure housing, the protracted and uncertain process of bankruptcy or foreclosure, or, as is most relevant to unlimited homestead and tenancy by the entirety protections, the loss of one's particular residence. Certainly, the short-term process of foreclosure is unpleasant, and there is evidence of increased depression, anxiety, and psychological distress during this period (Pollack and Lynch 2009; Vásquez-Vera et al. 2017, 202).

Psychology research suggests that adaptation, or the tendency of people to return to their baseline levels of well-being, may mitigate the harms from home dispossession in debt and bankruptcy cases. Research on adaptation has found that most people return to prior levels of happiness in a relatively short amount of time following both negative and positive events (Gilbert 2006). Residential moves, including forced relocation, cause short-term stress but often do not affect long-term psychological functioning (Bolan 1997, 226). People tend to adapt to geographic change and report well-being and satisfaction similar to their premobility state in relatively short order (Cuba and Hummon 1993, 120, 123–27; Ward and Styles 2003, 353). Some research suggests that migrants settle and create new social ties in six to eighteen months on average (Carlisle-Frank 1992, 835–38). Migrants typically mitigate the personal disruption of relocation by maintaining traditions, re-creating social roles in the new location, and decorating their new homes in ways that express their identities (for a summary of this research, see S. M. Stern 2009). Some studies of relocation following natural disaster find ongoing psychological distress, though more recent research that controls for variables related to the disaster and preexisting mental health problems shows either no long-term effects or smaller negative effects (Salcioglu, Başoğlu, and Livanou 2008, 55).

The psychological meaning and effect of relocation may be more severe if the move is the result of intentional acts, not of necessity, targeted at a small number of people. This is often the case with government expropriation of land. Research on forced relocation at the hands of government suggests that it carries more risk of negative mental health effects, but for most people the long-term effects are limited (Steinglass and Gerrity 1990, 410–13; Fischer 2002, 179–81). For example, the late 1950s redevelopment of Boston's tight-knit immigrant community of the West End was one of the most disruptive mass relocations in the history of American urban renewal. West Enders experienced great upset at the bulldozing of their community and forced dispersion. Yet, even in this case, one of the most severe in its destruction of psychological attachments to home, identity, and social ties, two years later 75 percent of former West Enders had acclimated to their new homes and reported positive well-being (Fried 1966, 360). Approximately 25 percent reported that they still felt sad or depressed (as a baseline, around 7 percent of the general adult population suffers from depression) (Fried 1966, 360; National Institute of Mental Health 2018).

In addition to the mitigating effects of adaptation, it may be that relocation is not very disruptive to social relationships, which are a key predictor of psychological well-being. While property law sometimes assumes a rich web of neighborhood social relationships, most neighborhood social ties are weak or intermediate. This means that in most cases neighborhood residents talk occasionally, often recognize each other by face rather than name, and occasionally exchange favors (Campbell 1990). The average person has a few strong social ties to neighbors (strong social ties are more intimate, trusting relationships) (Hampton and Wellman 2003; see also Putnam 2000, 274–75). Contrary to legal theories attributing a deep social function to residential property, the evidence suggests that one's neighborhood provides familiarity and occasional help, rather than strong social ties or a deep sense of community.

Given the moderate impacts of relocation, why does property law often assume the worst? The psychology research shows that people tend to overestimate the emotional consequences of preference satisfaction or preference frustration. This bias leads to systematic overestimation of the decline in well-being from negative events, as well as widespread overestimation of the increase in well-being from positive events (Wilson and Gilbert 2005, 131). It is possible, though not conclusively established, that loss aversion (the strong preference to avoid losses rather than acquire gains) occurs as a result of systematic overestimation of the impact on happiness from losses and systematic underestimation of the happiness bump from gains (Kerner et al. 2006, 649–53). These errors in what psychologists term "affective forecasting" apply to housing change as well. In a 2003 study, Dunn and colleagues found that students overestimated the degree of happiness or upset from their housing lottery results in significant part because they overweighted the physical features of their housing (room size, privacy, number of roommates, etc.) and underweighted social features that were less variable between housing units (Dunn, Wilson, and Gilbert 2003, 1429–30). There is also some evidence that involuntary relocation can provide psychological benefits, including residential satisfaction, employment, and personal growth (Fried 1966, 371–75).[21] Of course, it is not clear if such opportunities are available to owners who lose their homes as a result of creditor claims and thus are at increased risk of "downward moves" to areas of less opportunity.

The available evidence on the harms of forced relocation does not support unlimited exemptions or stay-put rights, but it may justify more moderate relief and protection (cf. Maciá 2016, 990–99). The fact that ill effects are often short-term does not necessitate concluding that no protection should be available. However, averaging psychological costs over time supports more moderate levels of protection as a starting place (later we will discuss vulnerable populations and their case for heightened protection). Another important qualification is that psychology research does not—and cannot—measure every injury. There may be injuries from loss that are not captured by the typical measures that psychologists use. For example, affronts to dignity and autonomy may inflict injury not captured by common psychological metrics.

Homelessness and Insecure Shelter

Thus far, our discussion has focused on relocation between residences. A different and far more serious situation ensues when people lack any secure shelter. Losing residential property to one's debts can leave debtors with inadequate capital to rent or buy a new dwelling. States with low-dollar-amount exemptions relative to housing costs, and prohibitions on debtors opting into the federal bankruptcy exemptions, run this risk.[22] Psychology research and public health studies make clear that homelessness or "underhousing" (grossly inadequate or unstable housing) is psychologically harmful (Lisa A. Goodman, Saxe, and Harvey 1991; Herman, Susser, and Struening 1998, 133–39). Concededly, these studies are challenging because mental illness is a major cause of homelessness. However, even in the case of preexisting mental illness, evidence suggests that homelessness intensifies mental health problems, likely due in part to barriers to medical care (Baggett et al. 2010). Some studies of children have found negative psychological and social impacts attributable to homelessness, such as withdrawn behavior, somatic complaints (e.g., fatigue), and lower school attendance, although the evidence is mixed (Buckner et al. 1999; cf. Harpaz-Rotem, Rosenheck, and Desai 2006 (finding no effect on children's self-reported emotional distress but large effect on school attendance)). Homelessness also raises the risk of psychologically pernicious experiences such as criminal victimization, trauma, and employment loss.

Implications

Turning first to homestead exemptions, the psychology research calls into question extending unlimited or high-dollar-value homestead exemptions based on the psychological value of maintaining one's particular home. The psychological harms to attachment, identity, and well-being from relocation appear moderate, or in some cases modest, in size and time-limited. Accordingly, partial homestead exemptions, which exempt a specified amount of home equity from creditor claims, appear to be a more proportionate response to psychological injury. It may be that nonpsychological harms provide better support for unlimited homestead exemptions, such as the economic harm to property values of neighboring homes and the risk that foreclosures will spread across neighborhoods as a result. However, unlimited homestead exemptions are poorly designed to address such harms. Unlimited homestead exemptions typically extend to all homeowners rather than targeting neighborhoods with more frequent bank sales of homes or greater risk to neighborhood property values.

The partial homestead exemption provides money to homeowners in many cases (i.e., their exempted equity), which reduces the risk that they will have insufficient funds to procure other housing. Renters are less well protected from this risk, although they can elect federal exemptions that are sometimes more generous to nonhomestead property or, in some states, shift some of the unused homestead exemption to protect personal property. In light of the empirical evidence of harm from homelessness or underhousing, a global exemption amount—rather than a generous exemption available only to homeowners—might better protect renters from the risk that they will be financially unable to procure replacement shelter (and also reduce ex ante incentives to invest in highly protected property types). One shortcoming of a global exemption is that, unlike specific bankruptcy exemptions, it cannot be tailored to counteract tendencies to over- or underinvest in certain kinds of property (Lewinsohn-Zamir 2003, 1722–30). For example, debtors might systematically over- or underinvest in shelter to the detriment of other property and their psychological and financial well-being. Reasonable levels of category-specific bankruptcy exemptions (e.g., for homes, vehicles, household goods, books) can counteract these tendencies by protecting a diversity of property, but only when these laws require the debtor to retain the item of property itself or to purchase a substitute of the same type and if the government chooses a mix of property exemptions that actually safeguards well-being. Empirical research is needed to determine the comparative effects on well-being from allowing owners to freely choose which property they will exempt versus requiring them to retain a diversity of different, specified categories of property. Another alternative is to extend the homestead exemption to residential leases, with the exemption based on rental value.

The psychology research on the harms from lack of stable shelter also has implications for laws in several states that require debtors to reinvest proceeds from the homestead exemption in another homestead. These laws can raise housing costs for financially fragile debtors who might be better off renting or cohousing with relatives. It may be that such laws seek to encourage homeownership, which can have psychological and social value for communities. However, as Stephanie M. Stern (2009; 2011, 903–12) has described, the values attributed to homeownership are more modest than assumed and derive mostly from increased duration of residence. The benefits of homeownership are unlikely to accrue if financially unstable debtors purchase new homesteads only to find themselves at risk of losing their homes again. Extending the statutory definition of reinvestment in the homestead to include not only purchased homes but also debtors' subsequent rental leases, or offering exceptions based on financial hardship are options to address these concerns. Another option is for states to eschew reinvestment requirements, which many states have done.

The psychological evidence similarly does not support tenancy by the entirety's across-the-board protection of the nondebtor spouse's (and thus in practice the debtor spouse's) rights to remain in the house. Like unlimited homestead exemptions, the strong protection from tenancy by the entirety is outsized relative to the psychological harms of home loss, assuming the debtors are not left without shelter. Altering or eliminating tenancy by the entirety protections so that the nondebtor spouse receives the cash proceeds of her share of the home may provide a better calibrated response to identity and relocation harms. Another option might be to replace tenancy by the entirety with a right of first refusal for the nondebtor spouse, which would allow the nondebtor spouse to buy out the creditor's claim to the debtor spouse's interest (Lewinsohn-Zamir 2009, 1404–08).

In some states, courts have imposed common law limitations on tenancy by the entirety that seek a middle ground. For example, in *SEC v. Antar*, a federal district court in New Jersey partitioned the tenancy by the entirety (i.e., legally severed the tenancy by the entirety in order to eliminate protections from creditor claims) for the defendants' vacation home and commercial property in a securities fraud case, but retained the tenancy by the entirety protection for the marital home.[23] For the marital home, the court held that although the plaintiff creditor could not jointly occupy the home, the creditor was due one-half the rental value of the home. Levying the debt against the home made the creditor and married couple tenants in common, and the creditor was due a share of the occupancy value of the home.[24] As mentioned previously, the Supreme Court in *United States v. Craft* has also made inroads on tenancy by the entirety protection, holding that the federal government can attach a lien on tenancy by the entirety property in order to satisfy a federal tax debt.[25] The psychology research establishing a moderate psychological attachment to one's residence and limited psychological harm from relocation supports intermediate solutions, such as those described here, that deliver partial protection to homeowners. In addition, limited protections better advance the goals of keeping the cost of credit low for all borrowers and minimizing strategic behavior to evade debt collection.

Vulnerable Groups and the Psychological Value of Residential Stability

On average, the psychological value of owner-occupied residential property is more modest than assumed in property law, calling into question stringent, across-the-board home protection. However, there may be particularly vulnerable groups or demographics that experience higher levels of harm and less adaptation over time than the general population. For example, relocations may exact a higher psychological price based on income, age, family status, or even personality traits such as introversion (Oishi 2010). Due to steeper declines in welfare from residential dispossession, vulnerable groups may warrant stronger legal protections or prevention measures. This section considers property laws affecting two vulnerable groups: elderly homeowners and low-income renters. We consider the justifications for existing laws, as well as potential new reforms.

Preferential Property Tax Treatment for Senior Citizens

Real property owners, including residential owners, pay property taxes to local governments based on the value of their property. Property taxes fund local transportation, safety, and education services. When owners can't afford their property taxes (or desire a different ratio and mix of taxes to residential amenities), they relocate to a new town, downsize, or transition to renting. This has become a particular issue for senior citizens, who are more likely to be single, on a fixed income, and longtime residents. Many state and local governments have heeded the cry from senior citizens who wish to "age in place" by reducing property taxes for elderly homeowners. Apart from any psychological considerations, local governments have incentives to offer benefits that attract seniors who typically do not have school-age children to strain local school budgets.

State and local property tax laws that shield seniors from market-rate taxation take a number of forms (Christopherson 2005, 205–07; Babe 2005, 325–35). Property tax exemptions for seniors on their homes decrease the amount of the property's assessed value subject to taxation. A more generous variant, the assessment freeze, does not allow the assessed value of low-income senior citizens' houses to increase at all, translating into low and more stable taxes. Other jurisdictions use property tax credits that reduce the total property tax paid. While these programs increase affordability and the opportunities for seniors to maintain their homes, they also impose a variety of costs. These tax protections create tax benefits for elderly homeowners at the expense of families with children and distort mobility decisions by providing incentives for seniors to stay put. Tax advantages also stymie the goal of moving property to the highest-valuing users as elderly homeowners retain homes that they might have otherwise have sold. In addition, more whites than African Americans or Latinos benefit from these provisions because of the higher rate of white homeownership (T. M. Shapiro 2006, 67–68, 74; Coulson 1999).

Given these substantial costs, property law should have strong justifications for departing from tax neutrality. The psychology research suggests that the elderly may provide compelling rationales.[26] While owners as a whole do not seem to be psychologically devastated in the long term from dislocation, the research indicates that the elderly value their residence more highly and may be more vulnerable to psychological harm. Elderly individuals are the least mobile demographic group and report the greatest attachments to home and community, even when controlling for duration of residence (Sampson 1988, 774). The direction of causation is unclear. Does the psychological importance of home to the elderly depress mobility or does immobility promote attachment to the home? For the purposes of legal design, the end result is the same: higher psychological burdens on elderly residents. Compared with their younger counterparts, the elderly also report that the home is more central to their personal identity and report higher satisfaction with their homes independent of its physical condition (Belk 1987, 157–58). Unlike young and middle-aged individuals, who tend to value residential and home amenities most highly, home satisfaction for the elderly is due to memories, competence in a familiar environment, the value of independent living, and affordability (O'Bryant 1982, 359).

These psychological impacts underscore the need for property laws attentive to the elderly. However, it is not clear that undifferentiated tax benefits are the most desirable option. Currently, many states do not target tax benefits for the elderly based on income. California is one of the few states to adopt a graduated scale that varies the amount of tax exemptions between $75,000 and $175,000 based on age and income.[27] Other states have circuit-breaker provisions, which operate independently or piggyback onto other tax breaks for elderly homeowners and reduce the property taxes of senior citizens who fall within specified income limits (Christopherson 2005). From the perspective of psychology and policy, applying tax benefits to senior citizens who can afford market-rate property taxes is a windfall, not a legal protection targeted to the harms of relocation.

The psychology research suggests another way to fine-tune property tax laws: applying or adjusting property tax benefits to elderly owners based on their duration of residence. However, such reforms may fail to completely respond to the harms to the elderly. As mentioned earlier, senior citizens report additional attachment to home regardless of the length of time they have been in a residence, when compared with younger residents. For younger property owners, there is some empirical evidence that psychological attachment, including aversion to loss, increases over the time property is in one's possession (M. A. Strahilevitz and Loewenstein 1998). More research would be helpful to establish whether the duration in a residence similarly enhances the attachments of elderly residents to their homes, and also whether the owner's advanced age and his or her duration of residence interact to create larger psychological attachments and dependencies than either variable standing alone.

An interesting alternative to traditional tax relief is to enable senior citizens to pay their property taxes from their home equity. Approximately half of the states have property tax deferral laws that allow elderly residents to defer paying all or part of their taxes until the residence is sold or they die (Babe 2005, 330–31; Christopherson 2005, 207). The state then levies on the accumulated taxes owed plus interest. These deferment programs are underutilized in many states, seemingly due to a combination of poor marketing and, in some states, high interest rates (Babe 2005, 332). Private providers have filled this void in recent years. A lending product called a "reverse mortgage" allows homeowners to extract equity from their house (essentially lending to themselves) with the debt paid from the proceeds of their home's sale upon their death. While these products have sparked controversy due to concerns about deceptive marketing, reverse mortgages are nonetheless a rapidly growing market (Wang, Valdez, and Piggott 2008).

Reverse mortgages and state and local tax deferment programs avoid many of the distortions and distributional concerns of traditional senior tax reductions. Because owners self-fund their taxes, there is no loss of local tax revenues. These options also respond to the perennial problem of variability in psychological needs and preferences. Because owners have to opt into these products at the expense of their home equity, reverse mortgages and deferment programs identify owners with strong preferences to age in place and are thus more efficient than across-the-board subsidies such as senior citizen tax freezes (cf. Fennell 2005, 1401–05, 1450–51).[28] Of course, there are also limitations. Property tax deferral and reverse mortgages rely on home equity and appreciation, and thus cannot help homeowners who do not have substantial home equity or during severe housing downturns.

Eviction for Low-Income Tenants

While homeowners receive a breadth of legal protections for their residences, renters' protections are more limited in most American states. This appears to be due to a combination of factors. Psychological attachments to the owned home are more prominent in legal discourse and, as discussed previously, there is a cultural belief that homeownership promotes personal industry and civic participation (S. M. Stern 2009, 2011). Importantly, homeowners are on average wealthier and more likely to vote (DiPasquale and Glaeser 1999), which enhances their ability to lobby for legislation to protect their assets, including their homes.

Landlord-tenant law, which is a combination of private contract (the lease) and state law, governs the relationship between landlords and tenants. Eviction is a major topic of landlord-tenant law. Rental leases typically address the actions, or nonactions, of tenants that give rise to the landlord's right to evict, including failure to pay rent, property damage, and noise and disturbance. State laws specify the process of eviction, including the notice due to the tenant, the formalities the landlord must observe, and the tenant's rights of recourse and appeal. In many states, accelerated eviction processes give tenants only a handful of days to vacate their rentals. For example, California's landlord-tenant law allows landlords to serve tenants with a notice to cure a violation of the lease in three days or to vacate.[29] If the tenant does not vacate voluntarily, the landlord must bring suit against the tenant in a special housing court to continue the eviction. If the tenant has legal assistance or sufficient education and resources to learn the law and argue her own case (neither of which is common in eviction cases), there are a number of ways to prevent or delay eviction, including arguing that the landlord failed to maintain the property according to the lease or applicable laws or that the eviction is retaliation for the tenant exercising her legal rights (Singer 2017, 481–82, 484–86). If the landlord wins the eviction suit, the tenant must vacate within five days with very limited extensions for severe hardships (e.g., a grave medical condition that requires more time for the tenant to move).[30]

Sociologist Matthew Desmond has undertaken extensive research on the prevalence and effects of eviction on low-income tenants. Focusing on tenants in Milwaukee, Wisconsin, he and his coresearchers accessed court records of evictions, collected data on mental and physical health following eviction, and interviewed evicted tenants. His research reveals a massive, and previously underappreciated, eviction phenomenon among the urban poor. In an average year, tenants living in 3.5 percent of Milwaukee's rental units, and more than 7 percent of its rentals in impoverished areas, were evicted via formal legal process (presumably, many more were evicted informally, without resort to court process) (Desmond 2012, 97; for similar findings, see Edin and Lein 1997, 53). African American women are the most strongly affected, accounting for half of evicted tenants (Desmond 2012, 102). The most common reason for eviction was failure to pay rent (Desmond and Kimbro 2015, 297). A startling 94 percent of the people evicted in the Milwaukee eviction court study did not receive any form of government housing assistance, despite the vast majority having very low incomes (Desmond 2012, 101).

Using longitudinal data of 2,676 mothers and children from the Fragile Families and Child Well-Being Study, Desmond and his coresearchers found that eviction correlated with large increases in depression and parenting stress in the year following eviction (Desmond and Kimbro 2015, 312). In addition, the mothers who had recently been evicted reported poorer health for both themselves and their children and increased financial hardship and difficulty obtaining necessities (e.g., food and shelter) (312–16). While these effects shrank over time (similar to the relocation studies discussed earlier), the short-term effects appear more severe among evicted low-income mothers (317). Other research supports these findings, including work by Manzo, Kleit, and Couch (2008) that found that repeat moves, typically due to housing unaffordability and eviction, impose high psychological stress on low-income, urban residents. These effects do not appear to be due to preexisting mental or physical health conditions. In order to rule out that mental health or other health conditions, financial hardship, or other factors increased the risk of eviction (rather than eviction increasing the risk of mental health and other harms), Desmond and Kimbro (2015, 303–10) compared the evicted mothers to a set of nonevicted mothers otherwise matched along a wide variety of characteristics.

The empirical evidence of the psychological injury and other harms from eviction supports greater public investment in housing assistance for low-income renters. Housing assistance may take the form of subsidized vouchers for private rentals or publicly constructed housing. Such assistance has declined over the past thirty years relative to the numbers of needy tenants. The research calls into question the adequacy of private markets to provide stable housing to low-income tenants and establishes the psychological effects of eviction as a major cost to government nonintervention in housing provision. As an alternative to dedicated housing subsidies, cash assistance offers tenants more flexibility to prevent eviction or, in the event that this fails, to buffer the economic shock of relocation. Cash subsidies, however, are politically unpopular compared with in-kind housing assistance, such as public housing or vouchers for private rental housing (S. M. Stern forthcoming). Also, as we discuss in chapter 4, in-kind housing assistance may have countervailing benefits, including to better support the recipient's dignity.

Property law could also limit the public availability of eviction records. A record of eviction harms tenants' prospects for new housing. Lack of stable housing in turn hinders job seeking and employment. Desmond (2012, 91) compares the stain of eviction for African American women to the mark of incarceration that inhibits the long-term prospects of African American men. How do these records occur? Evictions secured through housing court generate records of the court judgments. Landlords can report the nonpayment of rent to credit bureaus and agencies (the unpaid rent appears as negative history in the credit report and lowers the credit score). Rental applications typically ask about a past history of eviction, and property managers often call past landlords to check references. The mark of eviction is thus many-layered and difficult to eradicate entirely. However, property law might limit its impact in a few different ways. For example, it is not evident why eviction for nonpayment of rent due to severe housing unaffordability should stymie one's chance to obtain government-subsidized housing— indeed, it might be evidence of a household's need for such subsidies. Yet, housing authorities often count a past eviction against applicants for subsidized housing units and programs (Desmond 2012, 119). Housing agencies might alter this practice so that evictions for nonpayment of rent do not affect one's prospects for subsidized housing. Alternatively, housing agencies could consider prior evictions, but exempt evictions that occurred when the applicant's prior rent or the area's average rental rate constituted a severe rent burden, typically measured as more than 50 percent of the renter's pretax income (this describes most evicted tenants).

With respect to the private rental market, property law might require eviction records to be sealed after a period of time has elapsed without an intervening eviction. Similar to debtors whose bankruptcies are deleted from their credit reports after seven to ten years, sealing or expunging eviction records after a period of time would eventually allow tenants a fresh start. This reform would not, however, resolve the short-term problems tenants face in finding new housing following eviction. It may also indirectly increase housing costs in tight rental markets by raising the costs for landlords, who must accept more risk in the absence of information about applicants' rental history. On balance, however, this is a modest modification that seems unlikely to have major effects on rental supply.

Another option to address the psychological harms of eviction is to make it more difficult, or slower, for landlords to evict tenants. However, there are potential harms from altering landlord-tenant law in these ways. Most US markets have rental undersupplies that enable landlords to pass the costs of additional legal protections on to tenants in the form of higher rent. Some landlords will opt to bypass the hassles of protracted evictions by converting their units to condominiums or other owned housing, thereby further shrinking supply and raising costs. Tenants in the United States are already severely cost-burdened (Joint Center for Housing 2017, 28–33; Collinson 2011). While a longer window of time to vacate would reduce stress and increase the opportunity for the tenant to find adequate new housing, these reforms might come at the expense of rental affordability. Moreover, these legal reforms primarily forestall, rather than prevent, eviction. Laws forbidding landlords from evicting nonpaying or otherwise defaulting tenants are vulnerable to claims that they are unconstitutional takings of private property under US law.

In closing, there is weak protection for residents of rental properties in the US legal system despite psychological evidence of the sizable effects of eviction on the well-being and life prospects of tenants, who are primarily low-income. Further research on which variables produce eviction's harmful effects would be helpful to property and land use law reform efforts. We currently do not know the comparative contribution of different facets of eviction to psychological and other harms. These variables include psychological attachment to one's home, disruption of social ties, underhousing or homelessness following eviction, and the difficulty of securing new housing with an eviction record. A firmer model of causation would better guide eviction law reforms.

Is Personal Property Less Psychologically Important Than Homes?

While residential property generally receives robust protection against dispossession, the treatment of personal property is more variable. Personal property, or chattel, refers to tangible property that is not affixed to land (we do not include securities, money, or other financial instruments or intellectual property in our discussion of personal property). Courts and legislators at times seem less inclined, or at least more divided, about offering special protections to personal property based on psychological or sentimental importance. For example, in some states, tenancy by the entirety protection is the default presumption for real estate held by married couples, but not for personal property.[31] Eminent domain jurisprudence also reveals tension about whether personal property merits a lower standard of protection. The Supreme Court noted in *Lucas v. South Carolina Coastal Council* that personal property does not qualify, as real property does, for constitutional protection against regulations that wipe out all of the property's value.[32] Subsequently, the Supreme Court heard *Horne v. Department of Agriculture* to correct the confusion wrought by *Lucas* over the treatment of personal property and held that personal property is due the same constitutional protection under the Fifth Amendment as real property (i.e., land).[33]

The meager rights afforded to tenants who store personal possessions in self-storage facilities provide one example of lower protection of personal property. Self-storage facilities for personal possessions are a booming market, with more than 1.875 billion square feet of leased storage units in the United States as of 2005 (Vanderbilt 2005). Self-storage statutes, which have been enacted in almost every state, create a landlord-tenant relationship that is typically less protective of self-storage consumers than the negligence and other standards applicable in bailment law.[34] Under state statutes, storage facility owners can create a lien, typically within thirty to ninety days of nonpayment or abandonment, and sell the storage locker contents at auction if the tenant fails to pay rent or remove his or her items (Jones 2011b, 1020–21, 1027–32). Nonpayment of rent can occur for a variety of reasons, including because the tenant cannot afford that month's rent; experienced a health issue, hospital stay, or fire; or made a mistake and forgot to pay the rent that month. Compared with residential eviction, there is no requirement of judicial process prior to reselling the tenant's personal property. Moreover, state statutes rarely require commercially reasonable efforts in these auctions, meaning that tenants often receive extremely low prices for their possessions (1015–16).

Another example of weaker protection for personal property is found in state bankruptcy laws. In some states, there is a disparity between the magnitude of protection for personal and residential property in bankruptcy, even accounting for the residence's greater value. State exemptions limit creditors' ability to take personal property such as household goods, books and photographs, vehicles, and clothing in order to satisfy debts. For example, Florida, which offers an unlimited homestead exemption, only protects personal property (i.e., household goods, books, instruments, and clothing but not including motor vehicles) up to $4,000 and does not allow a debtor to claim the personal property exemption if she is claiming a homestead exemption.[35] These laws align with personhood theory's attribution of higher psychological value to the owned home relative to many other forms of property; however, they do not hew to the theory's assertion that fungible property should receive less protection than personhood property. For example, state as well as federal laws offer exemptions for "tools of the trade" despite the fact that tools are typically easily replaced market goods (presumably lawmakers view this protection as enabling the debtor's financial fresh start).

While personal property often receives less protection than residential property, this is not always the case. For example, in the state exemptions in bankruptcy discussed earlier, some forms of property, such as the family Bible or photographs, receive absolute protection.[36] This means that a creditor cannot make any claim to that type of property. The high level of protection reflects not only the personal nature of goods such as Bibles or photographs but also the fact that creditors can use rights to repossess high-sentiment, very low market value goods to coerce or harass debtors over repayment.[37] Other states protect categories of property up to a certain dollar amount for each category;[38] a few states allow a "wild card" exemption for any personal property of the debtor's choosing up to a specified value.[39] In no case, however, are there unlimited exemptions for any financially valuable category of personal property such as we see with homesteads.

Contrary to the inconsistent legal protections for personal property, the psychology evidence shows that people typically have identifications with and attachments to personal possessions that are as strong as, and often stronger than, those related to residential property. For example, in one study, fifty college students sorted seventy possessions into as few or as many piles as they wished based on similarities in the source of why someone might value them (Prentice 1987, 996). Family heirlooms, diaries, photographs, and old letters were most strongly linked to self, while the family house was most frequently grouped with "everyday possessions" such as furniture (995–96). Another study asked 248 participants to sort cards representing persons, places, body parts, intangibles (e.g., feelings, memories), and material things into "self" or "not self" groupings and then to further sort the "self" group into "a little related to self" versus "a lot related to self" (Belk 1987, 153–56). Feelings and values were the most related to self, followed by body parts, family members, and skills and education. The next tier down for identity construction included items such as favorite clothes, favorite vehicle owned, favorite book, and two residential property items, dwelling and favorite room. Rated only slightly lower were items such as favorite jewelry, art, sporting goods, and family heirlooms.

Among items of personal property, people report particularly strong attachments to property received as a gift, possessions that link the owner to her past, and collections or creations (Belk 1988). Theoretical work in psychology suggests that possessions can become "an extended self" that represents, develops, and communicates the owner's personal identity (Belk 1987, 1988). Possessions support self-expression by enabling owners to concretely express their values, attitudes, personal history, identity, or social status (Belk 1988). In some cases, attachments to possessions can skirt the line between human and object relations. An intriguing study by Lastovicka and Sirianni (2011, 337) found that people not uncommonly develop feelings of love for consumer possessions more akin to love for a person than object attachment; loneliness appears to mediate, or cause, this level of emotional attachment to possessions. The psychology research also reveals substantial variability in the possessions that people form attachments to and view as part of their identities. Some owners list possessions that symbolize identity or memories as their most treasured possessions, while other people cite instrumental possessions such as vehicles or tools (Prentice 1987, 998; Csikszentmihalyi and Rochberg-Halton 1981, 84–85).

The psychology evidence suggests that many categories of personal property may warrant stronger legal protection on the basis of their relation to self-identity and the strong attachments owners hold. For example, self-storage laws could better reflect property attachments by allowing tenants more time to reclaim their possessions subject to paying back rent, creating fiduciary duties or other rules to increase the likelihood that auctions will fetch fair prices, or allowing postauction redemption periods during which tenants can buy back their property with the amount owed plus interest and back rent (similar to laws that offer postforeclosure redemption periods for residential real estate).

As another example, we might allow people to shift an unused portion of the homestead exemption in bankruptcy to protect personal property. The state of Maine has a version of this that allows an unused portion of the homestead exemption up to $6,000 to be applied to any property.[40] Some states offer global exemptions for any personal property up to a certain dollar amount or include wild card exemptions that can be applied to property of the debtor's choosing, split between property, or stacked on top of existing exemptions.[41] States could also allow a global exemption up to a certain dollar amount for all property, both homestead and personal. These approaches would respond to the psychological evidence that people vary in the particular items of property they develop psychological attachments to (Epley, Waytz, and Cacioppo 2007). However, a global exemption and, to a lesser degree, large wild card exemptions would not address tendencies owners may have to over- or underinvest in protecting certain forms of property in ways that are ultimately detrimental to their well-being (Lewinsohn-Zamir 2003, 1722–30).[42] A global exemption would also fail to reflect the symbolic and expressive values of government protection of certain types of property. For example, many state laws exempt personal Bibles or letters, yet it is uncertain whether creditors will seize these items in a debt collection, since Bibles and letters typically have low or no market value (though creditors may use the threat of seizure of these items to compel payment). Even if these exemptions do not strongly affect debt collection practices, they nonetheless play an important role for citizens by signaling government's respect for religious practice and solicitude toward citizens' personal memories and histories.

Legal approaches to protecting personal property should learn from, and avoid, the excesses of residential property protection, such as unlimited protection. There is evidence that people find ways to reassert personal identity in the face of possession loss (Belk 1988, 143) and that most possessions have a life cycle in which attachments grow, then wane, until eventually the possession is transferred or discarded (Ball and Tasaki 1992, 166). The psychology research reveals that personal possessions and one's particular dwelling are not the strongest contributors to psychological well-being. As we discussed previously, social relationships are more psychologically fundamental to well-being. Research also finds that experiences (e.g., a vacation, a concert) make us happier and are more intimately connected to self-identity than most consumer purchases and possessions (T. J. Carter and Gilovich 2010, 2012; Van Boven and Gilovich 2003).

An impediment to calibrating protection for personal property—and a reason for the current checkerboard of property protections—is that the law does not merely reflect psychological understanding or rational legal design. As we have discussed, special interests lobby for protective regulations that benefit them. Typically, there are more interest groups agitating for residential protections than for similar protections for owners of household goods, vehicles, family photographs, sporting equipment, or other chattels.

Next, we turn to damages under the common law of bailments as an example of some of the challenges of remedying the psychological dimensions of personal property loss. Bailments offer an interesting example, more insulated from political pressures than legislated property laws, of how psychology can inform courts tasked with determining compensation for personal property.

Bailments and the Psychology of Heirlooms

In property law, an owner can deliver personal property to another to keep for a specified purpose, without a transfer of ownership. Bailment law governs the relationship between owners of personal property who leave their property in the care of another (Burke and Snoe 2016, 45, 48–49). The owner is the bailor, and the transferee is the bailee. The bailment typically ends when the bailor retrieves the item. A common example of a bailment is a coat check. At the coat check, the customer does not transfer ownership of her jacket to the attendant. Rather, the attendant stores the jacket until the customer comes to collect it. Assuming the bailor has paid as agreed and not abandoned the property, the failure of the bailee to return the chattel is a conversion that is actionable in a civil lawsuit (Singer 2017, § 16.5).

A major issue in bailment is the measure of compensation for loss of property or damage to it while in bailment. Common law uses fair market value at the time of the loss; for damaged bailments, courts use the fair market value before and after the damage to the property.[43] In many jurisdictions, only if the property lacks a market value (e.g., a photograph of a family member) will courts utilize a measure of the subjective value of the property to its owner (Burke 2003, 214). Other jurisdictions will admit the property's value to the owner regardless of whether evidence of market value is available. Some include subjective or sentimental value explicitly, and other awards appear to implicitly include sentimental value as part of above-market-value compensation. One case has held that if the property has both market value and sentimental value, the plaintiff carries the burden of proving that basing damages on market value alone would be "manifestly unfair."[44]

The case of *Bernhardt v. Ingham Regional Medical Center* illustrates the market value approach.[45] In that case, a Michigan court of appeals judge rejected the plaintiff's claim that the sentimental value of her lost bailment was high enough to meet the required amount in controversy for subject matter jurisdiction. The plaintiff left a ring and a watch at the hospital after removing them to scrub her hands before holding her newborn son. She contacted the hospital, which told her that it had the items. When the plaintiff went to retrieve her jewelry, the hospital told her the items were lost. The plaintiff argued that because the ring was her grandmother's wedding ring and the watch had belonged to her deceased brother, they had sentimental value greater than $25,000. The market value of each item was $300. The court rejected her claim because the two items of jewelry had a readily ascertainable market value, and therefore the court held that it must use market value rather than subjective value.

Psychology research on attachments to personal property argues against this approach and may suggest a partial doctrinal path forward for common law bailment damages. It would be inefficient, and ultimately would substantially raise the cost of bailments for consumers, to offer premiums above fair market value compensation for every piece of property lost or damaged. The psychology research indicates categories of property that owners are likely to value highly. The research converges on property that is linked to memories as particularly psychologically meaningful and likely to be part of one's identity (Richins 1994; Belk 1988; Csikszentmihalyi and Rochberg-Halton 1981). As Russell Belk observes, "Integral to who we are is a sense of our past. Possessions are a convenient means of storing the memories and feelings that attach [us to] our sense of [the] past" (1988, 148). People similarly particularly value gifts that provide linkages to past relationships. For example, family jewelry or an engagement ring may fall into multiple categories of high personal value as linkages to the past, often gifts, that symbolize important relationships. Photographs are another example of a possession that can affix a memory (Csikszentmihalyi and Rochberg-Halton 1981) (though photographs may be less important in today's age of digital photo storage and social media). Possessions associated with bad memories are less likely to be valued by their owners at market value, much less above market value (Belk 1988). However, in some cases, an owner may value a possession that reminds her of adversity she has overcome or historical wrongdoing. If a plaintiff does place sentimental value, or an emotion akin to it, on property associated with a negative memory, she should be allowed to establish that value by offering testimony and other evidence of the special nature of her attachment to the property.

In addition to possessions linked to memories, there is evidence that people have strong attachments to property that they have created, gathered, or curated (Csikszentmihalyi and Rochberg-Halton 1981; Belk 1988). For example, Csikszentmihalyi and Rochberg-Halton's (1981) study of 385 Chicago households found that visual art, often created by members of the household, extended family, or friends, was one of the top three categories of possessions most prized by participants. Similarly, people attach heightened value to collections (Belk 1988). It is not clear if the high value attached to collections and creations is due to the labor involved, the property's strong expressive function, or both. More research would be helpful to replicate these findings, which are somewhat dated, and to contextualize them to judgments about damages for possession loss.

While injury from a possession's loss cannot be calculated with scientific precision in each case, possessions linked to the past and possessions that result from creative effort can be useful categories for judging common law damages. These categories are not the only types of possessions likely to carry sentimental value, but they offer a starting place for the common law of bailments and other cases involving damages for personal property. These categories lend themselves to the multifactor tests that common law courts routinely employ. Alternatively, courts might attach a default premium above market value for damages to property in these categories; this premium could be overcome by the defendant's evidence.

The psychology literature also suggests a different way to think about damages, as not only compensation but a potential means to repair injuries to identity. If we take seriously that some possessions have strong sentimental value, a reasonable question is whether money is an adequate substitute. In some contexts, monetary damages may be commodifying or insulting (for a general discussion of people's preferences with respect to monetary and in-kind remedies, see chapter 8). However, the psychology literature describes some potential benefits of money that are highly relevant to contexts such as lost bailments where recovering the possession itself is not an option. First, money can enable us to acquire new possessions that express or symbolize the aspects of the self that we had previously expressed through the lost or damaged property (Belk 1988). For example, we might replace a lost item of jewelry, given to us by a relative, with a similar piece of jewelry or a nice frame for a photograph of that relative. Second, Belk notes that "money enlarges the sense of self because it enlarges imaginable possibilities of all that we might have and do" (150). Thus, damages premiums for sentimental or deeply personal property may enable not merely second-best compensation but personal development. At this point, these are theories. Before we apply them to law, predictions about the role of money in identity would benefit from empirical testing and validation not only in the laboratory setting but also in field studies of litigation and insurance claims.

The psychology research does not resolve all issues of compensation for personal property in bailment or other areas of property law. There will always be variability among plaintiffs in their attachments to their possessions and the risk that plaintiffs will exaggerate personal attachments to garner more compensation. However, recognizing the sentimental value of property linked to memories and creative effort is more likely to accurately reflect personal losses than either a system of market value damages or across-the-board premiums for all types of possession loss.

Concluding Remarks

A close view of the empirical evidence in psychology suggests that property law has sometimes missed the mark in allocating psychological and sentimental value to different kinds of property. What has emerged in property law, as well as in some aspects of bankruptcy and commercial law, is a patchwork of overprotection of owned residential property and, at times, underprotection of personal and commercial property. Law has bestowed generous, and in some cases complete, protection on owner-occupied residential property. However, the empirical psychology research on homes suggests only moderate psychological importance to one's particular dwelling. At the same time, property law offers less consistent protection for personal, residential leasehold, and commercial property despite research indicating that people can have substantial psychological attachments to them, in some instances more so than to owner-occupied residential property.

PART II

State Interference with Property

3

Takings

Few issues in the field of property law have been as extensively debated as the "takings" issue. The popularity of this issue may be due to the fact that, customarily, a taking is regarded as *the* main interference with private property, and hence necessitates safeguards for owners. Thus, for example, the Fifth Amendment to the US Constitution requires that the taking be for a public use and that the government pay just compensation to the property owner.

For many years, legislators, courts, and commentators have strived to develop rules to determine whether an injury to property by governmental authorities constitutes a taking, thereby requiring state compensation. The existence of a taking is often difficult to determine because most actions by the state affect—either directly or indirectly—the value of some property. Obviously, the state would not be able to carry out its numerous legitimate public functions if it had to compensate for every adverse effect of its actions on property interests.[1] Therefore, legal systems must distinguish between injuries to property that are takings and thus prohibited unless compensation is paid, and losses that result from the operation of the state's police power (i.e., the general regulatory power to protect the safety, health, morals, and welfare of the public), which may be left uncompensated. The value of a parcel of land, for instance, may depreciate due to diverse events, such as expropriation of part of it for a road, restriction of its development rights, a change in its designation to a less profitable use (e.g., from an intensive commercial use to a low-intensity residential use), proximity of the parcel to a public project constituting a nuisance (such as an airport or major highway), or a new property tax. Losses in value that do not involve any physical invasion of the property are commonly labeled "regulatory takings" (Serkin 2016, 257), and the power to expropriate property is also known as "eminent domain."

Once an injury has been classified as a taking and therefore its compensation is warranted, another major issue arises: the *magnitude* of the required compensation. Controversy exists regarding the appropriate measure of compensation. While current legal rules frequently adopt the "fair market value" criterion (i.e., the amount that a willing buyer would pay a willing seller in the market; Dana and Merrill 2002, 169), some scholars have advocated measures that are either higher or lower than this value (see, respectively, Fee 2006, 814–17; Blume and Rubinfeld 1984).

Discussion of all matters pertaining to takings is not required for our purposes. Rather, we focus on key issues that can benefit from psychological insights. The chapter opens with a brief survey of the rules relating to identification of a taking and its compensation. Following this basic introduction, we address various factors that affect the perceived legitimacy of the taking and its adverse impact on property owners. The remainder of the chapter deals with two central topics from a behavioral perspective: (1) When should compensation be paid? and (2) what constitutes just compensation?

General Introduction

Legal systems have formed various tests to determine when an injury to property amounts to a taking. Here, we describe, in broad strokes, the most common kinds of takings and their compensation rules. One main test developed in American case law is "permanent physical occupation." Accordingly, a physical taking of land (or part thereof) or a physical invasion of the land is prohibited without compensation, notwithstanding the potentially small size of the invasion or the lack of substantial economic damages caused (Dana and Merrill 2002, 94).[2] Another test focuses on "harm prevention" and provides that when the injury is intended to preclude a harmful use by the property owner, no compensation is due. This test was used, for example, to justify legislation that required underground coal miners to leave pillars of coal in place to prevent subsidence of structures owned by others on the surface, or that prohibited construction in a flood area.[3] However, the authority cannot use the harm prevention test to totally destroy the value of the land, unless the activity in question is so harmful as to have been discontinued by the background rules of nuisance and property law.[4]

Most injuries involve no physical harm to the land and instead affect property rights through laws or government action. In the seminal case of *Pennsylvania Coal v. Mahon*, the court recognized that property can be taken in a nonphysical way, by economic regulation. Therefore, the court stated that "while property may be regulated to a certain extent, if regulation goes too far it will be recognized as a taking."[5] The question whether regulation has gone "too far" is determined by an ad hoc balancing test, which evaluates three factors: the diminution in value of the property attributable to the regulation, the extent of its interference with the owner's distinct investment-backed expectations, and the character of the governmental action (Serkin 2016, 258–63).[6] The case law reveals that relatively little protection is provided against nonphysical injuries, such as restrictions on the land's development rights. Frequently, even enormous reductions in the land's value are legitimized without compensation. Generally speaking, compensation is paid when the regulation has denied all economic viability or reasonable use of the property. Courts tend to evaluate the injury to the land in light of the parcel as a whole and its possible uses. They focus on identifying "what rights remain" to the owner, rather than "what was taken" from her, and suffice with the fact that some economic use remains (Dana and Merrill 2002, 121–39; Michelman 1967, 1191–93). Some scholars suggest that the borderline between compensation and noncompensation is a two-thirds reduction in the land's value, but there are cases in which even more severe injuries were not compensated (Radin 1991, 257; Sax 1964, 44; see also Alterman 2010, 51; Singer 2017, 743–44).

The treatment of nonphysical injuries is different from that of physical injuries, as the latter are compensated regardless of the fact that the authority took only a small part of the land or that the permanent physical occupation only marginally affected the property owner's enjoyment (Michelman 1967, 1184–86). While the disparate legal treatment of the two types of losses is more pronounced on the federal level than in the states (see Sterk 2004 (arguing that state law and state courts provide the primary protection against takings); Singer 2017, 758–61 (explaining that some states enacted laws that broaden the right to compensation for regulatory takings)), physical and nonphysical injuries still are not dealt with in the same way, and property owners receive greater protection against the former kind of injury than against the latter (A. Bell and Parchomovsky 2017, 2078–81, 2088–92).

Compensation rules that distinguish between physical and nonphysical injuries and afford less protection against the latter type of loss can be found in other countries as well, such as England (Blackhall 2005, 369–76), Canada (Schwartz and Bueckert 2010), and Australia (Sheehan 2010). In contrast, certain countries recognize a generous rule of compensation for nonphysical injuries to land. For example, Israeli planning and building law compensates value reductions caused by restrictions on development rights if the harm exceeds what is reasonable under the circumstances of the case or if compensation is required in the interests of justice.[7] Courts have interpreted these legislative provisions liberally, and noncompensation is clearly the exception. The planning authority must prove that special reasons justify noncompensation—for example, that compensating very small damages will disrupt the ability to achieve public goals or is impracticable due to high administrative costs. In practice, injuries to development rights that cause value reductions of 26 percent and even 12 percent were held to require compensation (Alterman 2010, 58–59; Lewinsohn-Zamir 1996, 125). Under German law, unrealized development rights receive wide protection for a period of seven years, beginning from the time that the authority granted them. Value reductions within this period are fully compensated unless they are insignificant, and courts have held that damage exceeding 10 percent of the land's value surpasses this threshold. After seven years, the property owner is protected only against severe restriction of development rights, such as a prohibition of construction on land that is suited for that purpose (Schmidt-Eichstaedt 2010, 275–78; Lewinsohn-Zamir 1996, 126).

Following this short survey of taking rules, we move to discuss the contribution of behavioral studies to the evaluation and critique of these rules.

The Legitimacy of Takings

Takings pit the strongly held belief in private property rights against the constitutional power of government. Politically, takings doctrine demarcates a line of separation between the rights of the state and the rights of its citizens. Equally important, government expropriation affects something citizens have direct experience with day to day—real property. Not surprisingly, takings doctrine has proven controversial among lawmakers, scholars, and citizens. Public opinion polls have consistently found a strong degree of opposition to government use of eminent domain (Nadler, Diamond, and Patton 2008, 290; Strother 2016, 341; Somin 2009).[8] Opposition to takings has been a driving force in the rise of "wise use" interest groups devoted to opposing government infringement on private property rights as well as a spate of state legislation restricting eminent domain.

There has been no legitimacy crisis for the flip side of government takings: situations where government action or expropriation confers benefits on individual owners. In a thought-provoking article, Abraham Bell and Gideon Parchomovsky (2001) describe this asymmetry and propose a system of charges to owners when government action increases property values. For example, a local government that takes land for a park may increase the property values of owners adjacent to the park. Shouldn't citizens be equally outraged that those owners have not paid the government for the benefit or "giving"? The psychological phenomenon of loss aversion may explain this seeming irrationality in public and legal response. A large body of research on loss aversion shows that people prefer to avoid losses rather than to acquire equivalent gains (Kahneman and Tversky 1984). As Eyal Zamir (2015, 136) observes, loss aversion predicts that citizens will be more likely to protest having their property taken than the fact that other owners have received benefits. The psychological insight here is descriptive rather than normative. There may be efficiency, fairness, or liberty justifications for regulation of government takings, but not givings.

Psychology sheds light on takings controversies and underscores that nonmonetary aspects of takings strongly affect how people view eminent domain. These views in turn shape citizens' perceptions about the legitimacy of government expropriation. The perceived legitimacy of government action is important because legitimacy affects the magnitude and kind of injury to property owners from a taking, increases citizen compliance with law, and preserves citizens' commitment to democratic or other forms of government. Legitimacy is a multifaceted concept, encompassing the lawmaking process and its political underpinnings, the law's aim, and implementation. Tom Tyler and other social psychologists conceptualize legitimacy as whether people think there is authority for the state action, perceive that legal authority as just, and trust that the law will be carried out in a fair and honest way (Tyler and Jackson 2013, 78–79). Of course, psychology studies and opinion polls do not speak to every aspect of legitimacy—psychological responses are an important marker of legitimacy, but legitimacy extends beyond public opinion. Most of the psychological research on eminent domain focuses on the perceived justness of the government's action and the citizen's reaction (e.g., anger or opposition). Accordingly, in this section we focus mainly on these aspects of legitimacy.

Kelo and the Fifth Amendment's Legitimacy Crisis

In June 2005, the US Supreme Court decision in *Kelo v. City of New London*[9] incited media attention and public outcry unprecedented in the history of takings cases. *Kelo* addressed the question of whether the city of New London's condemnation of property in a residential neighborhood for a private redevelopment project met the Fifth Amendment requirement limiting the government to takings for "public use." New London, hoping to reverse decades of decline, had planned an extensive waterfront redevelopment and a new pharmaceutical plant in Fort Trumball, a working-class neighborhood in the city. In order to assemble land for the proposed ninety-acre site, New London condemned a number of properties, including the plaintiffs' homes and investment rental properties, and planned to transfer the property to a private nonprofit corporation to construct and market the redevelopment. Seven property owners brought suit alleging that New London had not met the constitutional prerequisite that a taking must be for public use. To the surprise of property lawyers and legal scholars, the US Supreme Court opted to hear the case. This was unexpected because the low threshold for public use, encompassing government action that could conceivably produce a public benefit, was well settled by prior Supreme Court cases.[10] In a five-to-four decision, the Supreme Court in *Kelo* held that New London's economic redevelopment passed constitutional muster as a public use. The Court affirmed its past precedents deferring to state and local government judgment and the "broader and more natural interpretation of public use as 'public purpose'" (480). It did not matter constitutionally that New London was transferring the land to a private firm for such firms may be more skilled and efficient than government at redevelopment.

Kelo ignited a fierce debate among the American public, and their elected representatives, over the legitimacy of takings. This did not occur because of a radical change in the views of the American public or, as noted previously, in takings doctrine itself. Rather, the media publicity from *Kelo* made large numbers of citizens aware of something they had not previously realized (but might have objected to if they had). Their property, including their homes, could be lawfully taken by government against their will (Nadler, Diamond, and Patton 2008, 297). Studies of public opinion immediately following the *Kelo* decision revealed overwhelming public opposition, with a 2005 Zogby poll finding that 95 percent of Americans disagreed with the decision and a 2005 Saint Index survey recording 81 percent opposition (American Farm Bureau Federation Survey 2005; Saint Index Poll 2005).[11]

What factors precipitated this legitimacy crisis? *Kelo* entailed multiple evocative elements: longtime owners, residential property (homes), economic redevelopment, the sale of the condemned property to a private redevelopment firm rather than to a public entity, and rumors of corruption within the local government. Following *Kelo*, a number of psychologists and legal scholars set to work to identify the psychological concerns underlying the public reaction. While most of the psychology research to date has addressed eminent domain, a few studies have explored factors that affect opposition to regulatory takings.

The following sections consider nonmonetary factors that influence citizens' perceptions about the legitimacy, and palatability, of takings.

Purpose of the Government Taking: Economic Redevelopment

A number of studies have found that people perceive eminent domain for private redevelopment, like the *Kelo* case, as less just and more distressing. The most comprehensive work to date is Logan Strother's (2016) cluster of studies on economic redevelopment takings. Strother completed high-quality, representative surveys in New Jersey, Illinois, and Ohio. The surveys found that support for eminent domain to build a road was at least four times higher in all three states than public support for eminent domain to construct a shopping mall (Strother 2016,

348). Next, Strother confirmed these findings in an experimental study of 722 participants, who were randomized into groups that received different vignettes about eminent domain. The vignettes varied along the following dimensions: type of property taken (home vs. vacant lot), the purpose of the taking (road vs. privately developed mall), and imagined ownership (the property taken is "yours" vs. "someone's."). He found that twice as many participants (18.1 percent) supported the taking for the road as supported the taking for the shopping mall (8.2 percent). This does not mean that the majority supported eminent domain. Consistent with other studies and surveys, the majority in both the mall and road conditions opposed the taking. The participants in the shopping mall condition also reported more anger and expressed greater willingness to support a bill in Congress opposing eminent domain for economic redevelopment (Strother 2016, 350–51). This study did not ask participants their views on compensation.

Citizens appear especially opposed when the government intercedes in failed private negotiations for voluntary sale. Nadler and Diamond (2008, 738–39) conducted an experiment to investigate reactions to a vignette about a developer who fails to negotiate successfully to buy a property; subsequently, the government takes the property via eminent domain to move the developer's project forward. Respondents were strongly opposed when government undertook eminent domain after the developer failed to voluntarily negotiate purchase—far more so than when the local government initiated the eminent domain negotiation without prior contact from the developer (739–42). This finding presents a challenge for property law. Voluntary negotiation is preferable to avoid the coercion costs and demoralization from involuntary eminent domain. Yet, when private negotiation fails, at least on the part of a private developer, recourse to eminent domain appears to heighten the psychological injury to owners.

Interestingly, while people report more negative attitudes toward economic redevelopment takings, they do not consistently demand more compensation for such takings. In their 2008 study, Nadler and Diamond found that respondents were more positive and felt the taking was more moral when the end use of the taking was a children's hospital than when it was a shopping mall. However, the participants in the shopping mall condition (private economic redevelopment) did not demand more compensation than those in the children's hospital group (Nadler and Diamond 2008, 743). Metcalf (2014, 707–08) replicated these results using Canadian subjects, suggesting that this reaction is not unique to American culture. In a study of both students and businesspeople, Lewinsohn-Zamir found an interesting dichotomy. Students did not perceive government expropriation for use by the government as a better outcome than government expropriation for use by a private entrepreneur (Lewinsohn-Zamir 2012, 876). Businesspeople, however, viewed the transfer of land for use by a private business as a worse outcome than when the land was expropriated for use by the government. In both cases, the goal of the expropriation was to build a park (883). It may be that businesspeople are savvier about the potential profits to private enterprise from such transfers or more sensitive to private competitors gaining an advantage from government.

We don't yet understand *why* people consistently oppose economic redevelopment takings but may not always demand more compensation. Perhaps they are disinclined to monetize an act they view as wrongful or they lack information about how to value compensation. It may be that those who object to economic redevelopment takings prefer to use political protest, or "voice," to demand that economic development takings occur less frequently or not at all (Hirschman 1970). It is also possible that respondents believe that compensation should be comparable across different categories of takings. Applying the psychological research to economic redevelopment takings doctrine, the evidence raises a question of whether adjusting compensation for economic redevelopment takings will produce the redress people seek. The evidence discussed earlier is mixed and in some respects paradoxical. It may be that with more research, clarification or different conclusions may emerge.

Takings federalism may provide at least a partial response to citizens who prefer to prohibit or restrict economic development takings. The low threshold for public use leaves states free to adopt more stringent protection than the federal floor provides, through state legislation and state constitutions (cf. Sterk 2004). A number of states have restricted economic development takings to blighted areas, for example. These efforts have had mixed results, as states often fail to define blight with any precision and therefore maintain considerable discretion (Somin 2009, 2120–21). However, such legislation may still signal to agencies and local governments the state's preference for a conservative approach to economic redevelopment takings. States and localities can also respond to the strong sentiments of constituents de facto by engaging in economic redevelopment takings sparingly or only when public gains are very high.

The psychology research also has implications for proposed reforms to privatize economic redevelopment takings. Michael Heller and Rick Hills (2008) have argued for the use of land assembly districts (LADs) composed of owners within districts sought for development. The owners decide by majority vote whether to sell all of the parcels within the district to a government entity or to a private redevelopment firm, and the LAD bargains for price. The psychology research raises questions about this approach and flags the need for further research. If citizens feel anger and moral outrage toward government for expropriating their property, how will they feel about their neighbors deciding to do the same? The dissenting owners' ties to decision makers (i.e., their neighbors), the status of neighbors as equals, and the "up close and personal" nature of a LAD decision may heighten a dissenting owner's injury (Lewinsohn-Zamir 2012, 891–92). Weighing against costs to individual owners, LADs may deliver a social benefit of insulating government from opprobrium over takings and preserving government legitimacy. This protective effect will only occur to the extent that citizens focus on the private LAD as the responsible entity and not on the government role in creating and empowering LADs.

Nature of the Property Subject to Eminent Domain

How does the type of property (i.e., business, home, vacant lot) affect perceptions that a taking is just or moral? To our knowledge, only one study has addressed whether property type alters reactions to eminent domain. Logan Strother's (2016) research found no significant differences in responses between participants who received an experimental vignette about the expropriation of a home versus a vacant lot. Participants in both conditions reported similar levels of opposition to an economic redevelopment taking, anger at the taking, and willingness to support a congressional bill opposing takings for economic redevelopment. This is an interesting finding, and one that is highly relevant to proposals to offer greater protection from eminent domain or higher compensation to residential versus nonresidential property owners (for further discussion of this issue, see the section on just compensation). However, a single study, even one that is rigorous and well designed, should be interpreted conservatively. This is an area ripe for further research that would enable us to draw firmer conclusions for law.

While the type of property does not appear to matter, the *length* of ownership has emerged as a strong and consistent predictor of reactions to eminent domain. Two experiments by Nadler and Diamond (2008) and a replication study by Metcalf (2014) found a strong relationship between length of tenure and opposition to the taking. Participants asked to imagine that their house has been in their family for 100 years reported that they were entitled to more compensation and viewed the taking as less moral than participants told that the property had been in their family for only 2 years. Nadler and Diamond concluded, "The length of ownership imbues the property with subjective value that is not recognized by the fair market value standard that the law of eminent domain uses as the metric for just compensation" (2008, 743).

Unfortunately, no study has addressed more intermediate terms of ownership (e.g., 7 years or 15 years). The 100-years ownership condition represents an extreme and unusual case, and it is difficult to extrapolate the empirical findings to more common lengths of tenure. Another possible issue with the findings is that participants may think the vignette is informing them that the property has high subjective value—otherwise, why keep it in the family for 100 years? This inference is different than, though not necessarily exclusive of, the explanation of greater personal attachment to property owned for long periods of time. In sum, more research is needed to gain a better sense of how long-term ownership must be to provoke opposition and whether the length of ownership affects perceptions of eminent domain of vacant lots and business property as well as residential property.

Quick-Take Statutes and the Psychology of Procedural Justice

Quick-take statutes, adopted in a number of states, are perhaps the most controversial procedural law regulating eminent domain. Quick-take statutes allow the state or local condemning authority to take possession of the property without the owner agreeing to or being able to litigate the compensation in advance. In a quick-take, the condemning authority deposits probable compensation with the court and can then enter and take possession of the property. The owner can litigate the amount of compensation only after the government takes possession. For example, in Virginia, the condemning authority must engage in voluntary negotiation with the property owner.[12] If that fails, the authority can file a certificate of taking under the quick-take statute and obtain defeasible title that allows the authority to proceed with its project. The title becomes indefeasible if the authority and owner subsequently agree to compensation or when the court determines compensation at trial. The authority has six months from filing the certificate of taking to commence the just compensation trial process (after that, the landowner can file claims with the court regarding compensation).

Quick-take legislation typically addresses specific types of projects, such as roads and schools, where delays are expensive and can have other ill effects on the community. Quick-take is attractive to states because it limits the ability of a few "holdout" landowners to delay or stymie public projects or economic redevelopment. However, it also imposes steep costs on process and fairness.

Psychological studies on procedural justice shed light on why property owners, and their attorneys, find quick-take statutes highly objectionable. Tom Tyler has conducted extensive research over the past three decades on the psychology of procedural justice. His work, and that of other social psychologists, has shown that people care as much, and often more, about how they are treated during a conflict than about its outcome or their compensation. His studies reveal four factors as the primary components of procedural justice. These factors are (1) the ability to tell one's side of the story in a conflict, (2) the perception that legal authorities and officials are neutral (transparency is one practice that appears to promote belief in neutrality), (3) respectful and dignified treatment, and (4) cues about sincere or benevolent intentions of people with whom they are dealing (Tyler 2000, 121).

Quick-take statutes violate multiple aspects of the procedural justice model. First, quick-take allows plaintiffs their day in court but truncate meaningful input both into compensation and about the taking itself. In many states, compensation is the only viable legal bone of contention because the public use requirement is often set low. The landowner can argue about compensation at trial, but she cannot use the compensation conflict as a platform for telling her broader story about why government dispossession is unjust, burdensome, and so forth. Also, in states with more rapid quick-take, the plaintiff may not be able to participate meaningfully in the hearing over preliminary compensation. Such participation requires expert appraisal of property value, which may be difficult to procure in a short period of time.

Plaintiffs are also less likely to feel that they have received treatment that respects their rights when they have been rapidly dispossessed. This dynamic is even more pronounced in states that prohibit or limit the landowner from withdrawing the preliminary compensation. For example, in a controversial case, *San Jacinto Community College District v. Superior Court of Riverside County*,[13] the California Supreme Court upheld as constitutional a local government's conditioning the landowner's withdrawal of the preliminary just compensation funds on his agreement not to dispute the amount of the preliminary compensation at trial. California state law did not allow withdrawal of the money before final determination of the compensation amount. Thus landowners who need to draw against the preliminary compensation cannot do so unless they forgo their right to contest compensation. This presents a financially burdensome and potentially coercive situation that disrespects owners' (already limited) rights to legal process in quick-take eminent domain. Regardless of the final compensation they receive, owners subject to this treatment are likely to feel that the quick-take procedure was less fair and acceptable. These attitudes may spill over to how they—and others—view traditional (i.e., slow) eminent domain and other instances of government restriction of private property rights.

Singling Out and Inequity Aversion

Allocation matters to the legitimacy, and legality, of government interference with property rights. In *Lingle v. Chevron, U.S.A.*, the US Supreme Court rejected a prior precedent in *Agins v. City of Tiburon* that a regulation is a taking if it does not "substantially advance" legitimate state interests.[14] The *Lingle* Court held that the "substantially advances" test is flawed because, inter alia, it does not address the magnitude or nature

of the burden and how that burden "is *distributed* among property owners."[15] In other words, a small number of property owners should not
bear the substantial burden of regulation that benefits the public without just compensation. The *Lingle* Court's "singling out test" for takings
has become a centerpiece of lower federal and state court decisions in
takings cases (Pappas 2016, 129). This test cannot be solely explained
by the economic theories commonly applied to property law. The goal
of moving property to its highest-valued use may be achieved without
attending to distributive considerations, and a grossly unequal distribution of property rights burdens may nonetheless produce public benefits
in excess of costs.

The singling out rule is better explained by psychology research on
how people perceive equity and fairness. While standard economic analysis assumes that people assess outcomes in absolute terms, behavioral
studies have long indicated that people's assessment of outcomes, including their own position, tends to be reference dependent (Kahneman
and Tversky 1979). People judge their own position not only in comparison to their own previous position (the status quo), but also—and
sometimes primarily—in comparison to the position of other people
(Kahneman and Tversky 1984). Consequently, when something is taken
from a person or a small group of people against their will, they experience a greater loss than when the same thing is taken from all the people
in the pertinent reference group.

Furthermore, psychological studies have found that people are willing
to sacrifice their self-interest to achieve greater equity and that inequity
aversion takes two forms: disadvantageous and advantageous (Fehr and
Schmidt 1999; Fehr and Fischbacher 2002). Disadvantageous inequity
aversion occurs when individuals are willing to incur a cost to prevent
someone else from receiving a larger, inequitable share. For example, in
ultimatum game experiments, one person (the proposer) decides how to
divide a certain sum of money between herself and another person (the
responder), and the responder can either accept or reject the proposer's offer. If the offer is rejected, both parties receive nothing. Standard
economic theory predicts that the responder should accept any offer
above zero and that the proposer should offer just that. In practice, most
proposers offer responders a generous share of the pie (40 percent on
average), and responders typically reject offers that substantially deviate

from an equal split (Güth 1995, 331; Hoffman, McCabe, and Smith 2008, 411–28, 436–53; for further discussion of ultimatum games and their implications for the law, see chapter 7). In contrast, advantageous inequity aversion occurs when an individual is willing to sacrifice resources to prevent herself from receiving *more* than another party. It appears that people's dislike of unequal outcomes can also lead them to reject distributions in their favor (Loewenstein, Thompson, and Bazerman 1989, 438; Fehr and Fischbacher 2002; see also Blake et al. 2015 (showing that advantageous equity aversion is not found in all countries, which suggests it is a cultural concept)).[16]

Given people's aversion to inequity, it is not surprising that "singling out" has become such an important factor in determining whether a taking has occurred. True, the experimental studies just mentioned address decisions about how to divide resources between private citizens, whereas takings entail divisions between property owners decided by the state. However, concern about inequity should be at least as strong (probably more so) when the government is the decision maker as when private citizens distribute resources among themselves.

Framing of Property Entitlements: Thing versus Bundle of Sticks

Property scholars debate whether property should be regarded as a "thing" or as a "bundle of sticks" (Dagan 2011, 37–55; Merrill and Smith 2007; Penner 1996; H. E. Smith 2012). The former metaphor views property as a discrete object, whereas the latter portrays it as a package of distinct rights: to possess, use, exclude others from, dispose of, destroy, and so forth (for a summary of the literature on the two property paradigms, see Di Robilant 2013, 877–94; J. R. Nash 2009, 694–70).[17] This controversy is not a matter of semantics. Rather, the framing of property one way or the other can affect people's perceptions of ownership and, consequently, the legal protection that the state affords owners.

Specifically, some scholars have argued that the "thing" conception implies exclusive, unlimited control over assets. Accordingly, any restriction of this right is an injury to property, and such a perception might eventually lead to excessive protection of property owners at the expense of other social goals. A bundle of rights understanding, in contrast, draws one's attention to the limitations of ownership and to the interests of others. Consequently, state interference with property would be more readily accepted as legitimate under this formulation (J. R. Nash and Stern 2010, 451–55, 462–65; Singer 2000, 2–13).

As a theoretical generalization, these arguments seem somewhat puzzling. In principle, why can't people regard property as a thing conferring limited rights, or as a bundle of broad and unrestricted rights? Furthermore, one may conjecture that the two property perceptions would have an opposite effect. Indeed, in theoretical discussions of the takings issue, some scholars have asserted that if property is perceived as a thing, fewer state interventions would be considered to be takings. This approach is based on the assumption that under the "thing" conception, property is likely to be regarded as taken by the state only when it is physically expropriated (and thus literally "gone"), or when regulation renders it useless (albeit leaving it in the owner's hands physically). That is to say, as long as some reasonable use of the asset remains, the owner would not consider her "thing" taken from her. In contrast, so the argument goes, the bundle of sticks conception emphasizes each distinct right in the ownership package. As a result, eliminating any one of these sticks is likely to be viewed as a taking of that right in its entirety. Ackerman (1977, 113–67) first advanced this argument, claiming that laypeople ("ordinary observers") adhere to the thing conception of property, whereas legal professionals ("scientific policymakers") view property as a bundle of rights. Legal theorists including Michelman (1988, 1614–25) and Radin (1988, 1676–78) expressed similar views regarding the probable effect of a bundle of sticks understanding of property.

Recently, behavioral scholars have addressed the thing/bundle of rights debate. Jonathan R. Nash (2009) examined how the framing of a laptop computer as a thing or as a bundle of rights affected incoming law students' acceptance of restrictions on the asset. Participants were told to envision a scenario in which they had to purchase a laptop from the law school. Half of the questionnaires tried to frame the laptop as a thing (e.g., by referring to the acquisition of "a laptop") and the other half as a bundle of rights (e.g., by indicating that the participants purchase the right to use a laptop). In both cases, the students stated their attitudes toward the law school's proposed limitations on the use of the laptops—for instance, with respect to the hours and types of permitted uses. Nash (2009, 715–21) found that while all students expressed unfavorable reactions to the suggested restrictions, those who received the bundle of rights version of the questionnaire were more accepting of the law school's intervention than students who answered the thing version.

Jonathan Nash and Stephanie M. Stern (2010) replicated and further advanced the finding that the conception of property is not exogenous but can be manipulated, and that a bundle of rights framing weakens ownership perceptions and decreases resistance to regulation of the asset, by similarly using vignettes regarding students' rights in laptops purchased from their law school. They demonstrated, inter alia, that explicitly forewarning the students about restrictions on their rights had a similar effect to that of the bundle of rights framing, and that a combination of the two techniques resulted in the greatest reduction in students' expectations about their property rights (J. R. Nash and Stern 2010, 470–75, 484).

Both studies advocate reframing people's property perceptions from "thing" to "bundle" in various legal contexts, such as environmental regulation and conservation (J. R. Nash and Stern 2010, 492–94). In support of this recommendation, these authors claim that the public acceptance of zoning regulation—in contrast to the popular hostility toward eminent domain—is an example of successful bundle of rights reframing (481). However, one may argue that if property owners indeed view zoning as legitimate, then this phenomenon may be explained by the opposing theory as well: since laypeople typically perceive their property as a *thing*, they do not regard it as taken by the state if it remains physically in their hands and can still be used in economically viable ways.

These initial studies indicate that the framing of an entitlement matters to how people perceive their rights and react to restrictions on them. At the same time, further experimentation may be necessary before we can confidently suggest normative implications for the law of takings. For instance, since the laptops in the experiments were purchased from the law school at the outset (rather than from a third-party seller), the students may have viewed the restrictions as a "limited giving" of property rather than as a "taking" of initially unrestricted property, and consequently regarded the interference as more legitimate than they would have otherwise (on people's different reactions to takings and nongivings of similar magnitude, see A. Bell and Parchomovsky 2001; Zamir 2015, 133–37). One must also take into account that even if property conceptions can be manipulated successfully in experimental settings, this might not always be possible in real life. Nash and Stern (2010, 491–92) acknowledge that the bundle of rights framing may disappear in the real world due to prolonged, actual possession and use of the asset. Furthermore, in reality, people may not be aware in advance of restrictions on their property rights or may not actually experience them with respect to most of their property. Therefore, it might be difficult for policy makers to educate owners to perceive property as a bundle of specific and limited rights, rather than as discrete assets.

Finally, let us note that the importance of property perceptions should not overshadow other relevant factors. Plausibly, property conceptions are only one of the factors affecting owners' reactions to restrictions on their assets; the context and substance of these limitations are likely to be significant factors as well. Thus, for example, the magnitude of the decrease in the asset's value (large, medium, or small), and the extent of the distribution of the injury throughout society (i.e., whether it is inflicted on a small group of property owners or widely distributed among many) may play a central role in the probable impact of property restrictions (Lewinsohn-Zamir 1996).

When Is Compensation Required?

The common justification for compensating takings of property is based on both fairness and efficiency considerations (Shai Stern 2016, 724–26). Accordingly, compensation would avert the unfairness of inflicting costs on some people for the benefit of the public as a whole (Dana and Merrill 2002, 33–34; Singer 2017, 746); avoid the demoralization of property owners and others who would sympathize with their plight (Michelman 1967, 1214–18); encourage individuals to invest efficiently in assets without fear of losing their investment (R. A. Posner 2014, 40) or wasting resources on attempts to prevent the taking (Cooter and Ulen 2012, 175–76); and compel the governmental authority to internalize the costs of its actions to property owners, thereby preventing excessive takings (Dana and Merrill 2002, 41–46; Serkin 2005, 705–08).[18]

Notwithstanding the general justification for compensating property owners, legal systems often differentiate between types of injury despite their similar magnitude.[19] As explained earlier, in the United States (and elsewhere), a distinction is made between physical and nonphysical injuries to property; landowners are afforded wider protection against physical injuries (such as the taking of possession or the elimination of existing uses on the land) than against nonphysical injuries (such as the restriction of unrealized development rights or the prohibition of future uses). Thus, for example, if 25 percent of the land is physically expropriated for public use, compensation will be paid. Contrarily, if the height of permitted development is reduced from five-story to three-story buildings (downzoning), and consequently the value of the land drops by 25 percent, compensation will be denied. Furthermore, while even a slight physical injury requires compensation, very large reductions in value caused by restriction of development rights are often left uncompensated (Lewinsohn-Zamir 1996, 114–19).

The relative lack of protection for development rights is emphasized in the way compensation for physical injuries is calculated. Compensation for physical injuries is not limited to the value of the existing use of the land or its designation prior to the physical expropriation, but is calculated according to the highest and best use of the land that would have been reasonably possible were it not expropriated (Singer 2017, 769). In other words, compensation for physical injuries includes compensation for loss of existing and potential development rights. Contrarily, when *only* development rights are injured (as when zoning laws change the permitted use of an undeveloped parcel or its intensity), compensation is usually granted when no reasonable use of the land is left.

The disparate treatment of physical and nonphysical injuries is manifest in other contexts as well. Legal systems that afford limited protection for unrealized development rights commonly grant substantial protection to *existing* uses—that is, realized development rights. In general, injuries to existing uses are compensated. Various American states differ as to when vested rights are created, thus granting immunity from uncompensated harm. Some states require that the project reach an advanced stage, and others suffice with preparations for construction—such as contacting an architect or submitting an application for building permits (Serkin 2009, 1232–42, 1249–56).

Although the physical/nonphysical distinction is not universal, as countries like Germany, the Netherlands, and Israel recognize a broad right to compensation for both types of injury (Alterman 2010, 45–47,

53–61; Lewinsohn-Zamir 1996, 125–26), this differentiation is a common enough phenomenon that deserves scrutiny. This is especially so since justifications or explanations for the distinction typically rely on behavioral assumptions and intuitions. Let us critically examine two prominent examples.

Losses versus Gains

Some scholars have employed the endowment effect (EE) phenomenon and people's disparate reaction to gains and losses of a similar scope to justify the physical/nonphysical distinction. Numerous experiments have shown that people value an entitlement or object they already possess much more than an identical entitlement or object that they have an opportunity to acquire (Camerer 1995, 665–70; Kahneman, Knetsch, and Thaler 1990, 2008; Knetsch and Sinden 1984; see also our discussion in chapter 1). The main explanation for the EE is loss aversion. Parting with an entitlement is perceived as a loss, whereas acquiring the same entitlement is viewed as a gain. Since losses loom larger than gains, people's selling price is significantly higher than their purchase price (Kahneman 1992; Korobkin 2003, 1250–55; Zamir 2012, 835–40).

Based on this behavioral literature, Robert Ellickson has argued that a physical injury to land ordinarily would be viewed as a loss, whereas a nonphysical injury is likely to be perceived as an unattained gain. Because the former type of injury is much more hurtful to property owners than the latter type, it is worthier of compensation (Ellickson 1989, 35–38). In a similar vein, Christopher Serkin has claimed that people experience the elimination of an existing use differently from the prohibition of a future use—the former as an out-of-pocket cost, and the latter as a foregone gain. Consequently, existing uses receive more protection than prospective uses, like development rights (Serkin 2009, 1267–69). Both authors rationalize the physical/nonphysical distinction by tying restriction of development rights to people's psychological reaction to unattained gains. Put differently, the two explanations are based on the crucial assumption that, usually, nonphysical injuries are perceived as foregone gains. But is this indeed the case? Findings from behavioral studies cast doubt on this critical presumption.

As we have shown in our earlier discussion of possession (chapter 1), people's notion of possession tends to be broad. It does not necessarily require any corporeal manifestation and may extend to intangible entitlements, assets, and expectations. Consequently, one cannot assume that the impact of nonphysical injuries to property is qualitatively different and always smaller than that of physical ones. If individuals frequently experience nonphysical possession, why wouldn't landowners view downzoning of their parcel as loss of formerly "held" development rights? Such a perception seems perfectly plausible, for instance, when the land's purchase price reflects the value of the development rights. In any case, absent direct testing of the matter, one cannot presume one way or the other.

Furthermore, even if restriction of development rights is regularly perceived as an unrealized gain—and thus the injury to the landowner is smaller than if such restriction were regarded as a loss—the injury may still be significant enough to merit compensation. Likewise, even if individuals who physically possess property experience a greater loss than individuals whose possession is not physical, this difference alone should not settle the compensation issue. Importantly, we do not claim that physical and nonphysical injuries are the same, or that every regulation that adversely impacts property warrants compensation. Rather, we argue that the law should not draw too sharp a distinction between the two types of injury. The compensation issue should be decided according to several fairness and efficiency considerations, including the following: the magnitude of the injury, the extent of its distribution (i.e., whether it is concentrated on a small group or widely distributed), the costs of awarding compensation, and the existence of nonmonetary or reciprocal benefits that offset the injury (for theoretical discussion of these considerations, see, e.g., Dagan 2011; Ellickson 1977; Epstein 1985; Lewinsohn-Zamir 1996; Michelman 1967).

Personal Property versus Fungible Property

The distinction between personal (or nonfungible) property and fungible property figures prominently in Margaret Radin's (1982) influential personhood theory of property. This theory is based on Hegel's justification of private property as necessary for the development of people's personality. According to the personhood theory, property is classified as "personal" if its loss cannot be remedied by receiving its value or purchasing a replacement in the market (paradigmatic examples, according to Radin, are the home, a spouse's wedding ring, and a family portrait). A fungible asset, in contrast, is easily replaceable with a similar object (e.g., money, a wedding ring in the hands of a jeweler, a parcel of undeveloped land belonging to a contractor, or a commercial landlord's apartment). Generally speaking, Radin has argued that greater protection should be afforded to personal property than to fungible property. For instance, preventing even the compensated taking of a highly personal asset (such as the family home) may be justified. In contrast, monetary compensation should always suffice for claims involving fungible property, and sometimes no compensation is necessary (Radin 1982, 959–61, 986–88; 1986, 362–65; 1988, 1688–92).

Over the years, nonbehavioral studies have criticized these normative recommendations. Legal scholars argued, for instance, that property deemed personal according to personhood theory is granted excessive legal protection. Such protection has elitist and regressive consequences because it favors people with large quantities of expensive personal property, like luxury homes (Schnably 1993, 375–79, 397–99). Moreover, fungible property receives inadequate protection under personhood theory. The fact that money sufficiently compensates for injury to fungible property does not constitute a reason for denying monetary compensation (Lewinsohn-Zamir 1996, 121). However, the critiques of personhood theory were not based on psychological data.

In the context of takings, Radin has employed the personhood theory to explain the disparate treatment of physical and nonphysical injuries to land and, specifically, the rule that denies compensation for substantial restriction of development rights. She argues that noncompensation for severe value reductions stems from the fact that development rights are fungible property, and that the owner often holds the injured land solely for investment or commercial purposes. In other words, the injury is caused to property that is not "personal" (Radin 1982, 1007–08; 1988, 1691–92).

The personhood explanation for noncompensation of development rights is based on rigid definitions of what constitutes personal and fungible property. According to Radin's personhood theory, a person's home belongs to the former category, whereas her business belongs to the latter. Furthermore, once an asset is classified as fungible, its injury is assumed to be relatively insubstantial. However, it stands to reason that property used for commercial purposes may also be personal, from the perspective of the individual user. Many people spend most of their time and efforts on their business, and people's occupation is often central to their self-identity. Plausibly, individuals' well-being depends on their business's flourishing, through which they realize their talents, independence, and personal character.

Moreover, even if owners do regard commercial assets as fungible, jurists should be wary of relying on this fact to justify limiting takings protection in the absence of sufficient data supporting such treatment. Indeed, the existing psychological evidence suggests that people may form attachments to fungible property as well, and that the fungible/nonfungible dichotomy is overly rigid and might lead one astray. This understanding, in turn, casts doubt on the explanatory power of Radin's justification for the physical/nonphysical distinction. Thus, for example, Beggan (1992) has documented a "mere ownership" effect, according to which individuals are biased in favor of an object and rate it as more attractive just because they own it. He argued that people desire to maintain a positive self-image and therefore place higher value on the objects they own (Beggan 1992, 235). Importantly for our purposes, the ownership effect appears to be a general phenomenon—it was even found with respect to mundane and cheap fungible assets, such as a cold-drink insulator. Likewise, psychologists have discovered that people generally regard their possessions as part of their identity or extended self. This perception is not limited to objectively unique assets but extends to fungibles, such as electronic goods, sporting equipment, and furniture. Involuntary loss of such possessions—for instance, by forced disposition—causes trauma and loss of self (Belk 1988, 150–51, 155; Csikszentmihalyi and Rochberg-Halton 1981; for more detailed discussion of these phenomena, see chapter 1).

In sum, the type of injury to property is not an appropriate yardstick for distinguishing compensated injuries from uncompensated ones.[20] The fairness and efficiency considerations that determine the takings compensation issue are relevant, in principle, to both physical and nonphysical injuries.

Just Compensation

Once an injury to property is classified as a taking, the owner is entitled to receive just compensation. In theory, if compensation aims to make the property holder whole, it should be calculated according to her subjective valuation of the property.[21] In practice, however, it is extremely difficult to determine subjective value reliably since—as per one obvious example— owners have an incentive to lie in order to improve their position.[22] Consequently, takings compensation is usually based on the objective, fair market value of the property. Market value is defined as the price that would have been agreed upon between a willing seller and a willing buyer in a competitive market and is often determined by observing actual sale prices of comparable properties (Dana and Merrill 2002, 169–71).

The Standard Critique of Market-Value Compensation and a Proposed Solution

Scholars and practitioners have long been aware of the possible divergence between market value and subjective value. Plausibly, owners who do not value their property above fair market value would likely have sold it (Fennell 2004, 963; Singer 2017, 769). In particular, the literature has focused on the problem of undercompensation that arises when landowners with high subjective valuation receive only market value (A. Bell and Parchomovsky 2007, 885–86). Above-market valuation of owners is typically attributed to factors such as psychological attachment to the property, customization of the property to the owner's tastes or needs, and nontransferable benefits associated with the property's location (Dana and Merrill 2002, 173–74).

To address this problem, some have proposed that market value be supplemented by a "compensation premium" (i.e., a certain percentage above the market price of the land). Indeed, some American states adopted legislation that grants such premiums to property owners. However, these additional monetary awards are usually limited to *certain types* of property, and mostly to residential property. Thus, for example, expropriators in the state of Indiana are required to pay 150 percent of market value for parcels that are "occupied by the owner as a residence" (Ind. Code Ann. § 32-24-4.5-8(2)(A)). Michigan's constitution states that when an individual's principal residence is taken for public use, the compensation award must not be less than 125 percent of its market value (Mich. Const. Art. X, § 2). In the same vein, Missouri awards market value multiplied by 125 percent for a "homestead taking" and sets a multiplier of 150 percent for "heritage" property, defined as "property owned within the same family for fifty or more years" (Mo. Ann. Stat. §§ 523.039; 523.001(2)–(3); for a survey of American states that grant compensation in excess of fair market value, see Maciá 2016, 954–56). Legal scholars have likewise suggested that length of use serve as a proxy in takings law reform. For instance, John Fee (2006) advocated that the government pay homeowners market value plus an additional 2 percent per year for each year lived in the home, up to a total of 60 percent above market value; Thomas Merrill (2005) proposed adding 1 percent above market value for each year the owner has continuously occupied the property. Merrill's recommendation for supplemental compensation is distinctive, in that it is not limited to occupied homes but extends to occupied businesses and farms as well.

The findings of Nadler and Diamond (2008) support initiatives to compensate landowners in excess of fair market value, but they leave open questions about which types of property warrant a compensation premium and the appropriate size of the premium. As explained earlier, Nadler and Diamond conducted an experimental study about the expropriation of homes. Participants were asked to indicate the sum of money above fair market value that would be required for them to sell their home, with the understanding that if negotiations for a voluntary sale were to fail, the government would compel the transfer. It was found that respondents indeed required compensation surpassing market value and that the length of time the residence had been in the family (2 years vs. 100 years) significantly affected the difference between market value and the hypothetical sale price (Nadler and Diamond 2008, 729–30, 743–44; Metcalf [2014] replicated these results in the Canadian context). However, like most current legislation and nonbehavioral studies, both Nadler and Diamond and Metcalf limited themselves to the case of occupied homes. They too did not examine whether similar phenomena exist with respect to other types of property.

In sum, the common assumption appears to be that market value is a quite satisfactory compensation measure with respect to unpossessed or undeveloped land, as well as commercial property. This assumption, however, must be tested. In the following, we report on initial psychological studies suggesting that market-value compensation for takings might be undercompensatory for all types of property (for further discussion and critique of the enhanced protection of homes in diverse legal contexts, see chapter 2).

Additional Justifications for Above-Market-Value Compensation

A main reason for the general deficiency of market-value compensation stems from the involuntary nature of governmental takings. Lewinsohn-Zamir (2012) examined this factor. In that study, participants were asked to evaluate the goodness or badness of the outcome of events that had a similar end result but differed in another respect. For example, events producing the same bottom line could vary in how the end result was achieved (voluntarily or coercively) or in the identity of the relevant party (stranger or friend). The study revealed that both laypersons and experienced businesspeople perceive outcomes broadly and therefore do not confine the judgment of events to their end products. Certain factors are commonly regarded as part of the outcome and significantly affect its valuation, such as how an outcome was brought about (e.g., in a spirit of goodwill and mutual cooperation or not), the identity of the parties involved, the voluntariness or involuntariness of their behavior, and the intentionality of their acts or lack thereof.

One of the experimental scenarios in Lewinsohn-Zamir (2012) related to a real estate company that purchased an undeveloped parcel of land. Participants were told expressly that the value of the parcel to the company was equal to its market value and were asked to rate the outcome of three events. In the first event, the parcel was sold subsequently to a buyer who paid the company its current market price. The second and third events depicted an expropriation of the parcel in lieu of a sale—for the use of either the government or a private entrepreneur—compensated by a similar payment of its current market price. In all three events, the reason for the sale/expropriation was to build a park on the parcel (together with additional plots in the area). Even though the company valued the parcel at its market price and, in fact, received this very amount in all three cases, participants still believed that from the perspective of the company, the events produced different outcomes.

Specifically, the outcome of the voluntary sale was considered to be significantly better than that of both involuntary purchases. It appears that the very fact that an asset was transferred unwillingly inflicts a loss that is distinct from the owner's subjective valuation of the asset. Moreover, this phenomenon is not limited to occupied land or to homes but exists even in the case of a vacant parcel that is held by a firm as part of its commercial stock (Lewinsohn-Zamir 2012, 872, 876, 882–83).

This finding suggests that awarding compensation based on market price is inherently undercompensatory,[23] and in the long run may lead to inefficiency and the demoralization of property owners (Lewinsohn-Zamir 1996, 61–62, 65–66). Therefore, the experimental data raise the possibility that if we aim to make the injured party whole, a "coercion premium" may be needed in *all* takings cases. Interestingly, such a premium once existed in English law, which generally awarded landowners a 10 percent bonus above market value in cases of expropriation, to compensate for the compulsory nature of the purchase. This practice was abolished in 1919 (Corfield and Carnwath 1978, 3–4, 177).

Another factor that may adversely affect the adequacy of market-value compensation is its monetary nature. Lewinsohn-Zamir (2013) tested the common belief that people are indifferent between in-kind and monetary remedies of equal pecuniary value. It was found that both laypersons and experienced businesspeople strongly prefer in-kind entitlements and remedies over monetary ones. Importantly, a preference for in-kind entitlements and remedies existed even when the right holder was a firm, and even when the remedy was related to nonunique, easily replaceable assets whose market value was ascertainable. For instance, in a vignette depicting the expropriation of 10 percent of an undeveloped and unpossessed parcel to widen an adjacent road and sidewalk, participants clearly preferred compensation in development rights for the remainder of the parcel to monetary compensation of equal and even substantially higher value (Lewinsohn-Zamir 2013, 163–65, 171–74, 186–88). Thus, the commonly used monetary mode of compensation, in and of itself, may less effectively compensate landowners for the harm caused by the taking (for further discussion of people's preference for in-kind remedies, see chapter 8).

In this regard, it is worth addressing the argument William Fischel (1995) raises against above-market compensation. Fischel acknowledges that landowners may experience an endowment effect with respect to their land. Consequently, the owner would experience a subsequent taking of the land as a loss, which is greater than the sum that she would have been willing to pay in order to purchase the land in the first place (Fischel 1995, 207–09). Notwithstanding this point of departure, Fischel rejects the claim that the EE phenomenon supports takings compensation exceeding fair market value. This claim, so the argument goes, ignores the fact that taxpayers finance compensation payments and that they, too, may experience an EE when parted from their income (Fischel 1995, 209–10). Fischel's critique is problematic because in the absence of experimental evidence, one cannot assume that the two effects offset each other. The EE from the loss caused by a taking of land may be substantially larger than the EE from loss of money (especially when taxes are fully or partially hidden, as in the case of employers deducting Social Security payments from salaries; McCaffery 1994, 1874–86). A possible reason for such disparity is that the loss to the land relates to a specific asset, whereas a monetary loss from taxes affects a person's wealth in general. In addition, while the former type of injury typically affects only a certain group of landowners, the latter type is widespread across all taxpayers. If this is indeed the case, over-market-value compensation for takings of property could still be warranted.

In sum, initial experimental studies indicate that a compensation premium may be justified, to address various losses left uncompensated under the fair market value standard. In addition to dealing with owners' subjective valuation, a compensation premium could also take into account the injuries from the coercive nature of the taking and the substitutionary nature of monetary compensation.

How Much beyond Market Value?

Accepting that some premium above market value may be warranted, the thorny question is, How much? Admittedly, employing fixed percentages may result in over- or undercompensation. The risk of undercompensation, however, is smaller than it is under the fair market value formula, and the risk of overcompensation can be mitigated by limiting the size of the premium or by crafting different premiums, for example, for vacant and utilized property (on variable premiums, see also Shai Stern 2016, 742–43). Yet, a varying-percentage scale based on the number of years the owner has used the property seems somewhat rigid. We doubt that the injury to a person who has used her residence or place of business for twenty years is significantly smaller than the injury to a person who used such property for fifty years (incidentally, Susette Kelo—whose expropriated home featured in the famous *Kelo* case discussed earlier—had lived in it for "only" ten years). Notably, however, recourse to preset scales or multipliers considerably reduces administrative costs as compared with flexible standards.

Brian Lee (2013) offers a variant on the compensation-premium approach. Lee argues that premiums set as a percentage of the property's market value are discriminatory. Since the more valuable the land the higher the additional sum that would be awarded, this compensation method treats wealthy owners' autonomy and sentiments as more valuable than those of nonaffluent owners. Therefore, he advocates granting an equal, fixed monetary amount to every owner who has an equivalent amount of sentimental value in the property taken, regardless of its market value (Lee 2013, 634–49). Although this proposal appears to be more egalitarian, it is also more difficult and expensive to apply. First, we cannot be sure that no correlation exists between the magnitude of the injury to owners' autonomy and sentiments and the value of the property taken by the state. Indeed, behavioral studies have found, in various contexts, that economic damages may serve as a useful anchor for determining noneconomic damages, because the severity of the harm is a relevant factor with respect to both types of damages (T. Eisenberg et al. 1997; Hans and Reyna 2011; Sunstein et al. 2002). Second, how would we determine the appropriate, uniform "price tag" for the injury to autonomy that a taking involves, and how would we establish whether owners in a certain area have an equivalent or differential sentimental attachment to their land? Considerations of simplicity and practicality may thus tilt the scales in favor of percentage premiums.

At the same time, percentage premiums need not be uniform across countries and states. Plausibly, the various injuries that compensation premiums address are somewhat location-specific. Communities may differ from one another in various respects: they can be more or less close-knit, experience more or less geographic mobility, and so forth. Thus, it may be advisable to leave the detailed crafting of such premiums, including the determination of their size, to the local authorities (for a general discussion of takings by local governments and the justification for applying different legal rules to takings at the federal, state, and local levels, see Serkin 2006).

Concluding Remarks

Behavioral analysis suggests that prevailing compensation rules might be generally and systematically undercompensatory. Even when the land is undeveloped and not considered unique by its owner, market-value compensation may still fail to fully remedy the injury from the forced taking.

Admittedly, there may be countervailing considerations against adopting people's perceptions and preferences in this regard. Take, for instance, a person who is not willing to sell her land for any price, or who values it at three time its market price. Even when no strategic behavior is involved, catering to such intense preferences is problematic. It seems unfair to favor these individuals over those who exhibit more "ordinary" intensities, when choosing the location of public projects and spending from the government's limited budget (for a general discussion of intense preferences, see Lewinsohn-Zamir 2009). Thus, the unwillingness to satisfy excessive idiosyncratic preferences (Lee 2013, 620–25), the high administrative costs of tailoring compensation rules, and the fear that too high compensation levels will stymie socially beneficial development or impede political resistance to questionable projects (Garnett 2006, 138–43) may constrain the magnitude of increased takings compensation. However, if one holds that enhancing human welfare is a central goal of legal policy making, and if one espouses a theory of welfare that is concerned with preference fulfillment, it is important to be aware of the flaws of current compensation rules—and particularly their underestimation of "ordinary" property and assets used for commercial or investment purposes. The conflicting considerations discussed in this section justify placing a ceiling on the percentage by which compensation can exceed market prices. One can view such a ceiling as setting the limits to the socially acceptable valuation of land.

4

Redistribution through Property Law

Worldwide, many people agree that promoting equality in society should be a central governmental concern. Reducing gross inequalities between individuals may be viewed as good in and of itself, or as a means to ensure that every person enjoys an adequate level of welfare. Property is commonly regarded as essential for attaining this goal. Thus, for instance, theoreticians have claimed that the ability to decide for oneself and to act according to one's choices, as well as the freedom from interference and coercion of others, require ownership of sufficient property. Without enough material goods to guarantee both physical and mental health, personal independence and autonomous action are impossible. Similarly, lack of security in one's present or future condition significantly reduces the possibility of free choice. Property ownership assures us the enjoyment of assets (such as the home and household goods) through which we draw a protective boundary between ourselves and the rest of the world, including the state. Consequently, property enables us to attain and retain our capabilities to act, develop self-respect and aspirations, and maintain our independently chosen beliefs and convictions (Harris 1996, 303–05; Rawls 1993, 298; Reich 1964, 771; A. Sen 1992, 39–55).

Private property promotes additional values besides autonomy and liberty. Material resources enable individuals to acquire knowledge about themselves and about the world, to adopt and realize long-terms goals, and to fulfill their potential. Furthermore, the various items of property and their many uses constitute an important source of pleasure (for discussion of the importance of property for enhancing people's well-being, see Lewinsohn-Zamir 2003). In sum, a certain amount of property is necessary for people to be able to fare even modestly well. Property surpassing this minimum can raise people's well-being by affording them greater freedom from others, more opportunities for acquiring knowledge, additional means for pursuing long-term goals, and more possibilities for enjoyment.[1]

These theoretical arguments are supported by behavioral studies. Thus, for example, psychologists have highlighted the adverse effect of poverty on people's judgment and decision making. When individuals are preoccupied by scarcity, their minds continually return to it, and they have reduced mental capacity for other aspects of their life. That is to say, scarcity creates "tunnel vision" and hinders people's ability to process information, solve problems, and make welfare-promoting decisions (see generally Mullainathan and Shafir 2013). More generally, the various human needs may be classified into higher and lower ones (Maslow 1970, 35–58, 97–98). The most basic needs are the physiological, such as satisfying hunger and thirst. A hungry person will concentrate her thoughts and capacities on the fulfillment of this urgent requirement. Other needs include the following: the safety needs (security, stability, freedom from fear and anxiety, law and order), the belongingness and love needs (for a spouse, family, friends, and a community), the esteem needs (high evaluation of oneself, self-respect, and the esteem of others), and the need for self-actualization (self-development and realization of one's talents and potential). It is harder to satisfy the higher needs when one is preoccupied with more basic, lower needs. The realization of the higher needs produces more happiness, serenity, and richness of inner life than does the fulfillment of the lower, more basic needs. The higher needs, such as love and self-actualization, are less selfish and involve other people (Maslow 1970, 99–100). Private property can plausibly assist in the gratification of all types of needs, both high and low.

Discussion of all the issues pertaining to the legitimacy and efficacy of governmental redistributive measures clearly lies beyond the scope of this book. In this chapter, we focus on one of the major debates engaging the legal literature: the *method* that should be used to redistribute welfare. Specifically, much controversy exists as to whether redistribution should be attained solely through taxes and transfer payments (such as progressive taxation, negative taxes, unemployment compensation, and cash assistance to needy families) or also via substantive rules of private law, including property law (hereinafter, legal rules). In the following, we show how behavioral insights support the use of private law rules for redistribution (alongside taxes and monetary transfers), with applications to property law contexts.

The Redistribution Method Debate

Even people who believe that promoting equality is a legitimate and worthy goal of the state may disagree on which means should be used to redistribute welfare. Law-and-economics scholars have argued that legal rules should not be used for redistribution because they are more costly and less effective than taxes and transfer payments (Cooter and Ulen 2012, 7–8, 106–08; Kaplow and Shavell 1994; Polinsky 2011, 153–62). When legal rules redistribute income in favor of the poor, so the argument goes, they distort people's work incentives just as much as the tax system does. People would respond to the redistributive legal rule in the same way they respond to an increase in their marginal tax rates and may consequently choose leisure over labor. Legal rules, however, create an additional inefficiency that the tax-and-transfer system avoids—the distortion in the very behavior that the legal rules aimed to regulate. For instance, a 30 percent marginal tax rate together with an inefficient tort rule that redistributes 1 percent of wealthy defendants' income to poor plaintiffs would distort work incentives to the same extent as a 31 percent tax rate coupled with an efficient tort rule. The former regime, however, entails the additional costs involved in defendants taking excessive precautions and refraining from efficient activities. (This claim has been dubbed the "double distortion argument": Kaplow and Shavell 1994, 2000; for general discussions of redistribution through the law, see Fennell and McAdams 2016; Sanchirico 2017; Bagchi 2008.)

In addition, scholars have claimed that legal rules are less effective than taxes and transfers (i.e., they achieve less of the desired distributive outcomes). This is because in contractual settings (as opposed to circumstances in which bargaining is impractical), the market often responds in a way that wholly or partially offsets the redistribution (Kaplow and Shavell 2001, 993, 1126; Weisbach 2003, 448–49). Take, for example, the implied warranty of habitability, which is a mandatory quality standard in favor of tenants, requiring landlords to lease residential units that are fit for human habitation (on the implied warranty of habitability, see Stoebuck and Whitman 2000, 299–317). Increasing the landlords' costs is liable to increase rents and reduce the supply of low-rent housing, thereby harming the poorest tenants (R. A. Posner 2014, 654–58; Komesar 1973, 1186–92).[2]

In sum, the critique of redistributive legal rules appears to be powerful. It seems unreasonable to adopt a form of redistribution that is inferior to other methods available to the state—namely, one that affords the poor less or might even worsen their condition. This critique, however, relies on an implicit, crucial assumption: that the goodness of a redistributive outcome should be evaluated according to its end result, and that the *process* that generated the outcome is unimportant. Furthermore, it is presumed that a unit of increase in the quantity of a redistributive outcome achieved through method X is equivalent in every respect to a unit of increase attained through method Y. Accordingly, the comparison between redistributive methods is based on a technical aggregation of end results.[3]

As we shall see in the following sections, behavioral studies cast doubt on this simplistic assumption and highlight the unique advantages of redistributing through legal rules as well.

The Differential Effect of Redistributive Methods: Behavioral Analysis

One of the first attempts to apply behavioral insights to the redistribution debate was made by Christine Jolls (1998). Jolls relied on the robust finding that people are often unrealistically optimistic and underestimate the probability of negative events (see Baker and Emery 1993; Weinstein 1980, 1987). Taxation is a certain event, whereas an event triggering the application of a redistributive legal rule—such as being involved in a car accident—is an uncertain one. If potential defendants underestimate the latter risk, they will perceive its costs to be lower than they actually are. Consequently, a redistributive tort rule—which expands the liability of rich injurers for the benefit of poor plaintiffs—will distort the work incentives of the former less than a tax yielding the same amount of revenue for the government (Jolls 1998, 1658–63). More recently, Fennell and McAdams (2016) have claimed that since losses loom larger than gains in people's minds, the framing of a redistribution as involving either losses or unattained gains can affect the political action costs of enacting and maintaining it. In particular, they argue that tax-and-transfer mechanisms tend to highlight the "taking away" of something that a person previously had and are therefore likely to be perceived as inflicting losses. Consequently, taxes and transfer payments may be more cognitively painful and less acceptable politically than other forms of redistribution that less obviously entail losses (Fennell and McAdams 2016, 1093–98).

More generally, and importantly for our purposes, psychological studies underscore the importance of the source and mode of outcome production. As explained earlier, the economic argument assumes that the success of the redistribution should be evaluated according to the bare quantity of resources that people receive, regardless of the way they were obtained. However, numerous experimental studies have shown that the benefit people derive from resources depends on complex factors, including the acts that generate the resources and the source from which they are received. In particular, an object believed to be attained "as of right"—through effort or as a result of success—is valued much more highly than a similar object obtained through no entitlement, through chance, or due to failure.

Loewenstein and Issacharoff (1994), for example, tested source dependence in a pair of interesting experiments. In the first, they distributed mugs to students who excelled in a previously conducted class exercise. Half of the students were informed that they received the mug based on their performance on the exercise, and the other half were told that they were randomly selected to receive a mug. All mug receivers were asked to fill out a form on which they could choose between keeping the mug and trading it for some monetary sum. The remaining students in the class, who did not receive a high grade on the exercise, were given a choice between getting a mug or similar amounts of money. The authors found that the perception that mug possession was due to skill rather than chance substantially increased its valuation, by the same absolute amount as did mere possession of the mug (Loewenstein and Issacharoff 1994, 160–61). In other words, source dependence was found to be equal in magnitude to the well-known endowment effect—namely, that people value an object they possess more than a similar object that they have an opportunity to acquire (for discussion of the endowment effect, see chapter 1).

In the second experiment, the authors compared mug evaluations of students who thought that they have received a mug (or not received a mug) due to high or low performance on the exercise. In one class the low scorers got the mugs, and in another class the high scorers received them. The results revealed two interesting phenomena. First, students who received a mug due to their high score on the exercise valued it significantly more highly than students who obtained a mug due to their low score. A positively perceived source enhances the valuation of an object, while a negatively perceived source diminishes it. Second, low performers who obtained mugs did not value them more than high performers who did not receive mugs. That is to say, when the source dependence effect operated in opposition to the endowment effect, the former eliminated the latter. A possible explanation for source dependence is that people associate between causes and effects, so that contemplation of one evokes the other. Since it is pleasurable to think about success, this association increases the positive affect attributed to the thing obtained. This affect, in turn, provides an incentive for increasing one's valuation of the thing above what it would have been had it been received in a more neutral way. Similarly, since thinking about failure is generally unpleasant, the value of an object diminishes if it was obtained as a result of such an event (Loewenstein and Issacharoff 1994, 159, 163–64).

Additional behavioral studies reveal the existence of source dependence. A bargaining experiment by Hoffman and colleagues (1994) showed that when sellers felt that they earned entitlement to a sum of money (by scoring high on a preliminary general knowledge quiz, rather than by randomly receiving the sum), they were less willing to share equally the gains of the trade with buyers. Thus, notions of entitlement enhance the valuation of the resource. Likewise, Bühren and Plessner (2014) found a "trophy effect," whereby participants who won an item (a ballpoint pen) in a mathematics competition valued it much higher than participants who received the same item as a result of being unsuccessful in the competition or by lottery. Similarly, McGraw, Tetlock, and Kristel (2003) demonstrated that the identity of the relational source of an object or an income and its social meaning strongly affected its valuation and consequent decisions regarding whether to sell or spend (rather than save) it. Objects and windfall income received from family members or close friends were valued much more highly than objects or income received from different sources, such as from an authority (an employer or teacher) or in market relationships. In the former scenarios, individuals demanded much higher sums in order to part with the asset, and were much more likely to save the income than to spend it. Thus, the more positive the symbolic, historical source of an object or income is, the greater it is valued by the recipient. These results were replicated and expanded by Jefferson and Taplin (2012) to include additional relational sources (a raffle prize vs. a gift from someone close), variable values of the sale object (a watch of low or high value), and different types of potential buyers (a friend vs. a merchant). Further studies have demonstrated that money is not always regarded as fungible, and that people often attach different meanings and separate uses to particular monies (Zelizer 1997, 3, 5, 200, 209, 211; see also Thaler 2000, 259).

Studies in legal contexts revealed that factors such as how an outcome was brought about (with goodwill and cooperation or not), the identity of the parties involved (strangers or friends), the voluntariness or non-voluntariness of their behavior, and the intentionality or nonintentionality of their acts significantly affect its valuation by both laypersons and businesspeople (Lewinsohn-Zamir 2012; for more detailed discussion of this study, see chapter 3). Likewise, studies of procedural justice have shown that people care not only about substantive outcomes but also about the process leading up to them. The perceived fairness or unfairness of the process may affect how the outcome is accepted and how legitimate it is regarded to be (Thibaut and Walker 1975, 72–77, 89–94, 118–22; Tyler 1989).

This body of research indicates that the *method* of redistribution matters. All methods of redistribution—including taxes, transfer payments, and redistributive legal rules—can be classified as positioned somewhere along the continuum between the two extremes of "humiliation" and "reward." Generally speaking, taxes and transfer payments are more likely to be perceived as humiliating, whereas redistributive legal rules would plausibly be regarded as more respectful and empowering (for further discussion, see Lewinsohn-Zamir 2006, 353–74).

Public opinion surveys have found that taxes and transfer payments are often viewed as "charity giving" and as helping the undeserving poor (Kluegel and Smith 1986, 152–57, 163–65, 175, 293; Gilens 1999, 1–9, 60–79). In contrast, private law rules set the baseline for interactions between individuals, determine what each party has (or should have) at the outset of their relationship, and typically convey a message of entitlement (see also Jolls 1998, 1672; Singer 2000, 177). Consequently, a smaller quantity of goods obtained through legal rules may advance the recipients' welfare to a greater extent than the same or even a larger amount received through taxes and transfer payments. The implied warranty of habitability in landlord and tenant law, for instance, carries with it a message that the object of a lease can only be a dwelling fit for human habitation. Tenants therefore have a right to such housing, and a landlord complying with these requirements is fulfilling her obligations, not granting any favors. Furthermore, private law rules establish standards and guidelines regarding what is objectively good for *all* people, and do not directly refer to the interacting parties' wealth. Usually, the rules do not carry a banner of "help for the needy." To illustrate, although a rule requiring residential units to be habitable is mainly relevant for the nonwealthy (since rich individuals would only lease a high-quality apartment), the rule is addressed to all tenants, not only to poor ones. Furthermore, redistribution that is perceived as the recipient's entitlement and as setting the "rules of the game" is likely to encounter less resistance from nonrecipients than one that is viewed as a handout. These features of redistributive legal rules increase the goodness of their distributive outcomes and should be taken into account by policy makers and regulators (for further treatment of these ideas, see Lewinsohn-Zamir 2006).

The argument in favor of redistributive legal rules is supported by a unique psychological phenomenon—the identifiability effect—to which we now turn.

The Identifiability Effect and Redistribution

The identifiability effect is the tendency of people to react more strongly toward identifiable individuals than toward unidentified ones. People might, for example, think that a particular miner trapped in a collapsed mine should be rescued at any cost, but object to taxation to finance more cost-effective measures that would prevent such mining accidents from occurring in the first place. The particular miner is identified, whereas those who would benefit from preventive safety measures are not (G. I. Cohen, Daniels, and Eyal 2015, 1). Likewise, victims of natural disasters or individuals who are gravely ill usually attract more generous contributions from the public when they are identified by name and/ or photo, rather than being anonymous (Kogut and Ritov 2005b; Small, Loewenstein, and Slovic 2007).

One major line of research on the identifiability effect examined pro-social behavior, such as monetary donations. Researchers found that people are significantly more willing to help another person if the latter is identified rather than unidentified (Kogut and Ritov 2005a; Ritov and Kogut 2011). Importantly, identifiability can have such an effect even when it conveys no meaningful or individuating information about the recipient (see, e.g., Burnham 2003 (identification by photograph); Charness and Gneezy 2008 (identification by name); Small and Loewenstein 2003 (identification by number)). To date, the identifiability effect has been observed mainly with regard to human beings, although one study found this effect in relation to endangered animals (Markowitz et al. 2013). Another line of experimental research explored the effect of identifiability on the reaction to blameworthy behavior. It was found, for example, that when an individual is seen as responsible for her plight (for instance, a person who contracted AIDS as a result of drug use), identifiability leads to a decrease in willingness to help (Kogut 2011). In sum, depending on the specific context, identifiability causes people to react either more generously or more punitively towards others.

Psychological studies have further shown that at least under certain circumstances, the identifiability effect occurs only with regard to a single identified person and does not extend to a group of identified people (Kogut and Ritov 2005a, 2005b).[4] This phenomenon has been named the "singularity effect." Other factors that affect the incidence and scope of the identifiability effect are perceptions of group belonging and the existence or absence of intergroup conflict (Kogut and Ritov 2007; Ritov and Kogut 2011). Among other things, it was found that in scenarios perceived to involve intergroup conflict, identifiability increased generosity toward an individual from the *opposing* group. Thus, for example, when eliciting donations for someone from a rival group—such as a member of another political faction or a fan of a competing soccer team— identifying the beneficiary increased people's willingness to contribute (Ritov and Kogut 2011).

The chief source of the identifiability effect is the stronger emotional reaction elicited by an identified individual (Kogut and Ritov 2010;

Markowitz et al. 2013). In the context of helping behavior, empathic emotions—such as sympathy, compassion, and distress at the plight of another—are preconditioned on adopting the other person's perspective and imagining how he or she feels. Such empathy is more likely to occur toward an individual who is identified, rather than anonymous or statistical. Similarly, when blameworthy behavior is involved, people may find it easier to attribute responsibility or feel anger toward an actual, identified person than toward abstract individuals (Kogut and Ritov 2005a; Kogut 2011).

The identifiability effect is potentially relevant to any decision concerning others, including decisions about everyday situations. Although most psychological experiments on the identifiability effect have examined it with respect to life-threatening events, some have documented it occurring when no risk to life or health was involved (see Kogut 2009 (decisions of school educators); Sah and Loewenstein 2012 (advice in situations of financial conflict of interest); Ritov and Zamir 2014 (support for affirmative action)). Moreover, an initial experimental study by Lewinsohn-Zamir, Ritov, and Kogut (2017) directly tested for the existence of an identifiability effect in legal contexts. Specifically, this vignette study examined participants' choices with respect to private law remedies and fines in two types of lawmaking—comparing the judgments they make as policy makers, formulating rules for *unidentified* people, with their judgments as decision makers concerning *identified* individuals. The identifying information in the decision-maker scenarios was minimal—merely the first names of the parties to the conflict. Participants had to determine, for example, whether to order specific performance or damages for breach of contract; to coerce a libeler to apologize or order additional monetary compensation; to order demolition or suffice with compensation for an encroaching building; or whether (and to what extent) to reduce a damages award for injury to property because the injurer is poor. It was found that participants in the role of decision makers were more lenient toward wrongdoers and more considerate of their interests than were participants in the role of policy makers. Thus, with respect to the preceding examples, decision-makers (who were faced with an identified wrongdoer) were more willing than policy makers to refrain from ordering specific performance, to avoid ordering a libeler to apologize, to refrain from demolishing an encroaching building, and to reduce a damages award due to the poverty of the injurer (Lewinsohn-Zamir, Ritov, and Kogut 2017, 519–32).[5]

The identifiability effect is highly relevant for the redistribution debate and lends support to the earlier argument regarding the probable effect of different redistributive methods. In particular, the identifiability effect points to another advantage of redistributive legal rules over taxes and transfer payments, that supports the use of the former alongside the latter. Private law rules set the baseline for fair dealing, cooperation, and real-life interactions between nonanonymous, identified individuals: a landlord and her tenant, an employer and her employee, spouses, and so forth. As explained previously, identifiability increases people's generosity toward others and their willingness to help them. Even if a certain landlord, for example, has several tenants (rather than just one), there is still a one-on-one relationship, in reality, with each tangible and identified tenant. Identification is expected to cause a beneficial effect in this context, rather than a detrimental one, because legal rules cultivate notions of entitlement and therefore are not likely to be associated with blameworthy behavior on the part of the recipients. Moreover, as mentioned, experimental studies show that identification is particularly beneficial in situations that are perceived to involve intergroup conflict. In such cases, the identifiability effect enhances the generosity toward an individual from the *opposing* group. To the extent that the parties to a tenancy, employment, or consumer relationship regard themselves as belonging to rival groups with conflicting interests, identification has the propensity to increase feelings of sympathy and relatedness to the other party. Thus, the identifiability effect suggests that redistributive legal rules are likely to be more successful than commonly believed. By deploying such rules, the state can harness this psychological phenomenon to promote prosocial behavior and enhance the public's support for redistributive measures.

In contrast to legal rules, taxes and transfer payments lack identifiability—namely, they do not involve day-to-day interactions between identified persons. People interact with the government, which functions as a taker or a bestower of money, rather than among themselves. Thus, the "link" between the individual givers and recipients of the redistribution is severed, and the recipients remain anonymous. No notions of entitlement in mutual relationships can be formed, and no patterns of cooperation, fair dealing, or commitment can emerge. Likely, under such circumstances, transferors would feel not only less sympathy toward the unidentified recipients but also less responsibility or confidence that they can effectively help them.

It is not surprising, therefore, that nonrecipients and recipients alike often perceive taxes and transfer payments as a form of charity—other people's money being transferred to possibly undeserving beneficiaries (for criticism of this common perception, see Murphy and Nagel 2002, 31–37). Thus, direct income transfers—the method of redistribution recommended by standard economic analysis—encounter the greatest resistance. Such transfers typically conflict with the widespread belief that people control their fortunes. In contrast, the public widely supports efforts to aid the "working poor" (e.g., through job creation), because such measures are seen as correcting market failures and providing equal opportunities for work and achievement (Kluegel and Smith 1986, 152–57, 162–63). In general, studies of attitudes toward distributive justice have found that although people want to eliminate extreme poverty and guarantee everyone some minimum meeting of basic needs, they strongly believe that subject to this floor society should allow and promote inequalities that result from individual ability and hard work (Miller 1992; Lewin-Epstein, Kaplan, and Levanon 2003). Similarly, Bergh (2008) argues that people's responses to inequality are governed by two conflicting norms: social sharing and property rights. While individuals are inclined to share equally resources that they feel no prior entitlement to, they are less likely to be willing to share resources generated by effort (Bergh 2008, 1793–94).

To the extent that these perceptions and reactions are widely entrenched and unlikely to change, we must take them into account when contemplating the optimal way to redistribute. For one thing, it would be difficult to sustain welfare programs over time in the face of unsympathetic public opinion.

Is it possible to change this state of affairs and increase public support by *identifying* the recipients of taxes and transfer payments? Alas, probably not. In almost all studies of the identifiability effect, participants were able to help a particular individual—that is, the recipient was the identified individual herself, and not a representative of recipients in general or a member of some recipient group.[6] Furthermore, as mentioned earlier, studies of this effect show that at least under some circumstances, this phenomenon is largely limited to single individuals and does not extend to groups. Another relevant consideration is whether identifying a recipient might backfire and actually weaken public support for the redistributive measure. This can occur if the beneficiaries of taxes and transfer payments are regarded as "undeserving poor," since identification may be detrimental when the identified individual can be blamed for his or her condition.

For all these reasons, it is doubtful that identifying a particular recipient of welfare payments by photo and name, for example, would suffice to enhance public support for such monetary transfers. It would hardly be credible for the state to claim that funds raised from certain taxpayers are earmarked for a particular individual's needs, as charities enable donors to assign their contribution to a specific beneficiary, and class actions feature a representative individual claimant who sues on behalf of herself and a larger group (for discussion of this unique feature of class actions, see G. I. Cohen 2015, 170–72). Moreover, actually implementing such a scheme in the context of taxation and other monetary welfare transfers would likely be prohibitively costly.[7] Another consideration against identification in this context is that it might stigmatize the identified beneficiary. Individuals may feel inferior or shamed when forced to reveal themselves to others as welfare recipients (cf. Lewinsohn-Zamir 2006, 394–95, who discussed this issue with respect to vouchers and food stamps).

In summary, while identifiability is a natural, inherent feature of redistribution through legal rules and may contribute to such schemes' success, it is lacking in the context of taxes and transfer payments. To be sure, various factors may militate in favor of or against any given mode of redistribution (cf. McCaffery and Baron 2005, 1781, who acknowledge that various redistributive taxes may differ in their public acceptability but argue that the inefficiency of psychologically pleasing taxes might be too high to justify their adoption). However, the identifiability effect lends additional support to the argument that legal rules are an important redistributive tool that should be employed alongside taxes and transfer payments. In addition, it would be worthwhile to examine whether identification of beneficiaries can, in practice, improve the low level of public support for the tax-and-transfer method of redistribution.

Policy Implications for Property Law

To demonstrate the fruitfulness of the behavioral analysis, this section discusses two applications: choice of a family property system and compensation for takings of property. As we shall see, psychological insights can be useful when choosing between different redistributive rules of property law and when deciding if a certain rule of property law is an appropriate vehicle for redistribution.

Choosing a Family Property System

Marital property is an area of law in which distributive concerns play a major role. It regulates the use, enjoyment, and division of property between spouses and must address the issue of inequality in spouses' property holdings (on people's inclination to favor equal division of property even when spouses are guilty of marital misconduct, see Braver and Ellman 2013). Generally speaking, there are two basic types of family property systems: joint property and separate property. A joint property regime (also known as "community property") holds that, in principle, both spouses jointly and equally own the property earned by either spouse during the marriage, notwithstanding formal title. Marriage is viewed as a partnership to which both spouses make an equally important—even if different—contribution. Each spouse has similar vested property rights in the marital assets, which can be exercised at any point during the course of the relationship. A separate property regime, in contrast, maintains that each spouse separately retains not only the property he or she possessed prior to the marriage or received during it by gift or inheritance (as is common even in a joint property regime), but *also* the property that he or she earned during the marriage. A more equitable division of assets is attained upon divorce according to factors like need, contribution in the home, health, and occupation. In addition, the poorer spouse may be awarded alimony or maintenance payments (Singer 2017, 394–95, 399–409).

The behavioral findings discussed in this chapter lend support for the superiority of the joint property regime as a redistributive device. Alimony and maintenance payments (like taxes and transfer payments) resemble charity giving. They imply that the spouse has no right to the property accumulated throughout the marriage but only has a claim to some of the other spouse's money to make ends meet. This type of redistribution may be associated with failure, thus diminishing the value of the thing received. Similarly, obtaining property rights in assets only after the divorce (under the separate property regime) might also convey a message of "no entitlement," because the poorer spouse has no property rights during the entirety of the marriage and cannot realize the advantages of having such rights throughout that period. Therefore, the subsequent transfer of assets upon divorce is likely to be perceived as a transfer of another person's property. The fact that the extent of the transfer is determined by factors like needs, rehabilitation, health, and skills may also solidify the association of the redistribution with failure and handouts to the needy. In contrast, joint ownership grants both spouses equal standing and rights in the marital assets throughout their relationship and therefore may foster notions of entitlement, responsibility, and sharing. In addition, having assets "as of right" and due to effort is more strongly associated with success, which increases the value of the quantitative outcome that the spouse receives (Lewinsohn-Zamir 2006, 385–89).

Undesirability of Redistribution through Property Takings

Psychological insights also point to contexts in which redistribution via legal rules is undesirable. A good example is takings compensation. When land or personal property is taken by the state for public use, its owner is entitled to just compensation (for a general discussion of the takings issue, see chapter 3). Should landowners' right to receive compensation be diminished, to some extent, due to redistributive considerations? Such redistributive rules were proposed by Dagan (1999), who argued that takings rules shape people's conceptions of what it means to own land, and thus their relationships with one another as landowners. Therefore, to achieve greater equality and social responsibility in the community, governmental action imposing a disproportionate burden on property owners should not be considered a taking if it complies with two conditions. First, the burden must not be overly extreme. This condition is evaluated by comparing the diminution in the property's value to the total value of the land affected and to the total holdings of the owner in the same surroundings. Second, the burden need not be compensated if it is likely to be roughly offset by similar benefits that the property owner will receive from other public actions (which harm neighboring lands). These countervailing benefits need not accrue immediately; suffice it that they would probably be conferred in the long run (Dagan 1999, 744–46, 767–81, 791).

According to the arguments raised in this chapter, compensation rules for takings of land are a problematic redistributive method, even assuming that we can carefully tailor them to ensure that they adversely affect only the relatively well-off. Curtailing the compensation right for takings may not directly advance the well-being of those who are worse-off. Rather, it mainly involves a "leveling down"—that is, a move toward greater equality by reducing the welfare of the better-off.[8] There is no guarantee that the money "saved" by noncompensation of landowners would be used in any project that benefits the poor, or that the welfare of the latter would be promoted in the long run by harming the former.

Moreover, even assuming that limiting compensation has positive redistributive effects in the long run, this method of redistribution shares the disadvantages of the tax-and-transfer mode and lacks the advantages of private law rules. Like the tax-and-transfer system, it severs the link between the coerced contribution and the subsequent benefits. The taking—as is indicated by its name—involves only the property owner and the state. Since there is no interaction between individuals across both sides of the redistribution, an identifiability effect is unlikely to emerge, and the educational effects of the limited-compensation rule—in terms of entitlements, fair dealing, and appropriate relationships between people—are likely to be weak. This, in turn, both reduces the value of the redistributive outcome to the recipients and increases the resistance and injury suffered by those from whom things were taken. In sum, it seems unadvisable to achieve redistributive goals by way of compensation rules for takings.

Concluding Remarks

Behavioral studies support the use of private law rules, including substantive rules of property law, as a method of redistribution. We do not claim that redistributive legal rules should substitute for tax-and-transfer schemes. Rather, we argue that the former offer unique advantages as a redistributive tool, and therefore should be allowed to complement the latter. Private law rules assist in forming notions of entitlement, which enhance the value of the goods that are distributed and, at the same time, decrease the givers' opposition to the redistribution and injury to their welfare. Taxes and transfer payments, in contrast, often imply charity giving, which in turn diminishes the goodness of the distributive outcome and its value to the recipients, and increases the resistance of those whose wealth is taken. While taxes and transfer payments are best suited to redistribute income and enable people to satisfy their preferences, they are much less capable of conveying valuable educational messages. Redistributive legal rules, in contrast, are best equipped to distribute in kind and to enhance attainment of objective goods (which have intrinsic value independent of whether individuals desire them). Thus, a good "division of labor" exists between the two methods of redistribution. We need them both and should not dispense with either.

PART III

Real Estate Transactions

5

Transacting Property

A major function of property law is to move property in markets through buying, selling, and financing (for discussions of leasing, see chapters 2 and 4). Law creates property forms, delineates the obligations of agents in transactions, governs liability for property defects, and regulates lending. Ideally, property law creates a legal infrastructure for markets that reduces the costs of property changing hands and increases welfare. This legal infrastructure encompasses statutory law, common law, and contract. In this chapter, we see how property law responds—or, as is sometimes the case, fails to respond—to cognitive and behavioral limitations that affect transactions.

In the model transaction, the buyer and seller attend and rationally respond to information, dispassionately price property, negotiate contingencies and compensation for defects, and make sound decisions about loans to finance purchases. Parties to real estate transactions must not only manage this information but also update their judgments throughout the transaction and financing process as new information becomes available (cf. Lefcoe 2016, 5–12). But is this how people behave in practice?

A wealth of research in psychology describes how people struggle to pay attention, process information, assess risk, update existing information as new data become available, and translate their decisions to action. As early as the 1950s, Herbert Simon described how people routinely fail to perceive full sets of alternatives, accurately estimate the expected reward or outcome of their actions given the actions of other players (the "pay off function"), order their own preferences, and calculate probabilities (H. A. Simon 1955, 102; 1957, 199). Instead, people depart from rationality in systematic patterns (biases) and use mental shortcuts or rules of thumb that focus on one dimension or a small number of attributes (heuristics) to simplify complex decisions (Tversky and Kahneman 1974). Social relationships, self-image, and emotional states also influence how we interpret information and make decisions (Fredrickson and Branigan 2005; Sah, Loewenstein, and Cain 2013). Even if we rationally attend to and process information, we may still stumble at translating that information into action. We might intend to act but find that willpower deserts us, or we fall prey to social pressures or emotions that unravel our intentions. These "bounds" on human rationality call into question the rational actor model in law and economics (Jolls, Sunstein, and Thaler 1998, 1477–79) and present challenges for real estate transactions.

This chapter considers how psychology can inform the laws governing real estate transactions. We examine the standardization of property forms, defect disclosure laws, regulation of dual agency for real estate agents, and lending regulation. Rather than attempt a broad survey, the chapter explores a number of psychological biases and heuristics in depth through illustrative applications to transactional law. We spend little time on commercial real estate or personal property transactions because contract law plays the leading role in those contexts. A theme throughout the chapter is the role of disclosure rules in responding to information-processing failures, and the capacity of psychology to improve information processing and risk assessment in property transactions. While disclosure laws are the most common response in real estate law to either lack of information or information-processing failure, disclosure can create a second-order problem of information processing: a disclosure may be subject to the same biases and cognitive blunders that it is supposed to correct (Ben-Shahar and Schneider 2014).

Property Forms as Schemas

Property law creates and defines the different forms of property and their respective configurations of property rights. For example, are you purchasing full and complete rights to property (fee simple) or the rights to use it for life (a life estate)? Are you obtaining shorter-term use rights with limitations on your ability to use or convey the property (e.g., a lease) or property rights that might accrue to you in the future (e.g., an executory interest)?

In an important article, Thomas Merrill and Henry Smith (2000) describe the *numerus clausus* doctrine. The *numerus clausus* limits property to a fixed number of forms, each defined by certain characteristics. For example, fee simple absolute ownership and the lease are property interests within the *numerus clausus* (12–13). The *numerus clausus* doctrine is formalized in civil property law and influential in common law courts. To illustrate the doctrine, Merrill and Smith offer the example of two parties attempting to create a time share in personal property, a watch, where one uses the watch on Mondays and the other has rights to the watch the balance of the week (27). The parties must create this division through contract because property law in the United States recognizes time shares only in real, not personal, property (other countries, such as Israel, do not recognize time-sharing as a property right in real or personal property). Merrill and Smith argue that a limited set of standardized property forms reduces information costs for subsequent buyers. If a buyer and seller exchange property that has an idiosyncratic form, other buyers must then expend time and resources to ascertain the property rights of that good or of similar items (25–27). Of course, on the other side of the balance, the *numerus clausus* doctrine may thwart the goals of participants in an exchange by restricting customization. Merrill and Smith contend that the *numerus clausus* is a rough way of achieving optimal standardization that decreases information costs, while not chilling too many transactions.

Psychology research on schemas and information processing augments Merrill and Smith's account of the informational advantages of a standardized, limited set of property forms. Property forms consolidate multiple pieces of information about property rights into an overarching structure, making it easier for us to understand and recall those property rights. Psychologists refer to such knowledge structures as schemas and have studied them extensively. Schemas are linked mental representations that organize information into a functional unit (Piaget 2002; Wadsworth 2004). For example, one's schema for a lease may include the following aspects: the tenant can use the property for a period of time; the tenant cannot sell the property; the tenant cannot alter the property without permission from the landlord; and the landlord controls the timing of the tenant's exit via the landlord's right to approve or disapprove lease renewal.

Psychologist Jean Piaget (2002) was an early pioneer of the psychological concept of schemas, which he argued are the basis of organizing knowledge for objects, actions, and concepts. Psychologist B. J. Wadsworth (2004) has described schemas as index cards that are filed in the brain and tell people how to react to stimuli or information. In a similar vein, research on "chunking" has found that dividing information into groups increases recall (e.g., remembering the word "rat" is easier than remembering the three letters *r*, *a*, and *t*) (Shiffrin and Nosofsky 1994). Without schemas or chunking, people can remember only a small number of discrete units of information that are presented at one time.

Property form schemas are also helpful when we encounter unfamiliar property forms. People can use existing schemas as the foundation for understanding an unfamiliar form by contrasting and comparing, retaining some aspects of the prior schema, and inserting new attributes in order to construct a new schema. As David Axelrod explains, "When new information becomes available, a person tries to fit the new information into the pattern which he has used in the past to interpret information about the same situation" (1973, 1248). For example, suppose a seller is willing to convey his land, Purpleacre, only for the buyer to use for the duration of her life. In property law, this form is a life estate, and its key characteristics are that the life estate holder's use rights end with her life, the life estate holder can convey the use rights only for the duration of her life, and the life estate holder is subject to common law duties to future rights holders not to decrease or "waste" the property value. A buyer or recipient of a life estate may not have heard of a life estate, but she likely has schemas in place for owning and renting, which are common property forms. The buyer may reason that, like a renter, she cannot damage the property and will not be able to sell the property outright, but, similar to an owner, she has significant (though not unlimited) control over how she uses the property, and she can sell her life estate property interest.

Property form schemas can improve cognitive processing of transaction information that is not directly related to property rights as well. Merrill and Smith assume that parties to the transaction will not need to judge much new information about property rights because the forms are a standardized and closed set. This point is debatable, and some scholars have challenged the *numerus clausus* perspective on the grounds that in practice a great deal of property rights "customization" occurs (Hansmann and Kraakman 2002). Even if we put aside the debate about the degree of customization of property rights, it is inevitably the case that a great deal of *other* information occurs within transactions. A property form schema allows buyers and sellers to devote the cognitive resources that would have been spent determining and understanding property rights to other information, such as physical attributes of the property, its valuation, financing, and the timing of the property transfer.

Bounds on Information Processing: Property Conditions and Defects

A major function of transactional real estate law is to regulate the flow of information between buyer and seller. Psychology research sheds light on why information, the sine qua non of market transactions, can suffer from information processing failures and cognitive unavailability. Information-processing failure refers to deviations from rationality in searching for information and weighing it to make a decision. The cognitive demands of paying attention (i.e., psychological search costs) may be too high, which truncates information gathering (Malhotra 1982). The most common response to a complex decision is for people to selectively attend to information by choosing a small number of salient characteristics or decision-making points on which to focus. This is in some respects adaptive: if people attempt to process too much information, they may show declines in cognitive performance and the quality of decision making. However, selective attention and biased assimilation of information can cause buyers and sellers to neglect highly relevant information and focus on less important or even irrelevant factors (H. A. Simon 1978, 13–14; Lord, Ross, and Lepper 1979). We consider here the psychology of information processing in the context of defects in residential real estate.

The Psychology of Caveat Emptor

Caveat emptor is one of the oldest common law doctrines in property and contract law, dating back to early Roman law and sixteenth-century English law governing the sale of chattels (Hamilton 1931, 1156–64). Caveat emptor, or buyer beware, provides that the buyer is liable for all defects in a product, including real estate, after the sale closes (Grand 1986, 44). The only exceptions to caveat emptor are when the parties allocate liability by contract or the seller has committed a fraud. Caveat emptor is a bright-line rule that provides ex ante clarity and certainty and reduces litigation costs. Yet, the consequences of caveat emptor can fall heavily on buyers who fail to research or pay attention to property condition. Today, caveat emptor remains the law in the United States for commercial transactions, where buyers have due diligence periods and greater expertise, and routinely negotiate and contract with sellers for contingencies, conditions, indemnifications, and insurance. But for the average residential buyer, caveat emptor has proven so challenging that the rule no longer applies to residential transactions.

The psychology research on attention and information search sheds light on some of the reasons that caveat emptor became unworkable as building construction became more complex. First, in the absence of information from sellers, buyers may show what psychologists term "inattentional blindness" (Chabris and Simons 2009). They may not see or hear what is directly in front of them if their attention is divided or focused elsewhere. In a famous experiment, participants counted the number of ball passes by three players in white shirts to three players in black shirts. While focused on the counting task, half of the participants did not notice a man dressed in a gorilla suit walk into the middle of the court and thump his chest, yet they maintained the "illusion of attention," or the mistaken belief that they would notice visible occurrences in the face of multiple stimuli (5–8). If people fail to see a gorilla in the middle of a ball game, it is easy to see how they might fail to notice cracks in a home foundation, water marks suggesting damage, or signs of wear on a heating system.

Second, information search failures may occur when the buyer has a preexisting inclination to purchase the property or trusts the seller or broker. "Confirmation bias" refers to the tendency of people to search for, and give disproportionate weight to, information that supports their preexisting beliefs (Nickerson 1998, 177–78). Interested buyers will tend to undersearch for information on property quality that might disconfirm their preexisting belief in the property's attractiveness. Home inspectors can increase the information available, but not the attention and decision-making weight buyers give that information. In addition, realtors, who have a stake in the sale closing, often refer buyers to favored home inspectors. This potential conflict of interest decreases the independence of the inspection and the quality of information inspectors provide to buyers.

Compounding the psychological challenges is a nonpsychological one: even if buyers became fully efficient information gatherers, not all defects are observable. The rule of caveat emptor worked relatively well in prior eras when buildings were simpler structures, lacking electricity, computerized home mechanics, extensive plumbing, and other features common to structures today. It may also be that caveat emptor was a more viable rule when populations were smaller and more dispersed, so that reputations for building quality and fair dealing by builders and sellers gave buyers a proxy for quality for features they could not access or see.

In the face of high search costs for information and human information-processing limitations, the caveat emptor rule can create a "market for lemons." In some circumstances, information asymmetries can harm individuals and markets through adverse selection. The market for lemons famously described by George Akerlof results when buyers cannot discern the value of a particular car and therefore will only pay the average value of the quality of existing stock (Akerlof 1970). Sellers then have an incentive to sell increasingly low-quality cars, or lemons, in order to turn a profit. Sellers of high-quality cars leave the market and hold onto their cars, causing average used car quality to decrease further. In addition to the effects on price and quality, information asymmetries or other forms of information failure also frustrate widely shared social and psychological preferences for fair processes and dealings (cf. Tyler 1988).

The Cognitive Psychology of Latent vs. Patent Defects

Given the failings of human attention and cognition and the practical difficulties of acquiring property condition information, it is not surprising that over time the common law began to shift from caveat emptor to a limited rule of seller disclosure. Following World War II, caveat emptor began to erode in the United States as building complexity, tastes for consumer protection law, and concerns about the chilling of real estate investment increased. For commercial real estate, caveat emptor remains the common law default. In residential real estate transactions, however, caveat emptor has fallen in favor of a bifurcated common law rule that enables buyers to recover for certain kinds of nondisclosure. Under the common law rule of latent defect disclosure, sellers must disclose material latent defects, but not immaterial or patent (i.e., visible) ones in the property. A latent defect is hidden or concealed and thus not apparent to the buyer. As the court in *Lingsch v. Savage* explained, "Where the seller knows of facts materially affecting the value or desirability of the property which are known or accessible only to him and also knows that such facts are not known to, or within the reach of the diligent attention and observation of the buyer, the seller is under a duty to disclose them to the buyer."[1]

The disclosure rule for latent housing defects raises two issues highly relevant to psychology. First, is the standard of diligent attention and observation an unrealistically demanding requirement? Second, even if a buyer discerns a defect, should we expect her to make rational estimations of the risks and costs of that defect? Turning first to the issue of attention, the latent/patent rule is an improvement from the information-gathering demands of caveat emptor. However, it still requires buyers and sellers to gather and encode complex information (i.e., to move information from observation to conscious recognition and processing) while they simultaneously juggle other aspects of the transaction. It is difficult to square the "diligent attention" required of buyers under the latent/patent rule with the findings in psychology that the majority of people cannot recall even arresting events when there are competing demands on their attention (Simons and Chabris 1999). The effect of emotions on attention also introduces variability. Negative emotions may narrow the attentional field and decrease information gathering (Fredrickson and Branigan 2005). Buyers who are stressed, impatient, or angry as they confront the minutiae of a real estate transaction may pay less attention to property condition. There is also an emerging line of research that suggests that people in good moods may have more expansive, but in some studies less accurate, visual attention (Vanlessen et al. 2016).

The psychology research suggests that the latent/patent common law rule does not reflect how people perceive the world. What is latent or patent depends on the context and number of stimuli competing for the observer's attention, not on visibility or accessibility as the common law prescribes. The latent/patent distinction illustrates the illusion of attention where most people believe they have attentional capacities far in excess of their actual capabilities (Simons and Chabris 1999). Through the latent/patent rule, courts have formalized this bias into the common law by assuming that buyers, or their agents, will be able to notice patent defects.

Buyers' psychological foibles in attention, as well as their lack of construction expertise, have birthed the profession of home inspection. Professional property inspectors, once rare, are now routinely used in real property transactions. While property inspectors are not immune to issues of cognitive load and inadequate attention, there are reasons to believe they are less affected. Unlike buyers, property inspectors focus only on one aspect of the transaction, the condition of the property, and are not emotionally invested in the transaction outcome. Because this is their livelihood, checking various aspects of a property becomes habitual. Habits free cognitive resources for other tasks such as analysis or probability estimation. Of course, home inspection is not a complete curative to information failure. Despite their comparative advantage in information processing, home inspectors may overlook defects, individual inspectors may lack experience, or certain kinds of defects may not be observable. Moreover, as noted earlier, many inspectors depend on repeat referrals from real estate agents, which can bias their search or their characterization of risks. Also, inspectors cannot control how buyers and sellers apply the information from the inspection to decision making and price negotiation.

The research on heuristics and biases suggests that even when people overcome bounds on information gathering, they tend to misestimate risks and generate inaccurate pricing information. In addition to confirmation bias, discussed previously, we are subject to optimism bias that causes us to systematically overestimate the likelihood of positive events. People expect longer lives, job success, talented children, and lifelong marriages more than the base rates of these occurrences support (Sharot 2011, R941–42). This bias appears to occur because people selectively update their beliefs more often in response to positive than negative information. Optimism bias is widespread, with approximately 80 percent of the population holding optimistic estimations (the remaining 20 percent include individuals with depression, who as a population do not show optimism bias) (R942). People are less likely to display optimism when the decision involves a risk to their lives or events that will soon occur (and be subject to evaluation), or when they are exploring goals or options prior to decision making (Armor and Taylor 2002, 339).

As a result of optimism bias, buyers and sellers may persist in transactions even as costs and risks accumulate. Optimism bias can create value for markets because it greases the wheels of transaction for both parties and may counteract sellers' tendencies toward loss aversion. However, for individual buyers and sellers, optimism bias can have negative impacts because it causes them to overvalue gains and underestimate risks from a purchase or sale. Based on the research showing that optimism bias is lower at the predecision stage, buyers should display higher rationality at the early stages of property search and more optimism bias as they lean toward a purchase decision or make commitments.

The availability heuristic also hinders rational processing of information about the risk of defects. Availability causes people to weight the probability of something happening based on how easily they can call such examples to mind (Kahneman, Slovic, and Tversky 1982, 11–14). Rather than statistics, people rely on salience and familiarity to predict probability (11). As a result, people base probability on factors such as vivid imagery or narratives, familiar or famous people or events, and recent occurrences (11–12). Availability can lead people to overestimate certain kinds of risks and fear them disproportionately, while neglecting larger risks that are not top of mind. For real estate transactions, people are likely to overestimate property risks related to events that have received recent mass or social media attention. For example, buyers are likely to overestimate the risk of termites, mold, or flooding because those issues occur in news stories as well as in frequent advertisements by home repair businesses. By contrast, they may under-fear structural problems or noncompliance with building codes. In some instances, availability can increase demand for regulation (Sunstein 2003, 757–58), as has occurred with indoor mold following media attention and a spate of high-profile court cases.

The latent/patent rule has left disgruntled buyers in its wake who failed to notice, or understand, the risks of patent defects. The psychology literature on attention and visual processing calls sharply into question the common law assumption that there is a crisp, or even dis-cernible, distinction between what people view as latent and patent. The number of stimuli and the consequent fracturing of attention, rather than the degree of visibility, predict what people see and observe. More comprehensive disclosure of both latent and patent defects is not the only way to ameliorate information failure—and indeed it may not be the best way given the evidence of bounds on information processing. From a cognitive perspective, it makes sense to reduce the number of disclosure categories and the amount of information so that people can focus on a small number of important variables. For example, a revised common law rule could allow legal action for concealment of "highly material" patent and latent defects to ensure that buyers receive infor-mation about the most serious defects (rather than a slew of information about lower-value aspects of property condition).

In lieu of disclosure, legal rules might impose short "cooling-off periods" or additional time for information gathering for buyers pur-chasing properties in poor condition. This could occur based on price-to-value ratios for the property or based on severity of the defects, with the highest risk categories of residential transactions allowing the buyer longer periods of time to withdraw from the transaction without pen-alty.[2] However, these reforms would burden freedom of contract and may raise the costs for buyers who wish to redevelop properties in poor condition by making them more expensive for sellers to market. Psycho-logically, it is not clear the degree to which more time will ameliorate in-formation processing. These options have not appealed to the real estate industry. Instead, brokers have successfully lobbied state legislatures to create state laws requiring comprehensive seller disclosures that cover both observable and unobservable defects (S. M. Stern 2005, 61). We turn next to these statutory disclosures.

Updating, Sunk Costs, and Statutory Disclosure

Most states have adopted comprehensive statutory disclosures that require sellers to disclose all material defects of the property. The disclo-sures cover structural, mechanical, and environmental issues. In some states, sellers must also respond to catchall provisions that require them to report any other defects that a prospective buyer should be aware of. The disclosures typically require the seller to report both latent and patent property conditions that the seller has knowledge of in existing residential real estate, but they do not affect new construction. For new construction, buyers may bring suit under statutes codifying implied warranties of habitability and workmanship or under those common law doctrines themselves. The implied warranty of habitability for new construction imposes liability for latent defects arising from faulty workmanship that substantially affect safety or habitability.

Disclosures provide some meaningful information to buyers—though, as we have discussed, less so than a rational model of information processing would predict. In practice, however, the positive effects may be muted by the timing of the disclosures, which back-loads the provision of defect information (S. M. Stern 2005; Zamir and Teichman 2018, 174–75, 316). The majority of states allow sellers to complete statutory disclosures following the buyer's offer to purchase, and one-quarter of states allow disclosure to occur after the seller accepts the offer (typically within three to ten days) (64–66). Thus, in most cases, disclosure occurs after the buyer has seen the property, negotiated a purchase price, secured preliminary approval for mortgage financing, and placed an offer. In the absence of law, market forces do not prompt early disclosure. Neither the seller's agent nor the buyer's agent is eager to advertise a property's flaws from the outset, realizing it is better to front-load positive information and cultivate a positive emotional connection between the buyer and the property.

People engaged in transactions or other forms of costly decision making are subject to psychological biases to follow through and complete the transaction. Both psychologists and economists have studied how psychological inertia leads people to persist in choices or behaviors even when better alternatives are available (Gal 2006; Polites and Karahanna 2012). Behavioral and decision-making inertia occurs as people seek to follow through on commitments, respond to costs that are already "sunk" and irrecoverable, or suboptimally adjust their judgments from earlier estimations. In addition, behavior and decision inertia may result from the need to minimize the "cost of thinking" by routinizing behaviors (e.g., creating a default rule of following an agent's advice in a transaction) or from automatic habits that are difficult to unseat (Polites and Karahanna 2012).

First, psychology research finds that people who make "behavioral commitments" in the form of an agreement, a verbal statement, a position, or a decision are more likely to persist with a course of action despite subsequent information about its costs. For example, in a classic psychological experiment, students who merely agreed to participate in a research study showed up for that study in higher numbers even when they subsequently learned the study started at 8:00 a.m., compared with subjects who knew from the outset about the early start time (Cialdini et al. 1978). The capacity of commitments to drive perseverance increases when the commitment is made in public or requires significant effort (E. Aronson and Mills 1959; Schlenker, Dlugolecki, and Doherty 1994). In real estate transactions, the buyer has typically expended significant effort prior to making a written offer to purchase, and that offer is made before the seller and any real estate agents. Although the buyer may legally withdraw from the contract based on new information about defects that becomes available after her offer to purchase, at this point in the transaction process there is considerable psychological momentum to persist.

Second, sunk costs effects may encourage the completion of purchases or sales despite late-coming information about property condition (Arkes and Blumer 1985; Garland 1990). Rationally, nonrecoverable expenditures of time, effort, or money should be irrelevant to decisions. Yet, in practice, people often "throw good money after bad" in their decisions and purchases. In an experiment on the sunk-cost effect, Donna Boehne and Paul Paese gave participants information about the amount invested in a commercial real estate project, the percentage of the project completed, and the future sale price (i.e., profit) and asked them to decide whether to complete the project (Boehne and Paese 2000). They found that participants who were told the project was closer to completion were much more likely to opt to complete it. As Boehne and Paese explain, "Individuals get caught up in the desire to complete what they have started, and as this completion draws nearer, information that might have been taken into account before choosing to undertake the project (e.g., cost/benefit ratios) becomes increasingly unimportant" (192). This effect holds even when researchers factor in participants' perceptions about the likelihood of success of the project (Arkes and Hutzel 2000).

Third, buyers are likely to "anchor" on the initial negotiated purchase price and suboptimally negotiate for price reductions or contingencies when they receive late-coming information about property defects. People do not adjust sufficiently from initial judgments in response to new information. Research by Daniel Kahneman, Paul Slovic, and Amos Tversky found that people who start with an initial value make subsequent judgments about value that are closer to the initial "anchor" or starting place than is warranted by subsequent information (1982, 14–18). Research on anchoring in negotiation has found that initial offers have a greater effect on outcome than either counteroffers or later concessions (Moran and Ritov 2002; Neale and Bazerman 1991). Thus, we should expect that in states that allow statutory disclosures to occur after the buyer's initial offer, buyers will negotiate for smaller purchase price reductions on average than in states with early information provision.

Is there a role for property law in reducing the magnitude of these biases and information-processing failures? In considering this question, we do not claim that disclosure is a total curative or eschew substantive regulation. Within the current framework of residential property law, disclosure is the central regulatory tool for property defects. At a minimum, psychology indicates that disclosure can be improved by adjusting the timing of information. States that require disclosures prior to the buyer making an offer minimize cognitive consistency, sunk cost, and anchoring effects. Early disclosure also reduces the costs of inspections, attorney consultations, or other expenditures that the buyer might not have pursued with up-front information about the property's condition.

Sellers and the Psychology of Deception and Cheating

In addition to buyer information-processing failure, seller deception is a major impediment to providing buyers with quality information about property condition. Seller deception can take two forms, self-deception (which is typically unconscious) and conscious cheating. First, sellers may deceive themselves about their property's condition through the use of motivated reasoning, a psychological bias that causes us to fit information to our personal goals. Motivated reasoning leads people to seek out information that supports a preexisting goal (biased search) and to credit evidence favoring their goal while discrediting information that is opposed (biased assimilation) (Kunda 1990). This "reasoning process is more like a lawyer defending a client than a judge or scientist seeking the truth" (Haidt 2001, 820). In real estate transactions, sellers may engage in motivated reasoning that causes them to underweight the magnitude of a property defect or the imperative to disclose it. For example, a seller may rationalize that leaking inside the house is "just seepage" common to all houses in the area and that there is no evidence of mold or other damage indicating a defect. With respect to information gathering, the seller is psychologically *and* legally inclined toward biased search. Not only do people have psychological tendencies to truncate searches before gathering negative or disconfirming information, but in the case of residential real estate there are also strong legal incentives for sellers not to investigate defects in order to avoid triggering the legal obligation to disclose.

Second, sellers may engage in conscious dishonesty, for example, by responding falsely on disclosure forms. Nina Mazar, On Amir, and Dan Ariely (2008) have found that most people cheat a little bit when given the opportunity. Using a series of math tests, the researchers found that most participants who could cheat did so. However, on average people cheated only modestly, at 13 percent of the possible magnitude they could have cheated (Mazar, Amir, and Ariely 2008, 637). The results suggest that there is a "magnitude range" for dishonesty. Below a certain level of cheating, people do not perceive themselves as having engaged in serious dishonesty that would threaten their self-concept. This can be a problem for markets: small amounts of widespread cheating have large cumulative impacts on transactions, businesses, and insurers. In real estate disclosures, we should anticipate that sellers will routinely engage in low to moderate levels of dishonest reporting of property condition.

It is possible that buyers assume this will occur and therefore price modest levels of dishonesty into price negotiation. However, psychology research indicates a surprising level of bias toward trusting others. While we might anticipate that people should not trust strangers at all, instead people show surprisingly high levels of trust when they act or trade (Dunning et al. 2014; Johnson and Mislin 2011). Although people can be cynical in their assessments of the trustworthiness of others, in experimental games requiring cooperation, the majority of people in practice elect to trust strangers (Fetchenhauer and Dunning 2009). A recent study by David Dunning and his colleagues suggests an explanation: people trust strangers and nonintimates due to a sense of duty to respect others (Dunning et al. 2014, 137). This body of psychological research suggests that even a buyer who recognizes in the abstract that a real estate seller or agent may not be trustworthy may nonetheless display outsized trust during a transaction.

Are there ways to reduce dishonesty in transactions? While law focuses on the severity of punishment, the psychology research indicates that the magnitude of punishment does not have a robust effect on cheating and lying (Nagin and Pogarsky 2003). This is particularly true when the probability of facing consequences is low, as is the case for housing defects that may not be evident to new owners until months or years after closing. Instead, psychologists have found that individualizing (making individual identity more prominent) and cuing morality can increase honest reporting (Mazar, Amir, and Ariely 2008; L. S. Shu et al. 2012). In a classic experiment, trick-or-treating children left unsupervised with a pile of candy were more likely to take only one candy, as the experimenter had instructed, when they had previously given their name and address to the experimenter and faced a mirror positioned behind the candy (Beaman et al. 1979). The mirror did not affect the amount of candy taken by a second group of children in the experiment who had not given their name or other identifying information. In another study of individualization and moral cuing, Shu and coresearchers found that a prior pledge of honesty by insureds significantly decreased dishonest reports of odometer mileage on annual insurance policy review forms (L. S. Shu et al. 2012). Partnering with an insurance company, the researchers sent annual policy review forms to more than 13,000 customers, with one group receiving a form that began with "I promise the information I am providing is true" and a signature line at the top, whereas the other group received a standard form that asked for the insured's signature at the bottom. The authors concluded that signing before reporting made morality accessible whereas signing at the bottom of the form gave people time to "engage in various mental justifications, reinterpretations, and other 'tricks' . . . that allow them to maintain a positive self-image despite having lied" (L. S. Shu et al. 2012, 15197).

In view of this research, state agencies creating real estate disclosure forms might consider modifications to enhance individualization and moral cuing. A simple change would be to revise state disclosure forms so that sellers sign at the top of the page following a statement that they pledge the disclosure to be honest, as was done in the Shu et al. study with the insurance policy forms. Displaying a photo of the seller on the disclosure form would likely have an even stronger positive effect on honesty, as imagery makes individualization more vivid and therefore salient. This could be an option in the future if disclosure forms become digital and linked to photos (perhaps from social media accounts that one uses to sign into government sites). Of course, these proposals assume that statutory disclosures do not primarily aim to protect the brokers who lobbied for them, but also to enhance consumer protection to buyers. In addition, there is a countervailing question of whether truthful disclosure is efficient. It is possible that in some cases a small amount of cheating facilitates transactions or overcomes irrationally high risk aversion (assessing a risk at greater than its statistical expected value) on the part of buyers so as to create net welfare gains (cf. Slovic 2000).[3] This may be particularly socially desirable when real estate markets are sluggish or depressed.

Broker Dual Agency: The Psychology of Conflicts of Interest

Dual agency, a controversial topic in real estate law, refers to transactions where one real estate agent represents both the buyer and the seller. This representation strains the traditional boundaries of the common law fiduciary duties of loyalty and full disclosure owed by an agent to his client. An agent cannot fulfill these duties to buyers and sellers, parties on opposite sides of the transaction, simultaneously (Curran and Schrag 2000; Gardiner et al. 2007). Dual agency appears to affect sales prices and time on the market. The empirical evidence is mixed on whether dual agency increases or decreases sales prices (M. Carter and Brambila 2012). Presumably this varies based on local real estate market supply and demand and whether it behooves agents to focus on volume or to hold out for the highest sales price.

In the face of mounting lawsuits and real estate broker anxiety, states have codified brokers' duties in single and dual agency. Many states allow dual agency but require that real estate agents disclose the dual agency arrangement (Rohan, Goldstein, and Bobis 2018, § 3.21). In addition, half of the states have added a third category, a "transactional broker," who does not owe traditional fiduciary duties to either the buyer or the seller. An agent serving in a transaction broker capacity has no duty of loyalty or full information disclosure and only limited obligations of confidentiality (though they must disclose material facts). In some states, such as Florida, statutes make transaction brokerage the default unless the parties specifically enter into a fiduciary relationship.[4]

For real estate agents in a conflict of interest, such as dual agency, the unethical behavior that can result is most often due to self-deception—the most difficult form of deception to eliminate (Mazar and Ariely 2006, 124). When there are competing principles or narratives about fairness, people tend to favor versions that advantage their own interests (Messick and Sentis 1979). For example, brokers can rationalize actions against a buyer's or seller's interest by reasoning that ultimately the sale will be in the best interests of both. People also rationalize unethical behavior based on a "sense of entitlement" that prior sacrifices or hard work justify the behavior. A study by Sah and Loewenstein (2010, 1210) found that while 22 percent of physicians asked about industry gifts to physicians found them ethically acceptable, tolerance for industry gifts increased dramatically to 48 percent when physicians answered questions about the financial and lifestyle sacrifices of medical training prior to offering their opinion. The acceptability rating increased further to 60 percent for a third group of physicians who answered the sacrifice questions and read a rationalization (i.e., "some physicians believe that stagnant salaries and high medical school debt justify accepting industry gifts") (1210). Another bias that affects agents and advisers is the belief that professionalism will prevent the conflict of interest from affecting their advice (Sah 2017). People wrongly believe that while *other* professionals will be swayed by conflicts of interest, their professionalism and character will prevent them from succumbing. This rationalization is exceedingly difficult to correct because at its heart is a particularly robust bias, which psychologists call "self-serving bias." People tend to believe that they have superior capabilities to the average person and thus, while others may be biased, they are not.

In experiments, educating people about self-serving bias, forcing them to argue their nonfavored position, or penalizing them have all failed to remove self-serving biases (Babcock and Loewenstein 1997).

Even when researchers succeed initially in debiasing rationalizations and self-serving bias for ethics judgments, ethical fading typically undoes the gains over time. The term "ethical fading" describes the tendency for moral issues to fade into the background as black-and-white cost-benefit and business information (e.g., valuations, profit margins) takes center stage (Tenbrunsel and Messick 2004). As a result, it seems unlikely that professional training or accreditation is an antidote to conflicts of interest. Monetary sanctions, another potential legal response to conflicts of interest, can be counterproductive because fines recast ethical conflicts as cost-benefit decisions, or "the cost of doing business" (Tenbrunsel and Messick 1999). Education, incentives, and sanctions may all fail because they assume that unethical behavior is the result of conscious reasoning. The evidence shows that the biases that lead people into such behaviors are more often unconscious (Sah 2017).

Disclosure of dual agency is also unlikely to prevent behavior that advantages the agent at the expense of the buyer or seller. The psychology research suggests that such disclosures may not succeed at this aim due to information-processing failures, as well as some unexpected consequences of ethical disclosures. Disclosure of dual agency confronts the challenges that plague disclosures near universally. Buyers and sellers facing lengthy disclosures have limited attention and imperfect capacities to understand and recall information (Ben-Shahar and Schneider 2014; Zamir and Teichman 2018, 173–77). Disclosure forms often include complex language and "bury" negative information in the text where readers are less likely to notice or remember it. For dual agency disclosures, many states prescribe and produce the disclosure form that dual agents must use. These forms, such as the one developed by the Louisiana Real Estate Commission, describe the legal relationships but do not explain the risks of dual agency.[5] For example, the Louisiana dual agent disclosure form does not provide information about how the dual agency may affect the advice received from the agent or that buyers and sellers should verify, or discount, the advice of a dual agent.

There is also evidence from experimental studies and fieldwork showing that ethical disclosure rules can increase bias and facilitate conflict of interests. Disturbingly, studies have found that disclosure can lead advisers to give even more biased advice, possibly because advisers rationalize that they have fulfilled their ethical obligations by giving their clients the disclosure (D. Cain, Loewenstein, and Moore 2005, 7). There is emerging evidence that clients may feel social pressure to follow their adviser's or agent's advice to avoid appearing suspicious or obstructionist after they have been informed of and consented to a conflict of interest. This compliance effect occurs despite the fact that advisees report they trust the adviser's advice less following the disclosure (Sah, Loewenstein, and Cain 2013, 292–93).

Ultimately, the value of dual agency disclosure laws may not be in controlling ex post bias or self-dealing but rather in reducing the frequency of such arrangements ex ante. As we have discussed, the disclosures may not have a strong impact on buyers and sellers in dual agency arrangements. However, there is some evidence that disclosure laws may reduce the number of real estate agents who are willing to serve as dual agents. A recent study found that advisers are more likely to refuse to enter into a conflict of interest if they know they will need to disclose that conflict to their clients (Sah and Loewenstein 2014).

Thus far, we have discussed addressing broker conflicts of interest via education and disclosure laws. Another regulatory alternative for conflicts of interest is to legalize them by imposing minimal (or no) substantive obligations or disclosure duties on brokers. This is the approach some states have taken by adopting transaction brokerage laws. From a psychological perspective, state laws allowing transaction brokerage may promote unethical norms by legalizing conflicts of interest. These laws remove the moral and social weight from legal prohibition and instead suggest that such ethical conflicts are not serious or disfavored enough to merit laws restricting them. Recall that in a transaction brokerage, the real estate broker acts as an agent for the transaction without the traditional fiduciary duties to the buyer or seller. It is difficult to discern what this means, other than the loss of fiduciary duties. Indeed, it sounds reminiscent of the rationalizations that psychologists have found people use to justify conflicts of interest. Psychologists studying honesty and morality suggest that conflicts of interest are so difficult to debias that the most effective regulatory approach may be to prohibit advisers from entering into roles where there are serious conflicts of interest (Sah 2017; Bazerman, Loewenstein, and Moore 2002). Transaction brokerage does the opposite.

It is possible that transaction brokerage will create norms and ex-pectations over time that reflect its nonfiduciary nature and thus pose less potential for harm to buyers and sellers. For this to occur, however, buyers and sellers would need to know they are entering into a transaction brokerage, which is not the case in all states. In some states, buyers and sellers do not realize their agent is working as a transaction broker because the state does not require disclosure or makes transaction brokerage the default. Even if the client realizes that the agent is acting as a transaction broker, the compliance effect indicates that the social nature of the broker-client relationship may influence buyers and sellers more than the legal status of the brokerage (Sah, Loewenstein, and Cain 2013).

Nudge Laws and Psychological Contestation

One option for addressing the cognitive and psychological vulner-abilities that can harm consumers in property transactions is to utilize psychology to improve laws and to create "smart disclosures." In recent years, Cass Sunstein, Richard Thaler, and other advocates of behavioral "nudges" have explored how psychology research can improve disclo-sure, as well as harness the power of social norms and behavioral inertia to improve decision making (Thaler and Sunstein 2008). These nudges include resetting defaults to take advantage of behavioral inertia (e.g., making saving from one's paycheck automatic), disclosures created based on psychological and cognitive science, and other forms of "choice architecture" that guide consumers (Thaler and Sunstein 2008). Other "nudge" policies attempt to exploit psychological biases or limitations in order to lead people to make socially desirable decisions. For example, in 2010, the US Food and Drug Administration (FDA) unsuccessfully attempted to require the tobacco industry to place graphic visual images on cigarettes that would be likely to induce dread and increase the cog-nitive "availability" of smoking risks through vivid imagery.[6] The images created by the FDA included the corpse of a smoker, a person smoking through a hole in his throat made by a medical tracheostomy, and a pic-ture of diseased lungs. Not surprisingly given the influence such nudges can exert over individual behavior, there has been much controversy over whether nudges unduly impinge on liberty, autonomy, and even human development and learning from one's errors (Wright and Ginsburg 2012; Klick and Mitchell 2006).

Nudges are an important area of inquiry and potential reform for property law. One issue confronting nudge regulation in real estate transactions, however, is that regulated entities also have psychological expertise they can leverage to undermine or undo nudges. Tension can occur when psychological nudges aim to correct consumer abuses by businesses or other entities that are themselves adept at leveraging psychology (Willis 2013; S. M. Stern 2016). Lauren Willis's (2013) work on "slippery defaults" has described how businesses evaded a no-fee default rule for checking account overdraft protection for ATMs by manipulating borrower transaction costs and exploiting psychological weaknesses. Specifically, banks reduced the cost of opting out of the default with prepaid envelopes and one-click opt-out, flooded customers with marketing about overdraft protection until they agreed, and elicited loss aversion by framing opting out as retaining one's existing overdraft services (1185–1200).

In many respects, businesses are the original psychologists. Producers manipulated information presentation long before psychological salience research, gaming houses intuited the effects of variable ratio reinforcement centuries before behaviorism,[7] and interest groups and firms have long experience in eliciting, and even creating, group identities (cf. Skinner 1974; S. T. Fiske and Morling 1996). Business and other special interests have powerful, unified motivations to master psychological tactics—their survival in financial and political marketplaces depends on it. As a result, firms, as well as special interest groups, have been front-runners in formal and informal research on psychological persuasion. Businesses often win battles of psychological expertise against nudge laws and policies based on their superior proficiency in deploying visual imagery, narrative, and social media, as well as their ability to rapidly iterate (i.e., revise and improve) psychological techniques in the marketplace (S. M. Stern 2016). In contrast, law has traditionally hewed to the pallid dimension of written text.

How does nudge regulation fare in real estate transactions? We turn to an example of a lending reform, the Truth-in-Lending Act/Real Estate Settlement Procedures Act (TILA-RESPA), that used psychological methods and principles to improve standard lending disclosures. Past lending disclosures have buried consumers in voluminous pages of technical language, which is not comprehensible to the average borrower (Zamir and Teichman 2018, 163–65). Many borrowers were unable to even read traditional lending disclosures. In the United States, the average adult reads at an eighth- or ninth-grade level, and approximately 15 percent cannot read prose above a fifth-grade level. The numbers who cannot read at a basic level increase substantially for certain racial groups and the elderly (National Center for Education Statistics 2003).

The new federal TILA-RESPA Integrated Disclosure is a relatively brief, three-page form. It uses principles of visual and cognitive processing to improve the disclosure's impact. The most important information is found on the form's first page, and there is limited text on the page, simple yes/no questions for the lender to answer, contrasting headings and text boxes, and an overall high level of readability. To develop the form, the government applied psychological science and then refined the form incrementally following several rounds of focus group testing.[8]

While the new TILA-RESPA is undeniably improved, it is not clear how the new disclosure will fare in practice. Banks and lenders, which have developed their own psychological expertise, can undermine these laws. For example, a lending institution or mortgage broker may increase the amount of information provided, perhaps inundating the borrower with other paperwork at the first visit or sending additional e-mails or mailings directly following the disclosure. It may not take much to overwhelm buyers or dissuade them from careful review of the TILA-RESPA. While the form is simplified compared with prior lending disclosures, it is still not simple. Lenders can also use shaming, consumer confusion, and salesmanship to their advantage. In particular, lenders can leverage the personal and social context of the sale to encourage the borrower to trust the lender or mortgage broker as a proxy, or substitute, for reviewing the disclosure form.

Concluding Remarks

Each stage of the transaction process assumes that buyers and sellers are able to acquire, process, and update information. In some instances, such as the evolution of different forms of property and the fall of caveat emptor, property law appears to accommodate the limitations of human cognition. In a number of other cases, however, property law imposes overwhelming burdens on the average buyer's capacity to gather and process complex information. Property laws that allocate responsibility for defects in the property or loans often envision better attention, risk estimation, comprehension, and calculation than most buyers can muster. This is particularly true in residential markets. Commercial buyers work with a larger stable of experts who can tackle discrete tasks and have knowledge and expertise that lessen the cognitive demands of transacting property. In this chapter, we have seen how bounds on attention, heuristics and biases, the psychology of deception and conflicts of interest, and the psychological proficiency of regulated entities alter the effect of real estate laws on the ground and we have suggested avenues for legal reform.

6

Discrimination and Exclusion

The landscape of housing and land use law is stained by instances of exclusion and discrimination. In the United States, legal scholar Jeannine Bell (2007, 53–54) has documented "move-in violence" in the form of arson, vandalism, threats, and assaults experienced by racial and ethnic minorities moving into formerly white neighborhoods. A recent study of 1,086 Milwaukee renter households found that Hispanic households were twice as likely to be evicted when they resided in majority-white neighborhoods, compared with Hispanic households renting in predominantly nonwhite neighborhoods (D. Greenberg, Gershenson, and Desmond 2016). Discrimination in lending, such as racial differences in the extension of mortgages to applicants and refusals to extend home loans to low-income, minority neighborhoods, remains a serious national problem (Wyly and Hammel 2004, 1221–24).

One of the most formidable challenges confronting property law is how to respond to exclusion and discrimination. These actions compromise private property's role in securing autonomy and providing opportunities for life improvement (Nedelsky 2011; de Soto 2000; Alexander 2009). While the sine qua non of property is to create boundaries around a resource and grant the owner the power to exclude others (Merrill 1998, 730; cf. H. E. Smith 2002), these exclusion rights are fettered by statute, common law, and custom. A person's identity or membership in a group (e.g., an ethnic or religious group) is often an illegitimate ground for exclusion and discrimination. In the United States, the federal Fair Housing Act prohibits discrimination on the basis of race, color, religion, sex, familial status, national origin, and disability; several states have expanded protections to encompass discrimination based on sexual orientation.[1]

Beyond direct instances of discrimination, there is another contentious question for property law. To what degree should states and localities take affirmative actions to decrease segregation or increase the quantity of affordable housing? Federal regulations pursuant to the FHA require localities to "affirmatively further fair housing,"[2] and some state and city "inclusionary zoning" laws mandate or incentivize affordable housing, in part to promote residential diversity.[3] To the extent that inclusionary zoning or affirmatively furthering fair housing increases residential diversity and interaction between members of different groups, these laws hold promise for reducing prejudice. Psychologists have found that "contact" between members of different groups reduces prejudice toward the person one interacts with and toward their group (Pettigrew and Tropp 2006). The magnitude of prejudice reduction increases when the contact occurs under conditions of cooperation, common goals, equal status, and the support of law or other authority (751–52). Unfortunately, laws seeking to promote residential integration and diversity have encountered numerous obstacles to implementation (Mukhija, Regus, Slovin, and Das 2010; but see Powell and Stringman 2005). Localities have mounted legal challenges to their obligations to affirmatively further fair housing and to increase affordable housing, and in one recent case, falsified required reporting of the impediments to fair housing and the county's plan to overcome those impediments.[4]

Psychology research offers a nuanced, and in some respects counter-intuitive, view of the challenges of remedying discrimination and residential segregation through property law. There are two fundamental differences between how psychology and property law view discrimination and exclusion. First, while the dominant approach in property law is to focus on punishing intentional, overt acts of discrimination, psychology research suggests that prejudice most often occurs in the form of *unconscious* bias. Second, in property law, bias and stereotyping are conceived of as wrongs for law and residential integration to remedy. Yet, a long-standing literature in psychology describes bias and stereotyping as routine and adaptive cognitive mechanisms that arise from innate tendencies to categorize people and objects into groups in order to simplify a complicated world (Allport 1954; Bruner 1957; S. T. Fiske and Taylor 2017). This is not to claim that intentional animus does not exist, that all prejudice is of a comparable magnitude or character, or that biased behaviors and practices should not be addressed. Rather, psychology exposes a conundrum: the most prevalent forms of bias and stereotyping are neither pathological nor rare.

In this chapter, we introduce, and explore, three intersections of law and psychology. We do not aim to survey the vast ground of psychological research on prejudice or the myriad issues of discrimination in property law. Rather, we delve into key psychological findings, some of which have far-ranging applicability to property law beyond the laws examined here. We consider (1) the potential of disparate impact law to redress implicit bias in housing transactions, (2) how the federal FHA capitalizes on the psychology of social norms, and (3) the psychology of in-groups in state and local devolution of land use governance responsibilities to neighborhood associations. We focus much of our discussion on exclusion based on race, in part because of the vast quantity of seminal psychology research studying racial prejudice. Many of these findings should apply to other kinds of discrimination as well (e.g., gender or religious bias).

The Law of Disparate Impact in Housing and the Role of Implicit Bias

For acts of housing discrimination that are conscious and intentional, the legal process in the United States is straightforward: impose liability (in the form of compensatory and punitive damages or forcing the defendant to pay to correct the discriminatory condition), an injunction to halt the discriminatory practice, or a combination of these remedies.[5] But how do we address biases that are unconscious? As Anthony Greenwald and Linda Krieger explain, "Implicit bias poses a challenge to legal theory and practice, because discrimination doctrine is premised on the assumption that, barring insanity or mental incompetence, human actors are guided by their avowed (explicit) beliefs, attitudes, and intentions" (2006, 946).

At times, judges, advocacy groups, and legal scholars have suggested that disparate impact claims offer a way to address implicit bias (Equal Justice Society and Wilson Sonsini Goodrich & Rosati 2014, 251–52; *Texas Department of Housing and Community Affairs v. Inclusive Communities Project, Inc.*; cf. Anderson and Plaut 2012).[6] Disparate impact under the FHA applies to facially neutral policies that impose disproportionate harm on a protected class or perpetuate segregation, regardless of whether the defendant intended those effects. Indisputably, disparate impact law provides an avenue of ex post redress for plaintiffs who have suffered covert or unintended discrimination. But can disparate impact law also "debias" implicit biases or incentivize housing providers to adopt practices that reduce implicit bias's impact on decision making? As we shall discuss, disparate impact law faces steep psychological, as well as legal, hurdles to effectively debiasing or preventing unconscious discrimination.

The FHA does not explicitly provide a cause of action for disparate impact (unlike employment discrimination law).[7] However, the circuit courts have allowed disparate impact claims, with varying standards. In 2015, the US Supreme Court sought to resolve whether disparate impact claims are cognizable under the FHA and, if so, to set a uniform standard for disparate impact. The plaintiffs in *Texas Department of Housing and Community Affairs v. Inclusive Communities Project, Inc.* (hereinafter *Inclusive Communities*) alleged that the Texas Department of Housing and Community Affairs used selection criteria for awarding Low Income Housing Tax Credits (LIHTC) that perpetuated racial segregation in the Dallas metropolitan area by disproportionately awarding tax credits for construction of low-income housing developments in minority neighborhoods and disproportionately denying them for developments in white neighborhoods.[8] The Supreme Court held in a narrow five-to-four ruling that the FHA encompasses disparate impact claims. The Court remanded the case with standards for lower courts to use to assess disparate impact claims. A plaintiff must show a "robust causality" between the statistical disparity in effects on a protected class and a specific policy of the defendant. The defendant can prevail if he or she then shows that the policy is "necessary to achieve a valid interest." Pursuant to regulations by the federal Department of Housing and Urban Development (HUD), which were left undisturbed by the Court's holding, the plaintiff can still prevail by proving that the defendant's valid interest could be served by an alternative practice with less discriminatory effect.[9]

Echoing long-standing precedents, the *Inclusive Communities* Court endorsed disparate impact as a means to capture disguised or covert discrimination (Rutherglen 1987, 1303) and to redress distributional harms from discriminatory allocation of resources and opportunities (Primus 2003, 523–24; Fishkin 2014, 1465). The majority in *Inclusive Communities* also described a third rationale for recognizing disparate impact claims, one distinctly grounded in psychology. Disparate impact could provide redress for unconscious housing discrimination. Writing for the majority, Justice Kennedy explained, "Recognition of disparate-impact liability under the FHA plays an important role in uncovering discriminatory intent: it permits plaintiffs to counteract unconscious prejudices . . . that escape easy classification as disparate treatment."[10] In effect, the Court suggested that unconscious, or implicit, prejudice is an important category of discrimination for fair housing law and a form of unconscious "intent" subject to legal redress (Bagenstos 2016, 1134–35).

Implicit Bias in Housing and Land Use Law

Psychologists have intensively studied the unconscious discrimination that Justice Kennedy referred to in *Inclusive Communities*. Implicit bias refers to unconscious attitudes disfavoring some groups and preferencing others, often via stereotypes of different groups. Typically, people's implicit biases favor their own group or identity. These biases persist despite people simultaneously holding egalitarian beliefs and consciously rejecting negative stereotypes (Gaertner and Dovidio 1986). Decades of psychology research suggest that implicit bias is the most common form of prejudice (Gaertner and Dovidio 2005). While implicit bias is typically described as unconscious bias, it is more accurate to view consciousness as a continuum and implicit bias as occurring at lower levels of cognitive accessibility.[11] A related form of prejudice, termed "aversive racism" by psychologists Gaertner and Dovidio (2005), is characterized by ambivalence toward other groups and preferences not to interact personally with other groups (but, unlike implicit bias, these preferences may be conscious or unconscious).

Implicit biases may translate to behavior. For example, in a well-known experiment, Joshua Correll and his coresearchers created a first-person shooter video game in which participants had to make decisions as quickly as possible to correctly shoot armed figures and refrain from shooting figures carrying neutral objects such as a cell phone (Correll et al. 2002; Correll et al. 2011). They found that both African American and white participants were more likely to shoot unarmed African Americans than unarmed whites (they were also faster to shoot armed African

Americans compared with armed whites). Shooter bias did not appear due to the explicit biases of participants, measured by psychological assessments of participants' level of prejudice. Instead shooter bias correlated with a subtler variable suggestive of implicit bias: participants' awareness of societal negative stereotypes of African Americans. Other studies have found that pediatricians who display a pro-white bias on implicit bias testing prescribed more painkillers to whites than to African Americans and that criminal defendants with more African facial features receive harsher sentences (Sabin and Greenwald 2012; Pizzi, Blair, and Judd 2005).

In the housing arena, implicit bias may lead lenders to offer women poorer quality loans, realtors to suggest house listings to Jewish clients in predominantly Jewish areas, and landlords to seek larger security deposits from minority tenants (Equal Justice Society and Wilson Sonsini Goodrich & Rosati 2014, 251–52). Only a small number of psychology and sociology studies have assessed implicit bias in the housing context. In an important study, Sampson and Raudenbush (2004, 336) found that the racial percentage of African American and Latino residents and concentrated poverty in neighborhoods more strongly predicted residents' and community leaders' perceptions of social and physical disorder (e.g., graffiti, public drinking, litter, disturbance) than the actual observed level of disorder. This held true for both African American and white residents. Presumably African Americans have less conscious and overt prejudice against predominantly African American neighborhoods than whites. Therefore, the comparable results between African Americans and whites suggest that implicit bias was at play. A recent study by Bonam and her colleagues (2016) found that the predominant race of a neighborhood predicted attitudes about siting locally undesirable land uses (Bonam, Bergsieker, and Eberhardt 2016). People expressed lower levels of opposition to a hypothetical siting of a chemical plant in an African American neighborhood than in a white one. These results held even when the experimenters controlled for explicit feelings and beliefs about African Americans, as well as the perceived socioeconomic status of the residents, the value of the housing described in the experiment, and the participants' level of concern for the environment.

Other studies have found bias in the housing or land use context but have failed to disaggregate implicit and explicit bias. In a recent study, predominantly white and Asian American participants assessed homes owned by African Americans less favorably than homes owned by whites (Bonam, Bergsieker, and Eberhardt 2016). These researchers also found that white participants rated African American neighborhoods as less desirable, dirtier, and more crime-ridden than white neighborhoods. Similarly, a study by Krysan and her coresearchers (2009) presented videos of neighborhoods with different racial compositions and socio-economic levels (see also Krysan 2008). White participants viewing the African American neighborhood gave lower ratings for the home itself, for neighborhood satisfaction with city services and amenities, and for the desirability of the neighborhood than when they rated the white neighborhood.

Implicit bias offers a possible explanation for a paradox in US housing and land use law: racial discrimination and animus have decreased, but the United States remains substantially segregated. Numerous studies have found a shift over time toward egalitarian beliefs about how people should be treated and a reduction in overt discrimination, beliefs that other groups have negative traits, and hateful feelings toward other groups (for a summary, see Gaertner and Dovidio 2005). Laws have forbidden explicit discrimination in housing transactions, and courts have struck down racial segregation in zoning laws and racially restrictive covenants (provisions in deeds, binding on successive purchasers, that prohibit a property from being purchased, leased, or occupied by members of certain racial or religious groups).[12] Yet, residential segregation persists, gaps in wealth between African Americans and whites are attributable in part to homeownership and credit opportunities, and the unmet need for housing for the disabled is growing (Pew Research Center 2011; Spader and Rieger 2017; Krivo and Kaufman 2004; S. K. Smith, Rayer, and Smith 2008).

Can Disparate Impact Law Reduce Discrimination from Implicit Bias?

An interesting question is whether disparate impact law can reduce implicit bias so as to prevent or reduce instances of discriminatory policies. Disparate impact law might do this by raising awareness among housing providers of their biases or by creating incentives for housing providers to adopt practices that reduce the effects of implicit bias. For example, the threat of legal liability might encourage housing providers to determine tenant selection criteria in advance and to enforce adherence to those metrics. Of course, disparate impact law can also impose liability directly or offer injunctive relief. However, in its corrective role, disparate impact law suffers from legal standards that make it difficult for plaintiffs to prevail, the expense of litigation, and a "count the bodies" problem where housing discrimination can only be remedied after it occurs. In light of these limitations, the notions of debiasing or preventing discrimination through housing law are intriguing possibilities.

To consider debiasing, let us divide the possible ex ante effects of disparate impact law into two categories of direct and indirect effects: (1) debiasing effects that we anticipate will reduce innate bias and therefore also discriminatory actions, and (2) the potential of legal liability to change the practices or decision-making procedures used by housing and loan providers. Psychology suggests limitations to the capacity of disparate impact law to achieve either of these aims. First, disparate impact lawsuits may raise internal awareness of one's bias but not translate into less bias or discriminatory behavior. Second, disparate impact may be a poor debiasing tool because it is not well tailored to implicit bias or the circumstances in which implicit bias is likely to arise (Oliveri 2015, 640; Krieger 1994–95, 1237). Third, fear of liability from disparate impact may lead housing providers toward revised practices, but not necessarily the right practices.

Let us turn first to the idea that disparate impact law can reduce implicit bias by raising awareness of one's own unintentional biases. It is tempting to believe that law can excavate our biases, make us conscious of them, and thus enable us to eliminate or at least reduce our prejudices. There has been much written about how law and norms are "sticky" and mutually constitutive (McAdams 2015). Examples abound, from seat belt laws to gay marriage, of how law has supported or accelerated changes in social norms. A major obstacle to debiasing through fair housing law, however, is that implicit bias is unconscious, or at least very difficult for the holder to cognitively access in day-to-day life. The psychology research reveals that making people aware of their implicit bias is quite challenging and that awareness alone does not seem to reduce implicit bias. Instead, the empirical evidence suggests that awareness of one's unconscious biases or habits may be necessary, but not sufficient standing alone, to ameliorate implicit bias (Monteith et al. 2002).[13]

Despite voluminous empirical research, there has been no intervention shown to substantially and stably reduce implicit bias. In a set of recent studies, Calvin Lai and his coresearchers (2014) completed an implicit bias "intervention contest" in which they independently tested seventeen interventions submitted by different social psychologists. Only eight interventions produced a statistically significant reduction in implicit bias (none reduced explicit bias). The effective interventions tended to be emotionally evocative, were relevant to the individual, or used exemplars of bad whites and good African Americans. They included interventions that could not be used in law, for example, exposing participants to graphic descriptions of gruesome crimes committed by a white attacker. The interventions where law or Supreme Court precedent on disparate impact might seem most applicable, such as encouraging people to reflect on egalitarian values or to take the perspective of the disfavored group, were not effective at all. The durability of bias reduction is also a problem. In a follow-up study, Lai and his colleagues (2016) measured the effects of the interventions that reduced implicit bias in the initial study several days after the intervention. None of the interventions retained an effect on implicit bias with the passage of time.[14] Lai and his coresearchers conclude that, based on the research to date, implicit bias may be "malleable" in the short term, but resistant to long-term change.

Even if we can effectively debias via disparate impact law, there is a baseline question of whether disparate impact cases primarily address unconscious bias versus strategic attempts to hide discrimination in a facially neutral policy. An example of conscious, strategic discrimination is when a landlord, knowing he cannot explicitly refuse to rent to individuals on the basis of disability, instead dissuades or restricts members of this group by requiring all renters to affirm on their rental applications or leases that they have the ability to live independently. While we lack empirical certainty, it appears that both unconscious and conscious discrimination by defendants give rise to disparate impact claims, but that the latter is more common (Oliveri 2015, 640).

If disparate impact law is unlikely to debias implicit prejudice, can it incentivize housing providers to adopt practices that reduce or eliminate the impacts of implicit bias on policy making? This notion, while more promising on the whole than disparate impact law as a debiasing agent, has a number of psychological and legal stumbling blocks. It is not clear that *Inclusive Communities* creates a substantial enough risk of liability to prompt housing providers to adopt different procedures or review systems. While *Inclusive Communities* affirmed circuit court cases allowing disparate impact claims, it created a causality standard that is too difficult for most plaintiffs to meet. The Supreme Court in *Inclusive Communities* required plaintiffs to establish a "robust" causal connection between a facially neutral policy (not mere discretionary action or a onetime decision) and a resulting statistical disparity adversely impacting the plaintiffs.[15] In practice, it is difficult for plaintiffs to prove such a high standard of causality and to refute a defendant's claims that other, nondiscriminatory factors (e.g., income, credit scores, or rental history) caused the disparity. Disparate impact housing plaintiffs have generally lost cases due to the causality prong following *Inclusive Communities* (Glassman and Verna 2016).

Even if housing providers are sufficiently motivated to reduce bias, redressing bias requires psychological expertise. It is not enough for firms to adopt practices; the practices must be effective. For example, mandatory diversity training to address explicit and implicit bias is ineffective, with any positive results disappearing in a matter of days; some studies show harm from mandatory diversity training in the form of hiring backlash against minorities (Dobbin and Kalev 2016). Another practice that some employers have experimented with, particularly in the European Union, is to "blind" applications so that race, ethnicity, gender, and so forth are unknown in the initial application stages. This has shown some promising effects, but it comes with costs. Blinding can make it difficult to evaluate applications and can cause decision makers to rely on problematic measures, some of which indirectly disadvantage the groups blinding was intended to protect (Rinne 2014). A landlord who collects blinded applications by removing any questions about race, gender, age, and disability but adopts a policy of renting only to high school graduates may adversely affect housing opportunities for racial minorities and individuals with disabilities. Also, since face-to-face contact frequently occurs in housing transactions when the prospective tenant or buyer views the residence, blinding only delays, but does not remove, the opportunity for bias.

Housing and home loan providers can also specify decision-making criteria in advance. Limiting discretion in decision making shows promise in theory, but it often breaks down in practice. To work effectively, the decision-making criteria and the steps must be specified and then weight assigned to each criterion—a complex and resource-intensive task often outside a housing supplier's expertise. For example, a landlord might specify in advance categories such as credit history, rental history, size of escrow payment, income, and work history and then criteria for awarding applicants points in each category. Rental decisions are then made based on applicants' composite scores. Many housing providers are ill-equipped to effectively design a weighted decision-making protocol. If such a system is adopted, individuals and firms need to ensure its implementation. In their research on increasing diversity in hiring, Dobbin and Kalev (2016) describe how managers and employees often selectively implement such systems so that they no longer accomplish their intended equity function. This happens when managers apply a decision-making metric only to some applicants and not to others, in ways that confirm the manager's initial judgments or stereotypes about the applicant's desirability.

In light of the ubiquitous nature of implicit bias and the barriers to debiasing, is finding a defendant's unconscious discrimination unlawful under the FHA too harsh a response? There are several reasons to think that it is not. First, as we have discussed previously, many defendants in disparate impact cases have engaged in intentional discrimination through carefully crafted, facially neutral policies, rather than unwittingly falling prey to implicit bias. It is not possible for courts to accurately differentiate intentional from unwitting discriminators in determining which cases should go forward. Second, focusing on the defendant's interests, rather than the plaintiff's, undercuts the FHA's statutory purpose to reduce discrimination and promote residential integration. It would be unfair to a plaintiff and contrary to the act's integrationist aims to offer no redress because a defendant experienced—or claims to have experienced—unconscious bias. Third, and perhaps most critically, the difficulty of debiasing implicit bias underscores the need for laws, including disparate impact, that revise and correct discrimination. If there are forms of bias that are difficult to expunge from our hearts and minds, an important purpose of property and housing law is to correct the discrimination that results.

While implicit bias should not remove defendants from the reach of the FHA, whether the discrimination was conscious or unconscious may be relevant to the remedies that courts elect. In theory, it would be desirable for courts to consider whether discrimination was unconscious in crafting remedies. If courts could reliably discern implicit bias, they might focus on correcting the discrimination rather than punishing defendants who discriminated unintentionally. For example, courts might apply injunctive remedies to unwitting discriminators (i.e., forcing them to correct the discrimination) while intentional discriminators would face monetary and punitive damages as well as injunctions. In practice, as noted earlier, it is infeasible for courts to ascertain whether a policy's disparate impact was the product of conscious or unconscious bias (and easy for defendants to make untrue claims about their intentions in order to obscure their discriminatory aims).[16]

In summary, it does not seem that disparate impact law is a highly effective "debiaser" of implicit bias or, standing alone, likely to prompt the types of practices that reduce the impact of implicit bias. The psychology research sheds light on the challenges of decreasing the prevalence of implicit bias through disparate impact and other laws. The research also underscores the importance of recognizing disparate impact claims. If there are forms of bias we cannot prevent ex ante, we should provide redress ex post. Upholding disparate impact claims under the FHA, as the Court did in *Inclusive Communities*, can correct the effects of implicit bias on housing providers' policies. This is not to suggest that implicit bias is the central justification for disparate impact litigation. The most critical rationale for disparate impact law remains its potential to redress actions undertaken to advance discriminatory ends but calculated to evade the FHA.

Regulating Discriminatory Speech in Housing: The Psychology of Social Norms

There are a number of options that property law systems can employ to reduce discrimination in housing markets. Legal rules can prohibit explicit acts of discrimination, regulate or prohibit housing practices that disproportionately harm certain groups, and incentivize residential diversity. As we shall see, the FHA adopts all of these approaches, with varying degrees of stringency. The FHA also includes another legal rule that regulates discriminatory speech related to housing. Section 3604(c) makes it unlawful to "print or publish . . . any notice, statement, or advertisement, with respect to the sale or rental of a dwelling, that indicates any preference, limitation, or discrimination because of race, color, religion, sex, handicap, familial status, or national origin." Section 3604(c) is a striking addition to fair housing law in view of the constitutional and political solicitude accorded to free speech rights. Its prohibition on discriminatory housing statements extends liability to publishers of discriminatory printed notices and advertisements and speakers of discriminatory statements, but not, as we shall discuss, to internet service providers for discriminatory housing advertisements posted by third-party users.

Section 3604(c) offers stronger protection than the provisions in the FHA governing explicit acts of discrimination (e.g., refusals to rent or sell, or discrimination in the terms and conditions of a housing transaction).[17] First, unlike most other provisions in the Fair Housing Act, section 3604(c) does not require actual discrimination to have occurred. For example, a landlord who publishes a discriminatory ad in the newspaper that states families with children should not apply for an apartment, but then ultimately rents to a family with a child, is still liable for violating the FHA. An investigation or lawsuit may arise following a complaint by a nonprofit housing organization or an individual about the discriminatory advertisement. Second, while other provisions of the FHA require that the discriminatory action occurred intentionally "because of" a protected status such as race, religion, or sex, section 3604(c) liability merely requires that the notice, statement, or advertisement for sale or rental indicate "any preference, limitation, or discrimination" based on a protected status. Third, unlike the provisions of the FHA addressing acts of discrimination in rental, sales, and lending, section 3604(c) does not exempt from liability owners of up to three single-family houses who sell or rent without using a broker, "Mrs. Murphy" landlords who occupy a room or apartment in their small rental buildings,[18] and religious organizations and private clubs.[19]

The strict regulation of discriminatory speech related to housing presents seeming paradoxes to the FHA. Why does a mere advertisement or statement occasion such vigorous legal response, particularly in light of the fact that liability for discriminatory actions, such as a refusal to rent or sell, is riddled with exemptions? What is the rationale for penalizing discriminatory housing statements, as section 3604(c) does, even when no housing discrimination was intended or ultimately occurred? Psychology suggests one answer: the role of social norms in prejudice (S. M. Stern 2019).

The Power of Social Norms to Alter Prejudice

Let us turn first to the FHA's prohibition on written advertisements and notices, which are typically in public view or available to large numbers of potential readers. From a psychological perspective, section 3604(c)'s publication provision reduces the *appearance* of prejudice and therefore the perception that prejudice is a widely held social norm. Knowledge of the attitudes of one's in-group or of widespread social norms can increase or decrease prejudice, depending on what people believe is their group's social norm (Sechrist and Stangor 2001; Stangor, Sechrist, and Jost 2001; Haslam et al. 1996; Wittenbrink and Henly 1996). This effect occurs even if the normative information is fabricated—it is perception of the norm, not the actual prejudice espoused by a group, that matters. The research does not establish whether the shift toward less stereotyped or racist beliefs indicates true attitude change or "mere" social compliance. From the perspective of ensuring fair housing, this distinction may not be important so long as social compliance lessens discrimination.

To illustrate, let us consider some key psychology experiments on the effect of group norms on prejudice. In a study by Stangor, Sechrist, and Jost (2001), a group of University of Maryland students estimated the percentage of African Americans who possess nineteen stereotypical traits, both positive and negative. They made a second set of identical ratings based on what they thought *other* students at the University of Maryland believed about African Americans. One week later, the experimenter shared information with these students about the percentage of fellow students who believed African Americans possessed each of the traits. While participants believed this was true information, in fact each received feedback about fellow students' beliefs that was substantially more positive than that individual's initial ratings. Then the participants provided a final rating of their personal beliefs by completing the same stereotype questionnaire used in the first session. The researchers found that participants reported fewer negative stereotypes and more positive ones after learning that University of Maryland students viewed African Americans positively. This pattern reversed when experimenters told a second group that their fellow students had negative beliefs about African Americans, with that group reporting more negative stereotypes (though not a lower probability of positive stereotypes). The magnitude of these shifts was substantial and, in the researchers' view, more effective than attempts to reduce prejudice through contact with members of other groups or appeals to morality (Sechrist and Stangor 2001, 645; cf. Allport 1954). One caution, however, is that the durability of social norm–induced attitude change is unknown, as there has not been significant long-term follow-up.

Other research has investigated whether social norms can alter attitudes in individuals who are highly prejudiced. Wittenbrink and Henly (1996) sorted research participants into "high-prejudice" and "low-prejudice" groups based on their scores on a psychological test called the Modern Racism Scale. One group of participants received biased response scales which indicated that others believe that a high proportion of African Americans have negative traits, while a second group received information indicating that others hold positive beliefs. After receiving positive information, the students who initially tested as high in racial prejudice reported more favorable attitudes toward African Americans as well as more positive evaluations of a hypothetical African American defendant accused of armed robbery (Wittenbrink and Henly 1996, 604). The low-prejudice group showed no effects from either positive or negative information, which suggests that attitude change is not driven solely by the need to conform (604–08).

An important question for fair housing law is whether social norms affect actions as well as attitudes. There is promising, but limited, research to date on whether interventions that promote less prejudiced social norms reduce acts of discrimination. In a 2001 study, experimenters told high-prejudice and low-prejudice participants that other university students shared their views about African Americans and then asked individuals to leave the room and take a seat in a nearby seating area while the experimenters remedied a computer malfunction (Sechrist and Stangor 2001). An African American student, recruited by the experimenters, was stationed in the seat closest to the experimental room that the participants exited (647). When high-prejudice students learned that other university students shared their stereotypes of African Americans, those students subsequently sat farther away from the African American student posted in the hallway than did high-prejudice students who had been told that fellow students did not share their views (649). Similarly, low-prejudice students who learned that fellow students shared their views sat closer to the African American student than low-prejudice students who learned that other students endorsed negative stereotypes (649).[20]

It is possible that strong affiliation with the group is necessary for norms to guide behavior. Research has shown that group norms affect intentions to engage in behaviors for participants who identify highly with the group, but not for low identifiers (Terry and Hogg 1996). The power of group identification to sway prejudice may also offer an explanation for why interventions to remove implicit bias by raising individuals' awareness of their bias have a disappointing record of success. Empirical work on the use of group identification and social norms to reduce discriminatory attitudes and actions in applied contexts such as housing transactions is a productive line of future research.

The Fair Housing Act's Publication Provision: Social Norm Regulation

The psychology of social norms suggests an important rationale for regulating discriminatory speech in housing—and regulating it strictly regardless of intent (S. M. Stern 2019). Housing providers are more likely to engage in housing discrimination if they see others doing so. More generally, those who read or hear about discriminatory advertisements from others may shift toward more negative attitudes toward members of the excluded group. As mentioned, the effects of social norms grow stronger as an individual feels greater affiliation with the group espousing that consensus (Sechrist and Stangor 2001; Pettigrew 1958, 40; Sherif and Sherif 1953). For example, a landlord perusing rental advertisements realizes that fellow landlords are discriminating as part of their rental business and interprets that as an acceptable norm among local property owners. Publication further strengthens the normative force of the message because the decision to print such advertisements suggests that the newspaper or website shares prejudiced views or at least does not seek to restrict them. Members of groups that are disfavored in advertisements are likely to infer that they are at risk of experiencing discrimination not only from the party publishing the ad but also from other sellers, landlords, or lenders. This may encourage them to seek out same-race or otherwise same-group neighborhoods (a practice inaptly referred to as "self-sorting").

If a goal is to reduce the perception that others are discriminating in housing, it is important that messages do not alter or dilute antidiscrimination norms. In the presence of conflicting messages about social or in-group norms, it is possible that the reader or listener will infer that a discrimination norm exists or that there is no agreed-upon norm. Thus, in view of the psychology of social norms, it makes sense that section 3604(c) does not provide exceptions for certain categories of speakers (such as the "Mrs. Murphy" exemptions that apply to discrimination in rentals) or quibble about the speaker's intent. The legal standard in a section 3604(c) publication case of whether an "ordinary reader" or an "ordinary listener" would perceive the words to indicate discrimination also supports an antidiscrimination social norm. In addition to effects on social norms, discriminatory publications may lead viewers to make erroneous inferences about the law. As Justice Ginsburg noted in a D.C. Circuit opinion in *Spann v. Colonial Vill., Inc.*, allowing discriminatory statements and advertisements could create "a public impression that housing segregation is legal, thus facilitating discrimination by defendants or other property owners."[21]

While the publication provision safeguards social norms emanating from printed advertisements, it of course does nothing for the unfortunate individual who responds to a nondiscriminatory advertisement only to find that a small-scale landlord may lawfully discriminate against him. While it is beyond this chapter's scope to address in detail the exemptions in the FHA for small-scale landlords, we note that these "Mrs. Murphy" exemptions have rightfully drawn criticism for countenancing discrimination and maintaining segregation (Failinger 2001, 383–85; Walsh 1999).

The research on social norms also illustrates the harms from declining to impose liability on internet service providers for discriminatory housing advertisements posted on their websites (S. M. Stern 2019). Appellate courts have interpreted the Communication Decency Act's provision that "no provider or user of an interactive computer service shall be treated as the publisher or speaker of any information provided by another information content provider" to hold that internet sites are not liable under section 3604(c) when they act as mere conduits for content posted by third parties.[22] The individual posters remain liable but are difficult to identify and expensive to litigate individually. Websites often do not collect identifying information for posters and frequently ensure anonymity via temporary, anonymous e-mail addresses for each post. The Communication Decency Act's liability shield for internet site providers and operators, and the resulting proliferation of discriminatory housing speech online (Oliveri 2010), pose substantial danger to social norms (S. M. Stern 2019). The normative impact of discriminatory housing speech online is especially concerning in light of the larger readership of internet postings compared with printed advertisements (Collins 2008; S. M. Stern 2019).

The ill effects on norms from discriminatory housing speech are made worse by the tendency of stereotypes and prejudice to spread across social, and social media, networks. Social networks are the configurations of direct and indirect ties that connect people to one another and to information. In field studies, researchers have found that recent migrants to New York City who met anti-Semitic people became more anti-Semitic, and white southern men in the 1950s who entered the comparatively more egalitarian environment of the army became less prejudiced against African Americans (Watson 1950; Pettigrew 1958). The transmission of social norms is also evident in the startlingly high degree of social accord about stereotypes, meaning the characteristics people believe to be most representative of different groups (Gaertner and Dovidio 1986; Karlins, Coffman, and Walters 1969; cf. Haslam et al. 1996). In most cases, people harbor stereotypes despite having minimal or no contact with members of the stereotyped group, suggesting that these stereotypes are the result of culture, not personal experience (Maio, Esses, and Bell 1994).

It is not clear whether the drafters of the FHA envisioned the normative force of section 3604(c). The legislative history for section 3604(c) is sparse and does not indicate specific rationales for the provision, other than for the FHA to reflect, and to broaden, provisions of Title VII applied to employment discrimination (Schwemm 2001). However, the legislative history of the FHA as a whole reveals that a major goal of the statute, emphasized by its supporters in the House and Senate, was to promote residential racial integration and address the problem of segregated ghettos.[23] This goal may have encompassed, at least implicitly, promoting antidiscrimination perceptions and norms via section 3604(c).

While social norms offer a powerful explanation for regulating discriminatory publications, there are still unanswered questions. As discussed earlier, more research is needed on the circumstances under which social norms ultimately reduce discriminatory behavior. There are also important concerns about the unintended consequences of restraining information. A recent study by Doleac and Hansen (2017) found that removing information about criminal history increased other kinds of bias. They found that in states with "ban the box" legislation that forbids employers from requesting information about criminal history (often in the form of a box that applicants check), employers interview and employ fewer young, non–college educated African American and Latino men.

Even with these caveats, promoting nondiscriminatory social norms through the FHA is an important strategy, particularly in light of the shortcomings of alternative approaches. A property law system that addressed only explicit acts of actual housing discrimination would reach only a tiny fraction of cases. Psychology research from both laboratory experiments and retrospective studies establishes that people who experience discrimination often fail to complain, with some studies finding that the majority of victims fail to report the discrimination (Kaiser and Major 2006, 812–18; Stangor et al. 2002).[24] This is not surprising given the societal reaction to discrimination claims. Individuals who report discrimination are judged harshly (e.g., on ratings of whether the person is sensitive, a troublemaker, or irritating) (Kaiser and Miller 2001; Garcia et al. 2005), even when the discrimination is blatant (Kaiser and Miller 2003; Stangor et al. 2003). As a result of negative attitudes toward complainants and narrow views of what constitutes discrimination (as well as steep evidentiary burdens), discrimination litigants have a very low likelihood of prevailing in court compared with other types of litigants (Eyer 2012, 1333). The barriers to success are so daunting that legal scholar Katie R. Eyer argues that the legal system should expand the use of claims that do not directly evoke discrimination, such as the tort of wrongful infliction of emotional distress, to handle these cases rather than employing discrimination law (1341–60). It is questionable whether this indirect approach is the solution for fair housing, in part because the FHA specifies an extensive framework for federal agency investigation, settlement, and litigation of violations of the act's provisions. However, Eyer's point that plaintiffs face steep barriers to litigation success supports the importance of leveraging social norms ex ante to reduce discrimination, rather than relying on remedies ex post.

The Prohibition on Discriminatory Statements: In-Groups and Stereotype Threat

The FHA also forbids oral statements that indicate discrimination or intent to discriminate based on membership in a protected class. For example, if a landlord tells a prospective renter during a face-to-face meeting, "We usually don't like to rent to Catholic people," this would violate section 3604(c). Unlike publications and notices, statements usually involve a speaker and one or a few listeners rather than a wide audience. If statements are made before one or a small number of people, they are seemingly less injurious to social norms. Social psychology supports two other rationales for prohibiting discriminatory speech in housing transactions and, surprisingly, finds that private statements can still affect social norms.

First, individuals seeking housing who hear discriminatory statements may infer not only that the particular speaker is prejudiced but that others in the neighborhood or area are likely to share those attitudes. This occurs because the landlord or seller often shares "in-group" membership or ties of common identity with other residents in the area (Dovidio et al. 2010, 9–10). Thus, "out-group" members may assume that attitudes are likely to be shared across the group. House-hunters may even conclude that such prejudice is widespread enough that they should limit their search to sellers, lenders, or landlords from their own group (e.g., same gender, same race, etc.).

Second, discriminatory statements may undermine the recipient's information-processing, negotiating, or other capacities, at least in the short term. Psychology research on "stereotype threat" finds that in situations where negative stereotypes may apply, members of stereotyped groups show degraded performance. Stereotype threat occurs "when an identity is linked to a negative stereotype, and the identity *and* stereotype are relevant in a particular situation" (Quinn, Kallen, and Spencer 2010, 382). For example, African American students who took a test they believed was "diagnostic" of their verbal abilities performed worse than European Americans given the same information (Steele and Aronson 1995). However, when experimenters told a second group that same test's purpose was to better understand the psychological factors involved in verbal problem solving, there was no difference between African American and European American students. Women taking math tests performed worse than men when told that research has shown gender differences in math performance between men and women, but they performed the same as men when told that the test had not produced gender differences (Spencer, Steele, and Quinn 1999). Asian American women score higher on math tests when experimenters cue their Asian identity than if the experimenters cue their gender identity (Shih, Pittinsky, and Ambady 1999). These effects do not appear to be due to an internalized sense of general inferiority but rather from the perception of negative stereotypes in a specific situation (researchers have found that "dominant groups" such as white men also experience stereotype threat if they receive information that Asian Americans outperform whites, see J. Aronson et al. 1999).[25] Researchers have not established whether stereotype threat generalizes beyond test-taking to other contexts. However, it seems quite plausible that stereotype threat, in the form of an explicit discriminatory statement, would permeate housing negotiations and contracting, which like tests call upon cognitive skills. This could affect those who experience discriminatory housing statements and possibly others who have not heard such statements personally but believe such statements, and the prejudice underlying them, to be common.

Third, discriminatory statements may still affect social norms, albeit less directly and potently than discriminatory publications. Psychologists have found that attitude change can occur even if a single bystander hears a single speaker make a discriminatory statement. In an experimental study, J. L. Greenberg and Pyszczynski (1985) gave white participants a vignette about a debate that either an African American or a white person won. Subsequently, participants overheard a racial slur about African Americans, a neutral remark, or nothing. They found that people who overheard the slur rated the skills of the African American debater who lost significantly more negatively than those who had not heard the slur (or those given the vignette where the African American debater won). An even more startling example comes from psychological experiments finding that merely overhearing that the assailant in a violent robbery was African American increased the perceptions of white students that African Americans are "hostile" and "antagonistic" (Henderson-King and Nisbett 1996). There was no change in attitudes about whites when the vignette specified a white assailant. These experiments did not assess long-term changes, and it is unclear whether these attitudes persist beyond the short term. If attitude change does persist, an individual's shift toward negative stereotyping or prejudice can affect social norms because, as we have discussed previously, prejudice tends to spread through social networks.

For the recipients of face-to-face discriminatory housing statements and slurs, there is also the question of remedy. Fair Housing Act cases have allowed recovery for emotional damages for discriminatory statements and racial slurs (Schwemm 2001, 305–14; Schwemm 2018). Providing a form of recompense is appropriate. The psychology research, as well as research in other fields, finds that stigmatization has grievous effects on life opportunities (for a review, see Major and Townsend 2010, 411–13).

Neighborhood Associations: The Challenges of Group Deliberation and Governance

From Elinor Ostrom's commons to collective water irrigation systems of the American Southwest, there are examples of residents or workers directly governing the allocation and rules of property systems. Self-governing property institutions have generated much interest and, in many circles, have abundant appeal. These institutions capture the regard of those who prefer a more limited centralized government, as well as those who strongly endorse notions of community or leveraging local "grassroots" expertise. Self-governance of property, with its reliance on social ties and direct participation, has been lauded for its capacity to build community and include a broader range of voices (for a review of this literature, see S. M. Stern 2013).

In law and political science, a number of scholars have endorsed the use of public "micro-institutions" at the block or neighborhood level to manage collective goods and solve local problems (Ellickson 1998; Ostrom 2010). In a bold proposal, Robert Nelson (2006) has advocated forming a nationwide system of neighborhood associations with the power to enact regulations, zone (e.g., specify which uses can occur in which areas, regulate density, and enforce other spatial and aesthetic requirements), and control development. Nelson proposes augmenting the large number of private homeowners' and condominium associations with legislation enabling associations in all neighborhoods. He envisions legislation that would delegate to local neighborhood associations responsibility for regulation, providing local services, and possibly transfer of ownership of public facilities (e.g., pools, parks).

In recent years, some localities in the United States have experimented with devolving land use self-governance power to neighborhood associations. These devolutions to neighborhood residents can range from modest functions, such as participatory budgeting in municipalities, to delegating zoning and spending power to neighborhood associations. For example, Los Angeles created neighborhood councils charged with hearing land use and zoning requests and managing limited funds for neighborhood improvement (Leighninger 2008, 7–8). Other cities, such as Portland, Oregon, have neighborhood associations that play an advisory role (City of Portland 2018).

The now-defunct Minneapolis Neighborhood Revitalization Program (NRP) was one of the most radical experiments in neighborhood self-governance. Under this innovative set of land use laws, the city delegated substantial powers to individual neighborhoods. The NRP required individual neighborhoods to form associations and then to create and implement plans for affordable housing and local revitalization. Neighborhood residents elected board members who, together with unelected committee members, chose and implemented neighborhood revitalization policies. Given the strong devolution of authority to the neighborhood level and the desire for innovation, there were limited constraints imposed by the city on the neighborhood associations.

In homogeneous, lower-income neighborhoods, the NRP worked relatively well. However, in racially and economically diverse neighborhoods, self-governance often fell short of its imagined benefits. Edward G. Goetz and Mara Sidney describe how in diverse, majority-tenant neighborhoods, relatively more affluent and typically white homeowners captured control of the boards and coordinated to exclude "undesirables" (1994, 327–31). Despite their mandate to increase affordability, these groups of owners increased owner occupancy by blocking the rehabilitation of multifamily buildings and funding condominium conversions, gutted a program of leasehold cooperatives, and disproportionately allocated funds to grants and subsidized loans for individual home remodeling projects. Goetz and Sidney found that low-income and African American residents were often shut out of boards and committees and had little decision-making power (329–30). Ironically, these effects occurred despite the fact that the neighborhood associations were constituted in part to improve housing affordability and ensure that local voices be heard.

How did self-governance, meant to capture the benefits of local community and expertise, lead to these effects? The psychology research sheds some light. Neighborhood associations, which operate with less formality and thinner legal and governance institutions than traditional land use decision-making bodies, depend on residents to trust and cooperate with one another. Psychology research shows that group formation, the process of deliberation, and economic competition frequently produce stereotyping and exclusion. This poses a challenge for self-governance of local land use—one that is often glossed over in the policy work and scholarship on the power of direct participation and neighborhood solidarity (cf. S. M. Stern 2013).

Group Selection Biases

Neighborhood associations in racially, ethnically, or otherwise diverse areas may systematically fail to reflect that diversity due to bias. Both psychologists and sociologists have found that social networks display homophily, meaning that people tend to interact with similar people (Gruenfeld and Tiedens 2010; McPherson, Smith-Lovin, and Cook 2001). Research has found that when people can voluntarily choose members of working groups, similarity is an influential criterion. In a study of how people select group members, Hinds, Carley, and Krackhardt (2000) assigned third-year college students to working groups to develop a computer-based information system. The researchers tracked via questionnaires the amount of interaction students had with one another and the perceived quality of the group project (as a proxy for quality of interaction with group members). The following year, the students were able to request up to five peers to work with on a second, similar project. The researchers found that students were more likely to request group members of the same race, as well as those with whom they previously had positive working experiences. In addition, reputation for competency, proxied by grades and similar measures, also increased the likelihood of being requested as a group member. It appears that people working in groups to complete projects strive to reduce uncertainty and increase predictability, sometimes at the expense of diversity (cf. Kets and Sandroni 2015). In neighborhood associations and other property self-governance systems where cooperation is vital and information about the behaviors, preferences, and competencies of others is thin, associations may use proxies such as socioeconomic status or race to select participants.

Working Together: The Psychology of Group Rivalry and Escalation

In some cases, the process of neighborhood self-governance reinforces both the motivation and the means for exclusion. The psychology research suggests three factors that may lead neighborhood associations to adopt discriminatory or exclusionary policies. First, psychology suggests that economic competition and prejudice are intertangled (Allport 1954). When groups are competing over resources that are zero-sum in nature, the ongoing rivalry to capture the resource can morph into intergroup hostility. In their famous Robbers Cave experiment, Sherif and his colleagues (1961) divided boys into two groups to play competitive sports to win a prize. Negative attitudes and bias developed rapidly and increased to the point of aggression, but reversed when the two teams then had to cooperate to earn a shared prize. This study suggests the problems that can occur when neighborhood associations enable certain groups to capture valuable resources, indirectly through zoning or directly through spending power. The Minneapolis neighborhood associations in diverse neighborhoods showed limited regard for the plight of renters and low-income residents as they conveyed home-remodeling grants to owners and decreased the supply of affordable housing.

Second, work demand may exacerbate these group dynamics to the further detriment of inclusion and nondiscrimination. Psychologists have found an increase in stereotyping and discrimination when people confront challenging, complex tasks (S. T. Fiske and Taylor 2017; Bodenhausen 1990). Recall our earlier discussion (in chapter 5) of how heuristics, or cognitive shortcuts, enable people to conserve decision-making resources in the face of high demands on information processing. Stereotypes can serve as heuristics to simplify decision making (Glaser, Spencer, and Charbonneau 2014). Neighborhood associations that have broad responsibilities including substantive decision making over zoning or spending, that are newly constituted, or that operate under thin, underspecified frameworks face a complex and uncertain decision-making environment. Given these demands, we should not expect bias to attenuate in this context and instead should anticipate it might worsen.

Third, as groups deliberate and work together, they can become more extreme in their positions and more hostile toward minority groups. Psychologists have found that group polarization frequently occurs over the course of deliberation as the members of a group become more committed to their initial position and that position becomes more extreme (Moscovici and Zavalloni 1969). Psychologists believe this occurs due to the desire for social acceptance by the group's majority and because the ideas supporting the majority view are repeated and influence attitudes, while divergent or contradictory ideas do not see daylight (Vinokur and Burstein 1974). More tight-knit or solidaristic groups are likely to have stronger polarization following deliberation, presumably due to their heightened desire to maintain social approval and more limited pools of information (Turner 1987; Sunstein 2000a, 92). A related concept, coined "groupthink" by Irving Janis (1971, 1972), occurs when a group's common identity grows over time, leading the group to adopt more extreme courses of action and persist in them despite strong indications to the contrary. Janis, who studied group think in political crises such as the Bay of Pigs Invasion and the Vietnam War, found that among the groups charged with those decisions, greater social cohesion increased "the danger that independent critical thinking will be replaced by group-think, which is likely to result in irrational and dehumanizing actions directed against outgroups" (Janis 1971, 43).

Of course, bias and exclusion also can occur in traditional, top-down local land use governance. From allowing racially restrictive covenants to discrimination in federal fair lending policy, there are many examples of how government has succumbed to bias. The point is not that bias is exclusive to self-governance, but rather that we should be wary of assumptions that neighborhood self-governance will organically generate greater inclusion (S. M. Stern 2013). Social ties and working together can reduce bias in diverse groups under certain circumstances (Pettigrew and Tropp 2006), but there is an equal, if not greater, risk that social ties in homogeneous groups, or diverse but inequitable ones, will create strong in-groups and polarization. Rather than an antidote to the failings of traditional governance, local self-governance may be particularly vulnerable to bias, or at least vulnerable in particular ways, due to its reliance on social ties and cooperation.

Using Psychology to Improve Neighborhood Associations

The psychology research does not profess that social ties, cohesion, and direct participation have no social value. They clearly do, particularly when they are subject to legal or normative constraints on exclusion and other forms of nonegalitarianism. What can local governments and neighborhood associations do to capture these benefits, while counteracting tendencies toward exclusion and discrimination? First, laws could encourage or require diversity of participation in self-governing local institutions. Ordinances and interventions that promote diverse neighborhood associations and working groups could range from efforts by cities to fund outreach to underrepresented groups and remind residents about the importance of diverse participation, as Oregon has done in its neighborhood associations (De Morris and Leistner 2009), to laws or ordinances regulating association composition. While specifying racial or similar quotas would run afoul of constitutional law, participation of underrepresented groups could be improved by requiring that associations contain a certain percentage of renters, a minimum number of positions for low-income residents, or representation from each block (segregated residential patterns mean blocks often cluster by race or ethnicity). Alternatively, states and cities could require that stakeholder groups representing these interests, such as nonprofits, tenants unions, or organizations devoted to underrepresented or underprivileged groups, have formal representation in neighborhood associations.

Legal rules and approaches that diversify local participation not only reduce exclusion but also may improve group decision making. Recent research highlights the value of diverse participation in deliberative working groups. In an experiment using mock juries, Samuel R. Sommers (2006) found that groups with African American jury members not only were less likely to find an African American defendant guilty but also made fewer inaccurate statements, contributed greater information, and were more open to considering the effect of racial bias on the prosecution than all-white juries. These effects emerged in advance of deliberation when the jury was merely seated together, as well as during deliberation (suggesting that the group composition effect is not entirely attributable to differences in information exchange in diverse working groups). These effects were substantially due to whites who altered their analyses based on the fact that their jury group included African American members (Sommers 2006, 606–07). There is a growing literature on group deliberations, and conflicting evidence has emerged on the effects of juror race on final jury judgments (Mannix and Neale 2005; Mazzella and Feingold 1994). More research also needs to be done outside the jury context to see how group diversity affects local deliberative bodies, urban neighborhood associations, and private homeowners' associations. While nuances remain to be resolved, the Sommers study suggests that groups, such as neighborhood associations, are likely to be more attentive to concerns of discrimination and more studied in their decision making when they are diverse and concerns about discrimination feature explicitly in the group's task.

Second, the psychology research underscores the importance of constraints on neighborhood associations, including legal rules and incentives. The Minneapolis NRP might have worked better in diverse neighborhoods if the city had specified a target number of affordable housing units and empowered the association to determine the means to accomplish that goal. Even then, additional specification or rules were likely needed to prevent concentrating affordable housing tenants or marginalizing them to less desirable parcels. Spatially concentrating low-income housing typically results in lower access for low-income residents to community amenities and higher crime compared with heterogeneous siting (see, e.g., Lewinsohn-Zamir 2008, 705–07; Fennell 2006, 1267–80).[26] The psychology literature, particularly the research on resource competition, also suggests that neighborhood associations may be more beneficial at addressing cross-cutting problems with a common goal shared by neighborhood residents (e.g., addressing a source of neighborhood pollution or increasing community policing) than at distributing resources.

Concluding Remarks

This chapter has considered how research in psychology can inform property and housing law. Implicit bias, social norms, and the dynamics of in-groups and out-groups affect housing and lending transactions, residential integration, and access to opportunities. An important role for law, as well as norms and morality, is to guide how we behave in response to our inclinations toward bias. In countries like the United States, where housing remains most citizens' primary source of wealth, housing discrimination has profound effects not only on residential living but also on long-term wealth-building and security. The psychology research sheds light on a puzzling provision in fair housing law, offers perspective on disparate impact claims, and reveals mechanisms of local exclusion.

PART IV

Remedies

7

Property Rules versus Liability Rules

One of the most fundamental issues every legal system must address is the form of protection that should be given to legal entitlements, including property rights. Since the publication of the seminal article by Guido Calabresi and A. Douglas Melamed (1972), this issue has been known as the choice between property rules and liability rules. An entitlement is protected by a property rule, that is, by the remedy of injunction, when no one can appropriate the entitlement without securing the owner's consent. The entitlement must be transferred through a voluntary transaction, with the owner-seller agreeing to its price. In contrast, liability-rule protection suffices with the remedy of damages, and thus enables a forced transfer of the entitlement. The coercing party need not seek the owner's consent but must only pay her the objectively determined value of the entitlement (Calabresi and Melamed 1972, 1092, 1105–07).[1] For example, a parcel of land is protected by a property rule when a buyer needs to acquire the owner's consent in order to purchase it and become the new owner. In contrast, the same parcel is protected only by a liability rule when the state can expropriate it for some public use, such as a road or a park, and the court determines the amount of compensation due (for a discussion of what constitutes just compensation, see chapter 3). To take another example, in the famous case of *Boomer v. Atlantic Cement Co.*,[2] the court refused to issue an injunction against a cement factory and required it to pay damages to the neighboring landowners who suffered from air pollution. As a result, the entitlement of the landowners to enjoy their property without interference was protected with a liability rule rather than a property rule. A major debate among legal scholars pertains to the choice between these two types of rules. We shall first summarize this debate and its underlying assumptions. Then we will show how behavioral studies offer important considerations that should influence the legal discussion.

The Conventional Wisdom and Its Influential Critique

Calabresi and Melamed (1972) offered a simple, elegant criterion for choosing between the two forms of entitlement protection—namely, transaction costs. Accordingly, property rules should be employed when transaction costs are low and the parties can bargain with one another to achieve desirable outcomes. In such cases, property-rule protection will induce parties to negotiate a voluntary transfer of the entitlement. Liability rules should be used when transaction costs are high and bargaining is impossible or difficult, such as when numerous or unidentifiable parties are involved (Calabresi and Melamed 1972, 1105–10, 1118–19, 1125–27).[3]

Although the transaction-costs criterion, with its attendant recommendations regarding the choice and content of legal rules, has garnered support in the literature (Chang 2015, 493–505; Craswell 1993, 8–9, 15; Krier and Schwab 1995, 450–51; Merges 1994; Morris 1993, 850–54; Ulen 1984, 367–70), it has also been subject to influential critique. Specifically, scholars have claimed that liability rules may be superior to property rules even when transaction costs are low and emphasized the risk that bargaining under property rules might fail. Such failure can occur, for example, in a bilateral monopoly situation with asymmetric information. If each party attempts to capture the potential gains from the trade (sellers by overstating their valuation of the good, and buyers by understating their valuation) and miscalculates the other party's evaluations and reactions, then potentially efficient transactions might not take place at all, or they may prove possible only after a costly delay. An advantage of liability rules in this regard is that they remove the entitlement owner's holdout power. Since under liability rules the transfer can be coerced upon the owner, these rules ensure the execution of efficient transfers (Ayres and Talley 1995, 1030–33, 1042–44, 1055–56; Kaplow and Shavell 1996, 717–18, 724–37; Shavell 2004, 87–91, 315).

However, the employment of liability rules is not without risk, since courts might err in assessing the entitlement owner's losses. Even advocates of liability-rule protection concede that the argument in favor of liability rules holds only if courts do not systematically underestimate compensation awards to entitlement owners (Kaplow and Shavell 1996, 720, 730–32). Thus, the superiority of liability rules over property rules rests on the judgment that the risks involved in employing the latter are higher than those involved in employing the former.

In sum, the case for increasing the use of liability rules rests on various explicit and implicit assumptions. An express assumption is the dominance of opportunistic behavior, which explains the concern that, under property rules, owners would fail to agree to efficient transfers of their entitlement to people who value it more. Another, implicit assumption relates to the belief that, under liability rules, courts would grant adequate compensation to entitlement owners. If losses are accurately assessed, owners would plausibly be indifferent between retaining the entitlement and receiving its equivalent monetary value. However, as explained later, behavioral findings question these assumptions, thereby strengthening the case for employing property rules whenever possible. Generally speaking, psychological studies invite more optimism about people's ability to reach mutual agreement under property rules and suggest that miscalculations of damages under liability rules may be a graver danger than presently realized.

Challenging the Dominance of Opportunistic Behavior

The fear that voluntary transactions under property-rule protection might fail rests on an assumption of extreme greediness. Accordingly, each party has a strong incentive to lie about her true valuation of the entitlement, in order to capture as much as possible from the surplus of the transaction. Although the incentive for strategic behavior can affect both sides to the potential bargain, it is the *entitlement owner's* incentive to behave opportunistically and "hold out" for greater profits that is emphasized in the context of property rules. Yet, an extensive body of research challenges this presumption. Individuals do not always exercise holdout power, and frequently cooperate with one another—hence succeeding in fairly dividing the potential gains from trade. People are not concerned solely with maximizing their own narrowly defined self-interest; considerations of fairness, solidarity, reciprocity, and altruism play a significant role as well (Bolton and Ockenfels 2000; Elster 1990; Etzioni 1988; Fehr and Schmidt 1999; Jolls, Sunstein, and Thaler 1998; Kahneman, Knetsch, and Thaler 1986; Korobkin and Ulen 2000, 1135–41; Lewinsohn-Zamir 1998; Mansbridge 1990; Margolis 1982).

Of particular interest for our purposes is the literature on the ultimatum game. In the basic form of this game, one person (the proposer) is asked to divide a sum of money between herself and another person (the responder). The responder is free to accept or reject the sum offered. In the former case, the proposed division is implemented. In the latter, neither player receives anything. The standard economic prediction is one of utmost opportunism: the proposer will offer the smallest amount of money possible in the game, and the responder will accept this sum, since any share of the pie is preferable to receiving nothing. Experimental results deviate dramatically from this prediction. Most proposers offer substantial amounts of money, often an equal split of the pie, and responders accept generous offers. Offers that deviate substantially from 50 percent (such as less than 20 percent) are typically rejected. Similar results were reached using relatively large sums of money and with numerous rounds (instead of one-period plays), thereby refuting the claim that high stakes or ample opportunity to internalize the logic of the game will drive results toward the economic prediction. The rejection of low offers is explained both by resistance to unfairness and by the desire to punish ungenerous proposers (for overviews of the vast literature on ultimatum games, see D. J. Cooper and Kagel 2015, 218–31; Hoffman, McCabe, and Smith 2008, 411–28, 436–53; Roth 1995, 253–348; Lewinsohn-Zamir 2001a; Thaler 1992, 21–35).

In the context of negotiations for the transfer of an entitlement, the responder in an ultimatum game may be compared to an owner whose entitlement is protected by a property rule. She may agree to an offer to sell her entitlement for the price suggested by the proposer-buyer, which represents a way of splitting the gains from the trade. The transfer, however, cannot be forced upon her. If the owner rejects the buyer's proposal, neither party would realize any gains. The results of ultimatum games question the conventional assumption that property-rule protection induces sellers to hold out for all the profits from the trade, and that such behavior either prevents the realization of efficient transactions or at least significantly increases their costs.

Most ultimatum bargaining is successful, and only a minority of offers are rejected for being too low. Proposers know in advance that they must acquire the responders' consent to enjoy any gains. Consequently, most proposers make offers that they expect responders to accept, and their offers are indeed accepted and efficient transactions carried out. In other words, property-rule protection may facilitate efficient bargaining by encouraging potential buyers to act fairly and offer some of the gains from the trade to the seller-owners. The rejection power afforded to responders does not induce extreme greediness but merely prevents proposers from trying to claim all the profits for themselves. As a rule, responders in ultimatum games do not reject offers between 20 percent and 50 percent of the sum at stake. They do not attempt to "educate" proposers to offer them 99 percent of the pie, calculating that the proposers will view any profit as better than nothing. Why, then, assume that owners in real life aim for the whole pie?

The simplicity of ultimatum games as compared with real-life bargaining strengthens the argument that the assumption of extreme greediness is misguided. Ultimatum experiments attest to the probable success of even onetime bargaining between complete strangers, who interact anonymously and are not troubled by considerations of long-term relationships, their reputation, and so forth. Negotiations in real life would plausibly be at least equally successful, because bargainers can communicate directly with one another and have an opportunity to discuss their disagreements and negotiate an acceptable compromise.[4]

True, the question as to what constitutes a fair division of the pie might be more controversial in real life than in a laboratory experiment.[5] In addition, the well-known phenomenon of self-serving bias might intensify real parties' disagreements regarding the fair division of the pie. For example, behavioral studies have found that people often assess fairness in a way that excessively favors themselves and that self-serving conceptions of fairness can sometimes obstruct successful negotiation (Babcock et al. 1995; Loewenstein et al. 1993). Nonetheless, recognizing the possibility of controversy regarding the division of the gains is far from being tantamount to an assertion that each party would attempt to extract most of these gains for herself. It is highly unlikely that people ordinarily feel entitled to all the profits of every transaction. Rather, they expect to receive a certain, acceptable share. Take, for example, the case of a parcel of land that is required for some public project. Is it reasonable to assume that the landowner would consider herself as deserving the lion's share of the profits of an enterprise she could not have executed on her own? Although a self-serving bias may potentially exist in every negotiation, property rules may mitigate its impact because they encourage parties to divide the gains from the trade. Owners know that they must compromise on the division of the potential profits if they wish to enjoy any profit at all (for a more extensive treatment of these ideas, see Lewinsohn-Zamir 2001a).

Furthermore, the argument that negotiations would likely fail under a property rule in low-transaction-costs situations, even when the seller values the asset less than the buyer, assumes that sellers are risk-seeking. Only a highly risk-loving person would stick to her holdout position in an attempt to extract more gains, especially if she does not know the exact size of these gains (which is usually the case). Interestingly, some behavioral studies have found that buyers outperform sellers in bargaining experiments. Specifically, sellers tend to be risk-averse (i.e., more concessionary and willing to compromise), while buyers tend to be risk-seeking (i.e., hold out longer for a higher future payoff) (see Neale and Bazerman 1991, 156–57; Neale, Huber, and Northcraft 1987). Note, we do not naively claim that opportunistic behavior does not exist or that inefficient holdouts never occur. Obviously, for example, if the government is planning to construct a major highway and needs to acquire small pieces of land from hundreds or even thousands of landowners, an exercise of expropriation powers may be unavoidable. We submit, however, that the dominance of the opportunistic motivation has been exaggerated. As experimental studies show, people are less greedy and more inclined to compromise in order to achieve favorable outcomes than standard economic theory is willing to admit.

The Impact of the Endowment Effect on the Property-Rule/Liability-Rule Debate

The endowment effect (EE) is the tendency of people to value an entitlement that they already have much more than an identical entitlement that they have an opportunity to acquire. Individuals demand a significantly higher price to give up an already owned entitlement than they would be willing to pay to purchase the same entitlement in the first place (for discussion of the EE in the context of ownership and possession, see chapter 1). Upon first thought, it seems that the EE phenomenon strengthens the case in favor of liability rules, by providing another reason why bargaining under property rules may fail, even when transaction costs are low. In fact, some legal scholars made such an argument. For example, Buccafusco and Sprigman (2010, 2011) argue that intellectual property rights produce in creators both an EE (as a result of ownership) and an additional "creativity effect," due to being the creators of the owned work. Consequently, the two effects make owners overly reluctant to part with their work (see also Jolls and Sunstein 2006, 220–22; Lemley 2012, 485–86).[6] In a similar vein, Peñalver and Katyal (2007, 1133–35) assert that the EE creates a conservative bias in favor of current property owners that hinders beneficial social changes in property law and the distribution of assets, to the disadvantage of nonowners. Likewise, Ayres (1998, 810–12) generally states that property-rule protection of entitlements creates an EE that impedes negotiations. According to this literature, an advantage of liability-rule protection is that it weakens or eliminates the EE. The reason for this, so the argument goes, is that entitling owners to monetary damages alone conveys a lesser sense of ownership than entitling them to an injunction against interference with their property (Rachlinski and Jourden 1998).

Although this application of the EE appears to be straightforward and plausible, it is actually quite problematic. Moreover, the use of the EE to strengthen the argument in favor of liability rules is particularly problematic in the context of property law. If the mere fact of having property creates a strong EE that obstructs efficient transactions, and if the solution is to protect property rights only with liability rules, wouldn't this undermine the whole idea of private property? The right of property owners to exclude others from using the property without their consent is considered a vital component of ownership (Epstein 1982, 1367; Merrill 1998). Adopting a general liability-rule regime would radically alter the current institution of private property, with detrimental effects in terms of efficiency and fairness.

In this context, it is worthwhile to address the results of a study by Rachlinski and Jourden (1998, 1559–72), who found that a stronger EE is manifested when entitlements are protected by an injunction (property rule) than when they are protected by a damages remedy (liability rule).[7] The authors observed participants' answers to hypothetical questionnaires (rather than their actual bargaining behavior or trades) and compared the elicited sale prices of entitlements protected *solely* by liability rules to the sale prices of entitlements protected *only* with injunctions. Both regimes greatly differ from any real-world property institution. In actuality, no entitlement is protected exclusively by one type of rule. Land, for example, is protected by a property rule when a person wishes to buy it for private use, and by a liability rule when the government wants to expropriate it for public use. Importantly, most parcels of land are voluntarily sold on the market, and expropriation is the exception rather than the rule. Consequently, an owner's natural reference point is her ability to refuse to sell her land, and the phenomenon of expropriation cannot alter this fact. Put differently, in reality, the occasional incidence of liability-rule protection will not suffice to alter individuals' perceptions of ownership and thus to eliminate the EE in the relatively rare cases where assets are taken from them against their will. In addition, all the questionnaires in Rachlinski and Jourden's study informed the participants that if they agreed to sell the entitlement, the purchase price could be used for acquiring a good substitute, and that this alternative goal could not be realized without a sale. The existence of an adequate replacement may have reduced participants' EE in the liability-rule scenario because the loss caused by the possibility of a forced transfer could be immediately remedied by a close substitute. In contrast, participants in the property-rule scenario may have felt that a sale was redundant, as they could achieve a similar outcome simply by holding on to their current entitlement (see also Korobkin 2003, 1284–85, who explains why the positive implications of the study might be limited due to its environmental context).

At any rate, the EE (fortunately) does not call for a drastic revision in our understanding of private property; this is because the magnitude of the EE varies greatly from one case to another. The argument in favor of liability rules relies on the general existence of the EE phenomenon. Yet the circumstances in which it is reduced or eliminated are ignored, though they are highly relevant for the property-rule/liability-rule debate. A major explanation for the EE is people's aversion to losses (rather than the enhanced attractiveness of an entitlement one owns) (Kahneman 1992; see also Morewedge and Giblin 2015). Accordingly, the pain of giving up an endowment exceeds the pleasure of acquiring it. Since losses loom larger than gains, if parting with an entitlement is perceived as a loss, then individuals will demand a higher price for it. Such feelings of loss, however, are not present in every transfer of assets.

Psychological studies have shown, for example, that goods held for exchange—in contrast to goods held for use—do not produce an EE; nor do money, bargaining chips, vouchers, or tokens that are valued only for their trading possibilities (Hoffman and Spitzer 1993, 78–82, 111, 113; Kahneman, Knetsch, and Thaler 1990, 1328–32, 1344; Novemsky and Kahneman 2005a; van Djik and van Knippenberg 1996).[8] Likewise, the EE is substantially smaller when an adequate substitute for the relevant good is available. Thus, Adamowicz, Bhardwaj, and Macnab (1993) found that differences between selling and buying prices for tickets to a National Hockey League game considerably decreased when a substitute for personal attendance—live television and radio broadcasts of the game—existed (Hanemann [1991] presented the theoretical claim that the existence of adequate substitutes decreases the magnitude of the EE).[9] Contrarily, the more difficult it is to compare the endowed item and its alternative, the greater the reluctance to trade (van Dijk and van Knippenberg 1998).

It is only natural that owners would be less reluctant to part with a good for which an adequate substitute is readily available and under circumstances in which they freely engage in market transactions. This is, in fact, the common denominator for all the cases in which no EE or only a small EE exists: bargaining chips, vouchers, and tokens are perfect substitutes for any good that their owner wishes to purchase with them. The case is basically similar for goods held specifically for exchange and goods willingly offered for sale by their owners.

Experimental studies have found that the EE is significantly weakened or eliminated when an owner *wants* to sell her asset. Thus, Mandel (2002) demonstrated that the motivation to bring about a potential transaction—which he labeled "transaction demand"—moderates the EE. As transaction demand increases, owners are more inclined to sell at lower prices, and prospective buyers are more willing to pay higher prices. In addition, when transaction demand was high for both sellers and buyers, the EE was reversed (i.e., mean buying price significantly exceeded mean selling price). Indeed, if transaction demand did not exist in the real world and "if motivational factors did not often override the effects of loss aversion on valuation, then far fewer transactions would be expected to occur than they actually do" (Mandel 2002, 745). Similarly, Simonson and Drolet (2004) showed that if a person decides that she wants to sell an item, no EE exists, and the market price becomes the primary driver of the owner's minimum asking price. In contrast, if a person is uncertain about her desire to trade, an EE is created. Liberman et al. (1999) likewise demonstrated that participants were reluctant to exchange an endowed good when they were in a "prevention" frame of mind (caused by priming that was unrelated to the subsequent exchange experiment), but not when they were in a "promotion" frame of mind. In sum, people's intentions determine their reference point and thus the framing of a situation as involving gains or losses.

These findings support the argument that the use of property rules may actually produce a weaker EE than the use of liability rules. Property-rule protection means that an owner will sell only if she has reached the stage at which she wishes to sell. A person desiring to sell is a person who intends to participate in the market and who believes that good substitutes exist for her entitlement. Put differently, property rules may induce a frame of mind that focuses on the profits of the exchange—the money or alternative good that can be bought with it—rather than on the good that is given up. As Novemsky and Kahneman explain, people's intentions may moderate loss aversion

> when there is an intention to exchange a good, the reference point is not the current endowment but rather the expected endowment at the conclusion of the exchange. In this case, giving up a good in an exchange would not involve loss aversion, because the good is not part of the reference point (i.e., the expected endowment). (2005b, 140)

(For a formal modeling of this insight, see Kőszegi and Rabin 2005).

One should not deduce from these studies that efficient transfers of entitlements should always be conditioned on the entitlement holder's consent. A transfer may be socially desirable even if an owner's refusal to sell is genuine and not strategic. For instance, a person may refuse to sell her home, even though the land is more valuable for a certain public use. However, behavioral studies help explain why bargaining under property-rule protection is likely to be more successful and less prone to failure than some scholars tend to assume.

Unlike property-rule protection, liability-rule protection signifies that an owner can be forced to transfer her entitlement. Even if the parties attempt to negotiate a transfer of the entitlement in the shadow of the liability rule, the owner is aware that refusal to sell will be of no avail. In any case, the entitlement can be taken against her will.[10] The power of coercion might evoke the role of an "unwilling seller" and an attitude of resistance. An individual unwilling to sell is an individual who prefers to keep the entitlement and who believes that adequate substitutes for the entitlement do not exist. Consequently, the EE may be stronger when entitlements are protected with liability rules (Lewinsohn-Zamir 2001a). This means that property rules—in comparison to liability rules—may expand the scope of potential efficient transactions. This is because the lower the owner's asking price, the larger the group of potential buyers whose maximum offer price equals or exceeds that price. The experimental data further suggest that damages awards under liability rules might systematically undercompensate entitlement owners. We turn to this problem in the next section.

The Adequacy of Compensation under Liability Rules

Once a transfer is coerced under a liability rule, the owner is entitled to compensation for her losses. Behavioral studies suggest that quantifying the damages award is a more complex task than is commonly assumed, and that existing compensation rules might fail to adequately address the owner's losses. There are various reasons for this potential adverse outcome.

Ordinarily, courts determine the amount of compensation according to their estimation of the competitive market price of the entitlement. Thus, for instance, compensation for the expropriation of a parcel of land will often be calculated according to the actual prices received in contracts for the voluntary sale of parcels as similar as possible to the one expropriated (Dana and Merrill 2002, 169–71). If indeed the EE is relatively small (and sometimes nonexistent) in ordinary, voluntary market transactions, and relatively large in coerced transfers, then determining compensation for the latter using empirical data relating to the former is likely to result in inherent undercompensation of entitlement owners.[11] Systematic undercompensation is unfair and would also create inefficiency in the long run by discouraging owners from investing in their assets.

Furthermore, the current compensation measure disregards the injury to owners from the very fact that the entitlement was taken from them against their will. Experimental findings show that people perceive outcomes broadly, and therefore evaluate the goodness or badness of events according to several variables beyond their end results. For example, a factor that exacerbates an injurious outcome is whether the injury was brought about intentionally (though without malice or intent to harm) rather than unintentionally. Another factor of relevance is the voluntariness or involuntariness of an act. Unwilling transfer of even exchange goods inflicts on the owner a loss that is distinct from her subjective valuation of the good (Lewinsohn-Zamir 2012; for further discussion of these findings, see chapter 3). Some evidence also exists that people prefer in-kind remedies over monetary remedies, and that this preference exists even with respect to fungible property, easily replaceable in the market (Lewinsohn-Zamir 2013; the general preference for in-kind redress is discussed in chapter 8). As a result, all assets are to some extent unique, in the sense that it is difficult to quantify the loss incurred by receiving only a monetary relief rather than an in-kind one.

Studies on the connection between possessions and self-identity, self-image, and self-development are also relevant in this context. Beggan (1992) found that overvaluation of owned objects occurs particularly when an owner's positive self-image is threatened (as a result, for example, of ego-injuring negative performance feedback). Belk (1988) showed that involuntary loss of possessions causes trauma and loss of self, but voluntary disposition does not. If forced transfer of assets through liability rules injures owners' self-image, this might increase their valuation of the taken assets and the loss that they would suffer. It is plausible that voluntary transfer through property-rule protection would not cause these detrimental effects at all (or cause them to a lesser extent).

Since exercise of liability rules entails intentional injury, coerced transfer, and monetary redress, there is reason to fear that the prevailing compensation criterion of "fair market value" may be inherently undercompensatory and lead to inefficiency and demoralization of entitlement owners (Lewinsohn-Zamir 1996, 61–62, 65–66). Even if we could alter the way we calculate damages under liability rules so as to address these additional losses, there would still be an advantage to using property rules: such rules bypass the need for complicated, potentially inaccurate, and more expensive damages calculations.

In conclusion, behavioral studies caution us against increasing the use of liability rules even when transaction costs are low and property rules are a feasible option. One cannot assume—as standard economic analysis does—that failed negotiations for voluntary transfers under property-rule protection are a greater risk than undercompensating entitlement owners under liability-rule protection. Current experimental data lend additional support to the elegant and simple Calabresi-Melamed criterion of "transaction costs" as the guiding rule for choosing between property rules and liability rules.

In-Kind Remedies versus Monetary Remedies

All legal systems must design remedies for rights violations, including property rights. In this context, one of the most common choices that must be made is between monetary and in-kind remedies. This issue only partially overlaps with that discussed in the preceding chapter, namely, the choice between property rules and liability rules. For instance, when a seller breaches a contract to deliver a certain asset, awarding the buyer specific performance (i.e., ordering the seller to deliver the promised asset) represents both an in-kind remedy and protection of the buyer's entitlement with a property rule. The alternative remedy of expectation damages embodies both a monetary remedy and liability-rule protection of the contractual entitlement. However, this alignment between type of remedy and form of entitlement protection does not exist in other cases. Thus, when a parcel of land is lawfully expropriated for some public use, the owner's entitlement is protected in any case with a liability rule, as the state has power to coerce the transfer. Yet, the remedy awarded to the owner may be either monetary (cash compensation) or in kind (e.g., a different piece of land).

It is widely acknowledged that money may fall short as a remedy when unique, irreplaceable goods are involved. At the same time, money is commonly believed to be an apt substitution for other entitlements in proprietary and commercial contexts. Specifically, legal practitioners, policy makers, and academics often assume that people are basically indifferent between monetary and in-kind remedies of equal pecuniary value. Notably, however, this strong assumption is mostly grounded on theoretical reasoning and intuitions, rather than experimental or empirical data.

The legal literature on this issue has focused mainly on remedies for breach of contract. Thus, law-and-economics scholars often claim that people ordinarily view a contractual obligation as an option to either perform in kind or provide monetary compensation (Markovits and

Schwartz 2011, 1948; R. A. Posner 2009). This claim is based on an untested presumption that promisees would prefer to afford promisors an option to perform or pay in return for a price reduction (Shavell 2006, 840–44). Some scholars have criticized this assumption (M. A. Eisenberg 2006, 574–75), but they, too, fail to support their claims with behavioral evidence. The relatively few experimental studies of contract remedies have not resolved this issue, since, for example, they informed subjects that a breach has occurred and focused on their moral judgments regarding such breach (Wilkinson-Ryan and Baron 2009),[1] whereas the option theory posits that promisees allow promisors to substitute money for in-kind performance (and therefore no breach has occurred). Outside of contract law, there was little examination of people's preferences with respect to different types of legal remedies.

In reality, monetary compensation is the most common form of redress for rights violations. This state of affairs may be due not only to the staunch belief in the adequacy of monetary remedies but also to their other advantages. For instance, a monetary remedy typically interferes less with the autonomy of the injuring party than an in-kind remedy and is comparatively easy to administer.

In this chapter, we question the conventional wisdom that people are ordinarily indifferent between monetary and nonmonetary remedies, focusing on remedies relating to property. Specifically, there is some experimental evidence that people prefer in-kind remedies to monetary ones, even when the remedy concerns nonunique and easily replaceable assets.

Which Type of Remedy Do People Prefer?

Lewinsohn-Zamir (2013) tested the prevailing belief that monetary remedies are usually a satisfactory substitute for in-kind redress by examining people's choices among different types of entitlements and remedies. In the experiments, laypersons and experienced businesspeople were asked to envision a scenario in which they could choose between an in-kind remedy (or entitlement) and a monetary one designed to equal the value of the in-kind option as precisely as possible. The vignettes used in the experiments referred to a wide array of rights from contract, property, torts, and labor law. For example, in a scenario where a person trespassed on vacant land purchased as an investment, participants could choose between full monetary damages for their losses and an injunction against the trespasser. Similarly, in a case depicting the expropriation of 10 percent of an owned but undeveloped and unpossessed parcel to widen an adjacent road and sidewalk, participants could choose between monetary compensation and additional development rights for the remainder of the parcel.[2] Respondents who opted for the in-kind alternative were asked a follow-up question: whether they would have been willing to opt for the monetary alternative had it been higher. Respondents who answered in the affirmative were then asked to indicate the sum that would be required for them to choose the monetary option.

The results revealed a clear preference for in-kind remedies and entitlements. Overall, across all the scenarios, 69 percent of the laypersons and 79 percent of the businesspeople preferred the in-kind option, and only 26 percent of the laypersons and 19 percent of the businesspeople chose the monetary one. Although the in-kind and monetary alternatives were designed to be of equal pecuniary value, only 5 percent of the laypersons and 2 percent of the businesspeople stated that they had no particular preference. Furthermore, close to half of the majority group who chose the in-kind option (46 percent of the laypersons and 40 percent of the businesspeople) said that they *would not* agree to opt for the monetary option, even for more money. Finally, many of those who answered the follow-up question in the affirmative conditioned the switch from the in-kind to the monetary alternative on the payment of an unrealistically high additional sum (Lewinsohn-Zamir 2013, 159–74). In the real world, this would be tantamount to rejecting the monetary option. Similar results were found when looking separately at the scenarios dealing with property rights. For instance, in the expropriation case, 68 percent of the businesspeople preferred to receive development rights to the remainder of a partially expropriated parcel rather than monetary compensation. Likewise, in the case of trespassing on a vacant parcel purchased for investment, 82 percent of this group preferred an injunction to full monetary damages (Lewinsohn-Zamir 2013, 171–72).

In sum, the initial experimental results indicate that people generally prefer in-kind remedies over monetary ones, even when the remedy relates to fungible, easily replaceable assets whose monetary value can be accurately calculated.[3] In the next section, we discuss this finding and offer some additional experimental support.

Further Psychological Data

The results just described suggest that people prefer to restore the very thing injured rather than obtain something else. It appears that in-kind redress may achieve the best fit between a loss and its correction and satisfy people in a way that monetary substitutes do not. In-kind relief may attain "restoration" in cases where monetary remedies afford only "consolation."[4]

This explanation does not preclude others, as more than one factor can explain a particular phenomenon. For example, Robert Ellickson found in his study of Shasta County that "when one ranchette owner's goat ate his neighbor's tomatoes, the goat's owner responded by helping to replant the tomatoes, not by sending a check" (1994, 235). Ellickson argues that monetary payment is perceived as cold and impersonal, befitting strangers rather than neighbors. In contrast, in-kind exchange signals solidarity and trust, reinforcing neighborly expectations of ongoing cooperative interactions. Note, however, that the remedy chosen by the ranchers was not just any nonmonetary form of relief. It was of the *same type* as the injury and resembled a restoration of the damaged asset itself. Therefore, anticommodification preferences alone cannot fully explain the chosen form of redress.[5]

The finding that people prefer to receive something of a similar type when it is not feasible for them to receive the thing itself accords with studies in social psychology. "Resource Theory," developed by Uriel Foa and others (U. G. Foa 1993; E. B. Foa and Foa 1976), classifies resources exchanged in interactions between individuals into six categories: love, status, information, money, goods, and services (E. B. Foa and Foa 1976, 103). Scholars found that the more similar two resources are to one another, the greater the likelihood that they would be exchanged (Brinberg and Castell 1982) and the greater people's satisfaction from the exchange (Converse and Foa 1993). Satisfaction from reciprocation is maximized when repayment is with the same resource; therefore, for example, satisfaction was lowest when love and money were exchanged (Teichman and Foa 1975). This phenomenon was found not only with respect to positive giving exchanges but also in cases of negative aggression exchanges. Respondents preferred to retaliate by depriving the injuring party of the resource that was the most similar to the one that had been taken from them. Thus, participants who lost love or status (by being personally rejected or derogated) preferred to retaliate by derogating or expressing dislike of their offenders rather than by making them lose money or goods, and vice versa (E. B. Foa, Turner, and Foa 1972). Those who retaliated with a dissimilar resource "compensated" for their dissatisfaction by increasing the level of retaliation. Moreover, the reduced effectiveness of the dissimilar resource led not only to a greater measure of retaliation but also to greater residual hostility, namely, a desire for further retaliation (Donnenwerth and Foa 1974).

An extension of Resource Theory that is most relevant for our purposes is a meta-analysis and new experimental study by Roschk and Gelbrich (2014). The authors focused on failed dealings between service providers and customers and examined which type of compensation is most effective in achieving recovery from a particular type of failure (in terms of consumer satisfaction, loyalty, and positive word of mouth). Thus, failure types could include monetary harm (such as an overcharge), flawed goods (e.g., shoes falling apart), faulty service (e.g., an overcooked steak), or lack of adequate attention (such as giving undue preference to other customers). Compensation type could be monetary, a new or exchanged good, a new or re-performed service, or psychological (an apology). It was found that recovery was the most effective when the exchanged resources were similar, that is, when the type of compensation was matched in form to the type of failure. It appears that the similarity of the two reinforced people's perceptions of justice, which in turn fostered positive consumer reactions. Specifically, the recovery effect of compensation was strongest when monetary compensation was provided for a monetary failure, new or exchanged goods were given for flawed goods, and new or re-performed services were granted for failed service (Roschk and Gelbrich 2014, 2002–06).

Importantly, these findings related to nonunique goods and routine services. The vignette study depicted, inter alia, an auto repair shop that was supposed to clean the soiled passenger seat of a customer's car but instead overcharged the customer, failed to clean the seat, or stained the car mats. The failure was regarded as best rectified when the repair shop, respectively, refunded the overcharged sum, re-performed the cleaning service, or exchanged the stained mats. In each of these scenarios, when the type of compensation was dissimilar to the type of failure, the recovery effect was lower (Roschk and Gelbrich 2014, 206–08). Note that monetary compensation was considered the most adequate remedy only when the injury itself involved money (rather than some nonmonetary asset). For instance, even though car mats are a perfectly fungible asset, the loss was regarded as best rectified when the injuring party gave the customer new mats rather than their monetary equivalent.

Finally, a study by Jane Beattie and Jonathan Baron (1995) lends additional support to the preference for in-kind solutions. Beattie and Baron compared what they called "in-kind" and "out-of-kind" penalties. Both types could be nonmonetary or monetary. For example, when a factory caused a fire that destroyed a nearby forest, participants preferred to order the factory to pay for the planting of new trees in a different state rather than to pay for purchasing land for a national park. Similarly, when a drug company manufactured a defective drug that caused blindness in children, the respondents preferred to require the company to fund a school for blind children instead of one for epileptic children. This preference for penalties that are compatible with the harm wrought can be viewed as a manifestation of the biblical "eye for an eye" (Beattie and Baron 1995, 140–43, 149). The authors' distinction between in-kind and out-of-kind penalties is not the same as the distinction between in-kind and monetary remedies. However, their results strengthen the argument that the type of redress matters and that people generally prefer remedies that resemble what they had lost.[6] We now turn to potential policy implications of the preference for in-kind redress.

Normative Implications of the Preference for In-Kind Remedies

Here, we address two contexts in which the preference for in-kind redress seems particularly pertinent: the remedy for wrongful interference with property, and land use planning and expropriation of property. But, first, a few general remarks are in order.

Even if people generally prefer in-kind remedies to monetary ones, this does not necessarily entail that the law should award in-kind redress. The choice of a remedy reflects numerous—sometimes conflicting—

considerations. Yet, as promoting individuals' welfare is a major (albeit not the only) concern, the notion that people derive greater utility from in-kind remedies is an important consideration. Absent overriding considerations, principles of both corrective justice and efficiency support the legal system's accommodation of these preferences. In-kind remedies are helpful in realizing the compensatory goal of many legal doctrines. They may also enhance efficiency because efficient deterrence requires that injurers internalize the full costs they inflicted on unwilling others.

Furthermore, awareness of the preference for in-kind redress is important even if other considerations eventually tilt the scales in favor of a monetary award. Specifically, nonfulfillment of this preference is a cost that should be taken into account. Consequently, just compensation and efficient deterrence may require that the injurer pay for the failure to provide in-kind redress. This may justify, in certain cases, an increase in the monetary award.

Remedies for Wrongful Interference with Property

The right of property owners to exclude others from using the property without their consent is considered a vital component of ownership (Merrill 1998, 730). Furthermore, this entitlement is often protected with a property rule, with injunctions being the typical remedy against trespassers on land (Stoebuck and Whitman 2000, 7). The case of personal property does not differ greatly from this. While according to the common law, the normal remedy for conversion of chattels is damages, the plaintiff usually has the option to recover the chattel itself (Dobbs, Hayden, and Bublick 2011, § 73). Furthermore, American state legislatures have recognized a general action for "replevin," which enables the recovery of personal property (Stoebuck and Whitman 2000, 8). Apparently, the uniqueness (or nonuniqueness) of the relevant property does not play a role in deciding whether to grant an injunction against the possessing wrongdoer and order the asset returned to the true owner.

Henry Smith (2004) has offered an information-costs theory to explain the preeminence of injunctions in this context. Assets commonly have multiple attributes that afford them numerous potential uses. Allocative efficiency requires information about the costs and benefits of these uses, but some uses are presently unknown and others are difficult to prove or to quantify in monetary terms. Property rules delegate to owners the function of gathering and acting on information about potential uses. This delegation is desirable because owners typically can produce the necessary information more cost-effectively than takers or courts (H. E. Smith 2004, 1753–78).

It is not surprising that Smith focuses on the example of land. Parcels of land may indeed vary from one another in their multiple attributes and uses—present and future, known and unknown. Therefore, land is the quintessential asset that requires costly information about its potential utilization. This problem is considerably less substantial when the asset wrongfully taken is a nonunique chattel, such as a family car or a cow. The information-costs theory cannot entirely account for why an in-kind remedy is generally available when assets are wrongfully taken. The experimental findings described earlier, in contrast, do provide such a general justification. Due to the value people place on in-kind redress, *all* assets may be regarded as unique, in the sense that it is difficult to quantify the loss incurred from receiving a monetary substitute rather than the thing itself. Since a monetary remedy unavoidably entails this difficulty, whenever possible it is prudent to bypass the need for complicated calculations.

Land Use Planning and Expropriation of Property

The experiments discussed earlier found that both laypersons and businesspeople generally preferred development rights to money as compensation for a partial expropriation of land. A plausible explanation for this result is that development rights restore the value of the injured asset itself, whereas money simply enables the landowner to regain her former level of wealth. Awarding development rights is the closest we can get to repairing the asset itself because it restores the land's development potential to its pre-expropriated state. Landowners cannot ordinarily use monetary compensation to purchase development rights for the remainder of their acreage.

In-kind redress may be superior to monetary redress in the land use context for another reason. Land use decisions typically entail both "winners" and "losers." Some property owners face expropriation or downzoning, while others see their land increase in value through favorable zoning provisions. Even if the injured landowners receive monetary compensation, they may still feel that they have been treated unequally. Since money is distinct from the land, a financial award may not eliminate the feeling of having been disregarded. In contrast, in-kind redress can approximate a repair of the injured property. Affected landowners may feel that, like their neighbors, they, too, share in the planning benefits. In-kind redress thus has an inclusionary, participatory aspect that monetary redress lacks.

Admittedly, in-kind redress would not be feasible in all circumstances. Compensation by awarding development rights to the remainder of a partially expropriated parcel is a practicable solution only when the original parcel was very large or a relatively small portion was taken. When granting additional development rights, the planning authority must consider the interests of the neighborhood as a whole. From a professional planning perspective, it would likely be problematic to grant large-scale building rights to the owner of a small parcel.[7] At the same time, adding development rights may be particularly appropriate when the authorities expropriate a servitude, such as a public right of way through one's land, rather than ownership. Ordinarily, servitudes do not substantially reduce the value of the burdened land. Hence, the new development rights are likely to be minimal.

The experimental findings are also relevant in those instances when a parcel of land is expropriated in its entirety. Indeed, such expropriation rules out compensation by adding development rights to the reminder of the property. However, the benefits of in-kind redress are not limited to a narrowly defined restoration of this sort. As explained earlier, people tend to derive greater utility from a relief that is of the same type as the injury inflicted, and they may prefer a substitute for the expropriated parcel rather than money (see also Parchomovsky and Siegelman (2004, 140–41), suggesting that when the government expropriates the land of an entire residential community, it may offer its members the possibility of resettling in an alternative site).[8] The in-kind option may be particularly attractive if a suitable plot can be located in the same area as the expropriated parcel. This would promote values like equality and community and enable the injured landowner to share the benefits of the new public use of her land. Other things being equal, when this option is available, it may be offered to the landowner.[9]

In the same spirit, the findings support the introduction of a planning tool that is used in some European and Asian countries (Alterman 1988; Hong 2007) but not yet in the United States, namely, land readjustment (reparcellation). This tool is particularly useful when the current subdivision of a commercial or residential area does not provide the necessary infrastructure (such as roads, schools, or parks). A readjustment process starts with the consolidation of the parcels in a certain area into a common pool. Later, a decision is made as to where the construction will take place, and the land is redivided (Davy 2007, 41). Owners ultimately receive smaller but more valuable parcels, thanks to the new infrastructure and the development potential of the post-readjustment plots. Whereas eminent domain procedures single out particular owners to provide the land necessary for the upgraded infrastructure—excluding them from the fruits of the project—readjustment facilitates the sharing of both burden and benefit among all owners. Compensation for the reduction in the size of the parcels is primarily given in kind, through mutual enjoyment of various planning benefits (Schnidman 1988, 250–51). The readjustment procedure may require that each new parcel be as close as possible to its pre-readjustment location, and that its value relative to the other parcels be maintained (Alterman 2007, 69). Land readjustment may thus realize the advantages of in-kind redress without sacrificing sound planning considerations.

Some Caveats Regarding In-Kind Redress

Notwithstanding the existence of a preference for in-kind remedies, one must take into account countervailing considerations. This section briefly discusses two considerations favoring monetary relief that are most relevant to property contexts: the autonomy of the injured party and the institutional costs of in-kind redress.

As explained previously, although the majority of participants in Lewinsohn-Zamir's (2013) study revealed a clear preference for in-kind remedies, some preferred the monetary option and some expressed indifference between the two. Such preferences certainly may be rational and informed. For example, a person may prefer the freedom that a monetary remedy enables, and instead of having a damaged asset restored to its former state, she may prefer to be given a sum of money that can be used for a different purpose altogether. Ignoring the minority's preferences would injure their autonomy and force them to bear costs of something that they would rather do without. Moreover, even those who in principle prefer in-kind redress may, under specific circumstances, opt for monetary relief. Thus, an owner whose property was damaged by a wrongdoer or a person who purchased a defective apartment might decide against seeking an order requiring the defendant to fix the asset. The plaintiff may doubt the defendant's ability to do the job well or be unwilling to deal with the wrongdoer. In her mind, a better solution may be to receive a monetary settlement to be used to hire a third party to do the necessary repairs.[10]

These considerations support the proposition that, ordinarily, in-kind redress should be optional, that is, available at the request of the plaintiff.[11] Only in exceptional cases should we consider mandating in-kind relief as the sole remedy.[12]

A different argument against in-kind redress centers on the institutional costs of granting such relief. Arguably, in-kind remedies are frequently more expensive to administer than monetary ones are. This important consideration is context dependent. Consider, for example, breach of contract. While specific performance of a building construction project may require very costly supervision, specific performance of a contract for the delivery of goods may actually be cheaper than enforcement of a damages payment, which may involve the seizure and sale of the breacher's assets. Specific performance also saves the court the task of quantifying the damages.

The additional costs involved in in-kind redress may sometimes be reduced. For instance, the institutional costs of compensation with development rights can be decreased if the necessary zoning changes to the remainder of the parcel are not dealt with ex post, but rather as part of the planned expropriation process. As described previously, land readjustment operates precisely in this manner. Designating land for public uses (such as infrastructure) and compensating landowners through enhanced development rights are elements of the same planning process. Hence, it stands to reason that the additional administrative costs are at least partially offset by the money saved by not awarding cash compensation for the land taken.

To conclude, psychological data point to an inherent disadvantage of the most common form of legal redress: monetary compensation. Damages might routinely fall short of providing adequate relief even when they pertain to nonunique, easily quantifiable assets. There is some experimental evidence that people derive greater utility from in-kind remedies, which are likely perceived as redressing the situation in a way that money does not. While these findings do not necessarily outweigh conflicting considerations in the design of legal entitlements and remedies, they should not be discounted.

Conclusion

This book has explored how psychology research can inform our understanding of doctrines, rules, and debates in the field of property. Specifically, we have examined how psychological research applies to four major areas of property law: acquiring, contesting, and protecting rights in property; legal rules governing state interference with property; real estate transactions; and remedies. These chapters have covered a broad swath of ground in property law. We have identified areas where psychological perceptions diverge from law, discussed reforms to property rules and real estate transactions, and offered novel proposals for remedies.

Empirical work in psychology enables us to test and evaluate the assumptions about human behavior, preferences, and attachments underlying property rules. In some cases, psychology supports a different rule or approach. Psychology research also cultivates a richer understanding of the underlying goals justifying the system of private property. For example, psychology adds nuance to the concept of individual utility in law and economics and calls into question personhood theory's claims about the psychological exigency of certain forms of property. Conversely, property law can enrich psychology by suggesting new avenues of research and sharpening psychologists' understanding of concepts such as possession and ownership. In the following sections, we discuss some of the implications of psychology for legal reform, as well as highlight directions for future research.

Applying Psychology to Property Law

As we have seen in this book, the applications of psychology to property law vary based on the specific property rule, circumstances, and societal interests. For example, the social, moral, and economic harms from housing discrimination support legal reforms to lessen prejudicial attitudes and their effect on housing participants. In other contexts, it is less apparent that law should seek to alter or "debias" cognitive errors or preferences. In some cases, legitimate rationales, such as preserving traditions or maintaining social ties, may animate preferences or decisions that seem irrational on their face. For example, reluctance to part with property at a profit or for more than the owner is willing to pay for the same item may reflect desires for control, status, or stability. Given the variability in context and motive, psychology cannot offer a single mode of legal reform for property law. Rather, the psychology research offers different applications. These applications include reforms to align property rules with psychological perceptions or needs, methods to offset or counteract welfare-eroding cognitive and social biases, and a growing body of empirical data to improve remedies. We review these approaches next.

Psychology-Informed Reform of Property Law

The empirical research reveals legal tension points where psychological perceptions do not align with legal rules. People may perceive property rights, or injuries to their property rights, that property law fails to recognize or remedy. Examples include the lower level of federal protection in the United States for regulatory takings compared with physical takings and, in some contexts, such as bailments, inconsistent protection or compensation for personal property. Such misalignments increase friction between citizens and the legal system and create losses and inefficiencies by failing to respond to preferences.

The empirical evidence illuminates possible avenues for reform. For example, the psychology research suggests that the common law rule for acquiring ownership in unowned property might productively expand its focus from physical possession and control to also consider factors such as effort, expectations, or proximity in determining ownership. The data on people's attachments and identification with individual items of property indicate that, in some cases, property and bankruptcy law have overprotected residential property and underprotected personal and commercial property. Regulatory takings law is another area where the psychology evidence to date reveals that people's perceptions of their property rights and the personal harm they experience from a regulatory taking are substantially stronger than the US Supreme Court's protections. Interestingly, state constitutions and state courts, which have closer contact with the sentiments of the state's citizens, often offer stronger protection than federal law by requiring less diminution in property value from regulation in order to find a compensable regulatory taking (Sterk 2004; S. M. Stern 2013).

Not all divergences between psychological perceptions and property law require legal reform. Sometimes psychology research supports an existing property rule. For example, the endowment effect supports common law and statutory "self-help" rules that enable possessors in certain circumstances to recover their property through their own intervention. This unusual rule makes more sense in light of the stronger endowment effects (EEs) of the recently dispossessed compared with weaker attachments of the dispossessor.

In other instances, it is not perceptions that are out of step with the law, but rather capabilities. As we have discussed, the law of real estate transactions imposes information-processing and other burdens on decision making that few individual real estate consumers can successfully shoulder. We can reduce cognitive errors by changing law to offer information about property condition or loan terms earlier in the purchase process and in more simplified terms. Such reforms lessen, but are unlikely to eliminate, information-processing errors. For example, disclosures provide information, but they do not address limitations on attention or systematic tendencies to misestimate risk. In addition, businesses may "capture" laws intended to improve consumer information processing by using complexity, distraction, and social pressures to mislead consumers and undermine information provision (Willis 2013; S. M. Stern 2016).

In all of these contexts, psychological factors are not the sole considerations, or necessarily the most important ones, for property law reform. The psychological costs and benefits of property rules must be weighed against a variety of economic, social, and political factors. For example, pressing environmental concerns may counsel against increasing protections for property owners against regulatory takings in order to maintain environmental regulations. Our goal in this book has been to explore psychological perceptions and attachments as important, but not exclusive, factors in determining property rules and legal reforms.

Debiasing Irrationality, Attitudes, and Behaviors

Rather than reforming property law, in some instances we may wish property law to "debias," or alter, property holders' perceptions, attitudes, or behaviors. Discrimination based on one's familial, sexual, or disability status, or membership in a racial, ethnic, or religious group offers a prime example. In these cases, it would be normatively undesirable to align laws with prejudiced attitudes. Instead, as we have discussed, property law can reduce discriminatory attitudes and behaviors by restricting communications that promote prejudiced social norms and offering safeguards against exclusion in property institutions (e.g., homeowners' and neighborhood associations).

Other instances in which property law might seek to change people's preferences or behaviors are more controversial. For example, if a societal goal becomes to encourage more sharing of property, property law might reduce the transaction costs of sharing, create default rules in favor of sharing property, or offer incentives for sharing. Such reforms have been of interest to scholars of the burgeoning "sharing economy" in transportation and housing (Kreiczer-Levy 2016; Dyal-Chand 2015). We can also employ psychology to promote redistribution or owners' willingness to accept limitations on their property rights, in service of societal goals, such as environmental protection or housing quality. Framing ownership rights as limited, or cuing obligations toward society and other individuals, can aid such efforts (J. R. Nash and Stern 2010). Debiasing poses opportunities, as well as challenges, for policy makers who must weigh its benefits against social, political, and moral concerns about altering citizens' preferences and behaviors.

There are also structural limitations to debiasing. In many contexts, people have limited interaction with the law. Many property conflicts are resolved voluntarily, often in accordance with social norms (Ellickson 1994). Even when people become aware of, or resort to, formal property law, their exposure to a law may be brief and readily forgotten. Effective debiasing is likely to require longer exposure and repetition, particularly if psychological biases or tendencies are deeply entrenched.

Rethinking Remedies

A major function of law is to adjudge compensation and remedies. Psychology research can inform law's goal of "making people whole" for injuries to their property rights. Research on the endowment effect, well-being, and preferences for in-kind remedies offers insight into the form remedies might take to accomplish this goal. For example, injunctions may be preferable to damages (i.e., property rules vs. liability rules) due to the difficulty of adjudging adequate compensation for the economic and psychological aspects of property loss (Lewinsohn-Zamir 2001a).

Psychology research can also help to innovate remedies beyond standard forms such as injunctions and monetary damages. For example, as we have discussed, emerging research suggests that people sometimes prefer to receive the same or a similar item of property to that which they have lost, rather than monetary damages (Lewinsohn-Zamir 2013). Psychology has also shown nonpecuniary forms of recompense to be valuable, including apologies and fair and respectful processes for compensation (Robbennolt 2006; Tyler and Lind 1988).

The Next Generation of Research

In this book, we have considered a wide range of research that intersects with property law. While psychological studies have generated an impressive body of data relevant to property law, unanswered questions and gaps remain. In this section, we discuss some promising directions for future empirical work.

Applied Psychology for Property Law

Most of the studies described in this book come from laboratory or survey work in controlled experimental situations. This form of research isolates causal variables by controlling a variety of factors and designing experiments that focus on the variable hypothesized to produce a certain effect. These studies often use hypothetical scenarios and a nonrepresentative pool of participants (university students are the most common). As a result, questions remain about external validity, which refers to whether a phenomenon identified in one context occurs in different settings, and with respect to other persons and groups. For example, if people respond to experimental vignettes differently from how they might respond if faced with an actual property conflict or injury, then those studies lack external validity. A productive avenue for future research is to conduct more studies of people engaged in property conflicts, transactions, litigation, and other real-world contexts of property. For example, studies assessing the psychological response of actual owners subject to a government taking of property, or the well-being of recipients of direct housing subsidies versus cash welfare, would advance our understanding of psychology's impact on property law.

Cultural Differences

Research in psychology and property law is at an early stage in exploring whether cultural differences shape perceptions of property rights and conflicts. Currently, there is a limited amount of research that considers whether the implications of psychology for property law vary across cultures. There is some evidence that the magnitude of the EE varies based on country, and cross-cultural studies suggest that citizens of different countries differ on measures of materialism (i.e., the attribution of life satisfaction to the amount and value of property one possesses) (Maddux et al. 2010; Ger and Belk 1996).

Many other questions remain to be answered. For example, does attachment to different kinds of property vary by culture (Gjersoe et al. 2014)? Another promising line of research is comparing the psychology of property between individualistic cultures and collectivist ones. Western culture is typically individualistic, meaning that the primary orientation is toward the separate and unique individual and the view of the self as internally based on one's own thoughts, emotions, and acts. In contrast, collectivist cultures perceive the self as defined by, and existing within, social relationships and emphasize connectedness and interdependence (Markus and Kitayama 1991). Do collectivistic cultures have different psychological reactions to property conflicts, such as those that occur in shared ownership, eminent domain, trespass, or landlord-tenant law? Do the moral dimensions of property law differ by culture? For example, the welfare-enhancing function of redistribution through property, such as housing, relative to cash payment may differ in countries where cash welfare has less stigma.

Ownership, Possession, and Dispossession

There is a need for more experiments and field studies investigating psychological perceptions of ownership and possession and conflicts between owners and possessors under different property rules. In particular, experiments assessing adult perceptions of ownership and possession and property conflicts would be a valuable complement to the substantial research literature probing these constructs in children. Other important avenues of study are the effects of lawful versus unlawful possession and short-term possession and ownership versus long-term possession and ownership on endowment effects, cognitive dissonance, and other psychological phenomena. The legal imprimatur of ownership and long-term contact with property may also intensify perceptions of property rights, emotional attachments, and the incorporation of property into identity.

For these questions and others, there are also gaps in the psychological evidence for certain kinds of property. While there is a sizable body of empirical evidence on homes and land, the research is sparser for chattel property, commercial property, and fungible property. This is particularly pronounced once one moves beyond the research on the EE (which typically uses chattel property such as mugs and pens) to psychological phenomena such as biases, heuristics, and subjective well-being.

With respect to dispossession, more empirical research on how people value and perceive appropriations based on cause, context, and process would provide firmer ground for legal conclusions. For example, do people respond differently to takings based on demographics such as age, rural versus urban location, or the type of process used to appropriate land? Questions also remain about what amount of compensation people perceive to be adequate for different types of takings (e.g., economic redevelopment, other physical takings, or regulatory takings). In cases of dispossession by creditors, such as property seizure or foreclosure, there is a limited body of research on the degree of psychological distress or loss of identity caused by dispossession of personal property. It would also be helpful to assess empirically whether the type or mixture of property one holds enhances well-being. For example, do bankrupt owners benefit from state laws that shield items from each of multiple categories of the debtor's property (e.g., household, tools of trade, books) from creditors, compared with states that allow owners to shelter any property they choose up to a specified financial limit?

Housing Discrimination

Psychologists have studied intensively the effects of debiasing efforts and social norm campaigns to reduce discrimination, particularly racial discrimination. This research is highly relevant to fair housing law and the effect of housing discrimination on racial minorities. Notably, however, the most common category of fair housing complaint is for discrimination based on disability (National Fair Housing Alliance 2018, 52). In light of this fact, it would be helpful to have a larger body of psychological research on attitudes toward the disabled as well as empirical research on the perceptions of landlords about the costs and risks of renting to tenants with disabilities.

Psychological research could also productively address methods to increase reporting of discrimination. Studies to date have established underreporting of discrimination, but there is less known about how to promote reporting (Kaiser and Miller 2001; Kaiser and Major 2006, 812–18; Stangor et al. 2002). Because the US Fair Housing Act is primarily a complaint-driven statute, complaints and reporting are requisite to preserving fair and open housing markets.

Remedies

Psychology research is just beginning to plumb the cognitive and social forces underlying litigants' and property holders' satisfaction with remedies. More research is needed to validate the emerging findings in this area. For example, studies that replicate the findings on preferences for in-kind remedies over monetary ones (Lewinsohn-Zamir 2012) are desirable, as is research to investigate the underlying motivations driving such preferences. Future research might also assess whether people prefer remedies that are in the same domain or that affirm similar aspects of identity. For example, if the same or similar property is not available, it may be that people prefer, for example, to receive other forms of real estate assets in compensation for a loss of real property rather than monetary remedies or other forms of property. In addition, little is known about whether the source of a remedy matters to property holders. Do people perceive the same remedy differently if it comes from a state court, private condominium board, or administrative proceeding? Empirical research could shed light on these questions.

Concluding Remarks

This book has considered the psychological dimensions of property law. We have utilized research from diverse fields of psychology, including social psychology, cognitive psychology, and moral psychology, and applied these findings to a number of important questions in property law. While we have presented a sizable body of psychological studies and considered a breadth of property law rules, there is still much to be explored. The intersections between property law and psychology raise novel research questions and opportunities for future exploration. We hope that this book offers a starting place for both research and policy making, based on the insights of empirical psychology for property law.

NOTES

INTRODUCTION

1 Property law derives from a mixture of statutes and regulations, common law judging, constitutional law and interpretation, and, in some cases, specialized courts. The US constitutional property laws of due process and government "takings" of property are interpreted by federal courts and the federal Supreme Court, as well as state courts that interpret their state constitutions. There are also some specialized state courts that address property claims, such as landlord-tenant courts, which account for almost one-third of state court civil filings (National Center for State Courts 2015).

2 For a classic case of the necessity doctrine, see Ploof v. Putnam, 71 A. 188, 189 (1908) ("A traveler on a highway who finds it obstructed from a sudden and temporary cause may pass upon the adjoining land without becoming a trespasser because of the necessity.").

3 See Fair Housing Act, 42 U.S.C. § 3601 et seq.

4 Notably, not all property rules accomplish this end, as described by Lee Fennell (2016) and by Eric Posner and E. Glen Wyl (2017) in their critiques of the monopoly power to block transactions accorded to classic, or "fee simple," ownership rights.

5 US Census Bureau 2018.

6 Statistics Portal, Volume of Commercial Real Estate Transactions Completed in the United States from 2001 to 2016 (in billion US dollars); National Association of Realtors 2018 (2012 data for commercial floorspace).

7 There have also been theories of a biologically or genetically based possessiveness or ownership "instinct." However, these theories lack evidence and remain challenging to prove (Beaglehole 1932).

8 See Integrated Mortgage Disclosures under the Real Estate Settlement Procedures Act, 78 Fed. Reg. 79,730, 79,742 (December 31, 2013) (codified in 12 C.F.R. pts. 1024, 1026 effective on August 1, 2015).

9 See Helliwell, Layard, and Sachs 2018; Constitution of the Kingdom of Bhutan, Art. 9(2), 2008.

10 See chapter 3; 42 U.S.C. § 810(b)(1) and 24 C.F.R. § 103.300(a).

CHAPTER 1. OWNERSHIP AND POSSESSION

1 Legal scholars have explored thoroughly the implications for legal theory of this discrepancy between individuals' selling price and their purchase price. For

instance, Russell Korobkin noted that according to the Westlaw database, by the year 2012, the terms "endowment effect" and "status quo bias" appeared in law journal articles 1,619 times. Korobkin 2014, 301.

2 But see Plott and Zeiler (2005, 2007), who argue that the EE is due to participant misconceptions caused by the specific procedures used to elicit valuations. For criticism of Plott and Zeiler's studies, see Isoni, Loomes, and Sugden 2011.

3 A related explanation for the ownership effect and overvaluation of one's possessions focuses on other-derogation rather than on self-enhancement. For example, Huang and Wu (2016) found that participants associated others' possessions more with negative attributes than positive attributes. A negatively biased view of other people's possessions can also result in a higher valuation of one's own possessions.

4 A cold-drink insulator is a plastic tube that holds beverage cans and keeps them cold (Beggan 1992, 230). The "mere ownership effect" is supported by experiments in which the purchase price of buyers who happened to own an object identical to the one they were offered to buy—such as a mug—equaled the seller's asking price. See Morewedge et al. 2009.

5 One study reported that when asked to name their cherished material possessions, individuals mentioned not only items like family heirlooms, photographs, and pets but also objects such as coffeemakers, cameras, sports equipment, cooking utensils, televisions, umbrellas, and boots. See Prentice 1987, appendix.

6 We revisit this issue in chapter 2, which discusses the dissimilar legal treatment of fungible and nonfungible property.

7 For an application of Belk's theory in the context of wills, see Gordon 2017.

8 For a study of self-extension and self-expression through workplace possessions, see Tian and Belk 2005. Note, however, that an excessive quantity of material possessions ("clutter") might create a disorderly and chaotic home environment, and consequently reduce the affected individual's well-being. See Roster, Ferrari, and Jurkat (2016).

9 Pierson v. Post, 3 Caines 175 (N.Y. 1805).

10 The strength of the interface-touch effect varied with the type of product involved. Thus, for example, it was stronger with respect to the purchase of a college sweatshirt than with respect to the purchase of a New York City walking tour. See Brasel and Gips 2014, 229.

11 Interestingly, a recent study has found that the EE extends also to goods owned by others who are intimately close—specifically mothers, romantic partners, and close friends (but not acquaintances). See Zhao, Feng, and Kazinka 2014. This finding also demonstrates that enhanced valuation of an object does not necessarily depend on its formal ownership or physical possession.

12 Feelings of possession with respect to intangible assets are embraced by both adults and children; see Shaw, Li, and Olson 2012.

13 Cf. Brenner et al. (2007, 375–76), who state that "the notion of possession is somewhat fuzzy" and that "it is no accident that statements like 'I *have* a headache' or '*My* commute is very long' use possessive verbs and pronouns."

14 Notable in this context is Ori Friedman's (2010) study. Friedman observes that people view the person who intentionally pursued an object and was probably necessary for the object's ultimate possession as the object's owner. For example, participants who read a story about a person who threw a rock to dislodge a gem jutting out from a high cliff, before someone else retrieved the gem from the ground below, judged the rock thrower to be the rightful owner of the gem (rather than the person who first took hold of it). Interestingly, Friedman does not regard the pursuer who failed to attain direct physical contact with the object as its "possessor." In fact, he interprets his findings as an alternative account to the one that establishes ownership upon first possession of an asset (this idea is further developed in Palamar, Le, and Friedman 2012). For a similar, narrow understanding of possession, in the context of conflicts between finders of an object and owners of the land on which the object was found, see DeScioli, Karpoff, and De Freitas 2017. The authors tested, for example, a scenario in which a person finds two gold rings on someone else's private land and observed that most participants granted ownership of the object to the landowner rather than to the finder who was first to hold it physically. However, as we explained earlier in the text, the findings of these experiments may be interpreted as supporting the argument that people's notion of possession is broad and not necessarily physical. Accordingly, in the preceding examples, the rock thrower is actually regarded as the first possessor of the gem, and a landowner is typically viewed as the initial possessor of an object found on private land not open to the public.

15 Unlike wild animals, the baseball obviously had a previous owner (probably the home team). However, the custom in baseball games is that if the ball flies into the stands, the original ownership is relinquished and the ownerless ball becomes available to the spectator who first establishes possession.

16 Popov v. Hayashi, No. 400545, 2002 WL 31833731 (Cal. Super. Ct. December 18, 2002). For discussion of the Popov case and, more generally, additional scenarios in which an entitlement is divided between the two parties to the conflict, see Parchomovsky, Siegelman, and Thel 2007.

17 Note that some reasons for respecting possession may be relevant only for physical possession. For example, Rose (1985, 81–82) argued that possession is socially useful because it gives clear notice of who the owner of the asset is, which in turn facilitates trade and minimizes resource-wasting conflicts.

18 To the extent that the possessor has improved the land, she may be reimbursed for these costs—at least in cases where the encroachment was in good faith. See Sterk 1987, 80–81; Somerville v. Jacobs, 170 S.E.2d 805, 807, 813 (1969).

19 In a similar vein, a field study observed that owners of iPhones and laptops who already picked up their purchase in the store were willing to pay a higher price for a warranty than owners who did not have a chance to touch the purchased item yet. See Chark and Muthukrishnan 2013.

20 Experimental studies have also shown that length of ownership increases the valuation of objects. However, the owners in these studies were also possessors

of the valued asset; thus, ownership and possession were not contrasted. See S. B. Shu and Peck 2011, 443–44; M. A. Strahilevitz and Loewenstein 1998. Jane Gradwohl Nash and Robert A. Rosenthal (2014) examined the existence of an EE in the context of a college housing lottery. They compared hypothetical selling and buying prices of students who were awarded or denied, respectively, their first choice of residence, at two points in time: immediately following the housing lottery and two months after the students experienced actual residence. The EE existed at both time points but was enhanced in the latter one. Although students at the first point in time were not yet in possession of their housing, at both points they were the owners of the housing entitlement. Thus, this study did not pit nonpossessing owners against possessing nonowners either. It does, however, indicate that actual possession can augment the effect of mere ownership.

21 In some countries, such as Israel, the property legislation itself grants a direct right to self-help. See Land Law, 5729-1969, 23 LSI 283, §18 (1968/69) (Isr.).

22 Holmes 1881, 213.

23 Land Law, 5729-1969, 23 LSI 283, §§101, 106 (1968–69) (Isr.).

24 For further elaboration, see Lewinsohn-Zamir 2008.

25 Continental law, in contrast, affords substantial protection to testators' children and other blood relatives by entitling them to a reserved portion of the estate. See Glendon 1989, 240–50.

26 Other examples of property rights that can be lost due to nonuse are trademarks and rent-controlled housing. See Lewinsohn-Zamir 2008, 650–55.

27 In contrast, American eastern states have adopted a "riparian rights" system that allows landowners only "reasonable use" of the water in common with others, and does not permit them to reduce the water to individual ownership. See Stoebuck and Whitman 2000, §7.4.

28 Various laws prohibit the destruction of specific assets, such as buildings designated for conservation (Lawson and Rudden 1982, 116) and certain types of currency (L. J. Strahilevitz 2005, 843).

29 The opposite behavioral phenomenon of overpessimism, or overestimation of risks, is expected to occur when a negative event that one cannot control (or affect) becomes highly salient, such as after wide media coverage of a nuclear power plant accident or a natural disaster. See Viscusi 1992, 150; Jolls 1998, 1662–63. Overpessimism is less likely to characterize ordinary contractual relationships—such as landlord-tenant ones—where both parties exercise at least some degree of control over the ensuing outcomes, and the relevant contingencies are unlikely to be very salient.

30 For our purposes, we need not take a stand on whether total deference to alienation-prohibition clauses is justified. One might argue, for instance, that both prohibition and conditioned-transfer clauses should be subject to a reasonableness test (indeed, such is the case in Israeli law; see Hire and Loan Law, 5731-1971, 25 LSI 152, §22 (1972) (Isr.)). However, if we believe that landlords should have the power to veto alienation by the tenants completely, sound psychological reason

exists to require that such contractual terms be phrased in an extreme and unambiguous fashion.

31 Abandonment renders an asset ownerless and enables another person to take possession and become its new owner. Abandonment ordinarily requires less effort on behalf of the original owner than destruction does.

32 Lior J. Strahilevitz convincingly argues that destructive acts often promote expressive values and that such acts should receive greater deference than currently afforded under law. Examples of expressive destruction include burning a flag or a draft card (L. J. Strahilevitz 2005, 821–22, 824–26).

33 Strahilevitz recommends solving this problem—with respect to destructive instructions contained in wills—by requiring owners, while they are still alive, to market the future interest in the property (i.e., the ownership of the property after their death). If the owner's minimum asking price exceeds the highest bid in an auction of the future interest, then she demonstrably values the property's destruction more than anyone else values its preservation, and consequently the instruction in her will to destroy the property should be honored (L. J. Strahilevitz 2005, 850–51). Note that Strahilevitz does not suggest a similar mechanism as a condition for permitting owners to destroy property during their lifetime. Thus, he appears to assume that the risk of inefficient antemortem destruction is too small to warrant legal intervention.

34 It is not surprising that nonuse does not in and of itself extinguish ownership of land. This is because ownership of land enables many potential and diverse enjoyments, some of which may be realized only in the future. It may very well be the case that land is presently unutilized because it is not yet ripe for development or because the owner is waiting for the time when a better use can be made. Thus, a use-it-or-lose-it rule might create inefficient incentives for premature development.

CHAPTER 2. PROTECTING HOMES AND OTHER TYPES OF PROPERTY

1 Other rationales for property protections include promoting efficiency by preserving property values and preventing harmful spillover effects, creating incentives to invest in property, and ensuring that debtors have sufficient resources to begin anew.

2 Debts may be "secured" by an interest in property. A secured creditor has a lien (i.e., a right to be repaid from the proceeds of the sale of a specific piece of property) and also has priority in satisfying claims for repayment compared with unsecured creditors. "Unsecured" debts arise, for example, from loans for which no property is pledged as collateral or from debts resulting from court judgments.

3 Chapter 13 is a less common form of bankruptcy employed by higher-income debtors to partially repay their debts. Cf. 11 U.S.C. §701 et seq. (2018) (chapter 7 bankruptcy); 11 U.S.C. §1301 et seq. (2018) (chapter 13 bankruptcy).

4 See 11 U.S.C. § 522(d)(1), (5).

5 See Ark. Const. Art. 9 §§ 3, 4, 5, 6; Ark. Code Ann. §§ 16-66-210, 212, 218; D.C. Code § 15-501(1)(14); Fla. Const. Art. X, § 4, § 4 Fla. Stat. Ann. §§ 222.01, 222.02;

Iowa Code Ann. § 561.16; Kan. Stat. Ann. § 60-2301; 31 Okla. Stat. § 31-1(A); S.D. Cod. Laws § 43-45-3.

6 Mass. Gen. Laws, Ch. 188, § 1; R.I. Gen. Laws § 9-26-4.1; Mont. Code Ann. § 70-32-104(1); Nev. Rev. Stat. § 21.090(1)(l).

7 For debtors filing bankruptcy, federal law limits the exemption to $136,875 for debtors who acquired property during the 1,215-day period preceding the date of the bankruptcy filing. See 11 U.S.C. § 522(p).

8 See, e.g., Ark. Const. Art. IX § 1 and 2 (exempting $500 of personal property for heads of families and $200 for unmarried debtors who are not heads of families).

9 See, e.g., N.Y.C.P.L.R. § 5206(e); Colo. Rev. Stat. § 38-41-207; Ariz. Rev. Stat. Ann. § 33-1101(c).

10 See Colo. Rev. Stat. § 38-41-207

11 Tenancy by the entirety provides protection not only from unilateral debts but also from one spouse's bankruptcy so long as that spouse elects to use state law exemptions. See 11 U.S.C § 522.

12 See, e.g., In the Matter of Horace G. Houghton, 75 N.J. 462 (1978).

13 See, e.g., N.C. Gen. Stat. § 39-13.6(b).

14 See 765 Ill. Comp. Stat. 1005/1c (2008).

15 See Tenancy by the Entirety States, www.assetprotectionplanners.com/tenancy-entirety-states/ (accessed April 10, 2018).

16 See, e.g., Fla. Stat. Ann. § 655.79(1) (2017) (extending tenancy by entirety protection to spouses' jointly held deposit accounts); Beal Bank v. Almand and Assoc., 780 So. 2d 45 (2001) (extending tenancy by entirety presumption to bank accounts acquired and held by spouses).

17 535 U.S. 274 (2002).

18 The 2005 Bankruptcy Act now limits this behavior by creating an exemption cap for filers who have committed a felony that indicates that filing was an abuse of the bankruptcy process, when the debt arises from violation of federal securities law, or in other specified instances of wrongdoing. See 11 U.S.C. § 522(q). Another provision limits exemptions if debtors have not been domiciled in the state for the preceding 730 days. 11 U.S.C. § 522(b)(3)(A).

19 See Texas Journal of the Constitutional Convention, November 5, 1875, 569–70 (submitted by N.H. Darnell).

20 Sawada v. Endo, 561 P.2d 1291, 1297 (Haw. 1977).

21 The evidence indicates that mobility is most beneficial to individuals who are living in neighborhoods that are in decline or in housing situations that are ill-suited to their personal needs (Massey, Condran, and Denton 1987, 52–54).

22 Creditors may have an option for the federal exemption in some but not all states. Opting for the federal exemption in a state with low-value state law exemptions can improve the debtor's position to start anew in the face of sparse state exemptions.

23 See SEC v. Antar, 120 F. Supp. 2d 431, 450–51 (D.N.J. 2000).

24 Id. at 451.

25 535 U.S. 274 (2002). The court held that the husband's tenancy by the entirety interest, as defined by Michigan state law, constituted "property" under the federal
tax lien statute, thereby enabling the lien.

26 Interestingly, children appear more resilient to moves. Children appear harmed
only by a high number of residential moves across childhood (a situation more
likely to affect renters), not one or two moves.

27 See Cal. Civ. Proc. Code § 704.730(a).

28 Reverse mortgages do not sort homeowners precisely because some homeowners may need to use reverse mortgages for other costs, such as health care bills,
despite their strong preferences for residential stability. Yet, even with these im-
precisions, reverse mortgages and state and local tax deferral programs are more
targeted, and less costly to localities, than merely basing tax benefits on age.

29 See Cal. Code of Civ. Proc. § 1161(2)-(3).

30 See Cal. Code of Civ. Proc. § 715.010(b)(2).

31 For example, this is the case in North Carolina, which by common law has a
strong presumption of tenancy for real estate but not for personal property. In
Florida, the issue was unsettled with the presumption for real estate but not for
personal property until the recent case of *Beale* applied the presumption to financial instruments.

32 505 U.S. 1003, 1027–28 (1992).

33 135 S. Ct. 2419 (2015) (holding that personal property has constitutional parity
with real estate and, accordingly, the government could not require raisin growers
to reserve part of their raisin crop to be destroyed or donated in a government
market stabilization program).

34 Most state statutes and storage facility leases also place the risk of loss or damage
on the tenant (Jones 2011b, 1015–21).

35 Fla. Stat. Ann. § 222.25(4) (2017).

36 See, e.g., Ala. Code § 6-10-6 (2016) (categorically excluding all apparel, family portraits or pictures, and all books used by the family from the bankruptcy
estate); Mass Gen. Laws. ch. 235 § 34 (2018) (fully exempting items such as
clothing, bedding, appliances, and two cows, twelve sheep, two swine, and four
tons of hay); N.D. Cent. Code §§ 28-22-02 and 28-22-03.1 (2018) (fully exempting
personal property, including family Bible, family pictures, and schoolbooks and
other books).

37 As another example, the US Federal Trade Commission's credit practices rule
protects household goods and appliances and certain forms of highly personal
property, such as photographs, wedding rings, and personal papers, if the creditor
has advanced money for the purchase of items other than those household goods.
See 16 C.F.R. § 444.2(a)(4); US Federal Trade Commission, Complying with
the Credit Practices Rule, www.ftc.gov/tips-advice/business-center/guidance/
complying-credit-practices-rule#SecurityInterestsinHouseholdGoods.

38 See, e.g., Ariz. Rev. Stat. § 33-1125 (2016) (exempting categories such as clothing,
books, and wedding and engagement rings up to differing amounts per category);

Colo. Rev. Stat. § 13-54(102)(a-f) (exempting clothing, family pictures, household goods, and jewelry up to a specified amount per category).

39 See, e.g., Wis. Stat. Ann. § 815.18(3)(d)(2018) (exempting household goods, furnishings, clothing, keepsakes, jewelry, appliances, musical instruments, firearms, sporting goods, animals, and other property held for personal use up to $24,000 in aggregate value for married couples); Del. Code Ann. tit. 10 § 4902 and § 4914(d) ($25,000 exemption for all personal property and real property other than the home, with full exemptions for Bibles, books, clothing, and a few other categories of personal property).

40 Me. Rev. Stat. Ann. tit. 14 § 4422(16) (2018).

41 See, e.g., N.C. Gen. Stat. § 1C-1601(a) (2018) (exempting animals, crops, books, clothing, appliances, and household goods up to $5,000 plus an additional $1,000 per dependent plus an additional $4,000); Fla. Const. Art. 10 § 4(2) (exempting up to $1,000 of any personal property); Me. Rev. Stat. Ann. tit. 14 § 4422(15) (2018) (wild card provision of $400 applied to property of debtor's choice); Ohio Rev. Code Ann. § 2329.66(A)(4), (18) (capped exemptions that can be applied to property of debtor's choice).

42 This theoretical study has suggested that ensuring that debtors can maintain a variety of forms of property (e.g., homestead, household goods, books, or instruments) may promote objective well-being. Additional empirical work would be useful to determine if debtors are better off with laws requiring diversity in the kinds of property the debtor maintains versus allowing debtors flexibility to allocate the exemption to their most valued possessions.

43 See, e.g., Dado v. Jeening, 743 N.E.2d 291 (Ind. App. 2001).

44 See Carye v. Boca Raton Hotel, 676 So. 2d 1020 (Fla. 4th DCA 1996).

45 641 N.W.2d 868 (Mich. App. 2002).

CHAPTER 3. TAKINGS

1 See also Pennsylvania Coal v. Mahon, 260 US 393, 413 (1922).

2 In the famous case of Loretto v. Teleprompter Manhattan CATV Corp., 458 U.S. 419 (1982), the taking consisted of requiring landlords to permit a cable television company to install cable equipment on its buildings.

3 See, respectively, Keystone Bituminous Coal Association v. DeBenedictis, 480 U.S. 470 (1987); First English Evangelical Lutheran Church v. County of Los Angeles, 258 Cal. Reptr. 893 (1989).

4 Lucas v. South Carolina Coastal Council, 112 S. Ct. 2886 (1992).

5 Pennsylvania Coal v. Mahon, 260 US 393, 415 (1922).

6 Penn Central Transportation Co. v. City of New York, 438 US 104 (1978).

7 See Sections 197 and 200 of the Planning and Building Law, 1965 (19 L.S.I. 330).

8 Most public opinion surveys of eminent domain have been done in the past decade, following a highly publicized Supreme Court decision, Kelo v. City of New London, which upheld the use of eminent domain to develop a site for a pharmaceutical company.

9 545 U.S. 469 (2005).

10 Two decades before *Kelo*, in Hawaii Housing Authority v. Midkiff, 467 U.S. 229 (1984), the Supreme Court held that a Hawaii statute empowering the government to take lands from private landlords, transfer the land to the state, and then resell it to the former tenants met the constitutional requirement of public use. Even earlier, in Berman v. Parker, 348 U.S. 26 (1954), the Court upheld the District of Columbia's use of eminent domain for an economic redevelopment project that, like New London's plan, aimed to improve a declining area through redevelopment by a private firm.

11 While opposition to *Kelo* is rigorous under any measure, survey responses change with question context and details. Notably, most polls asking whether private property rights or environmental concerns (e.g., protecting endangered species) are more important found that the majority of respondents rate environmental protection more highly (Nadler, Diamond, and Patton 2008, 291).

12 Va. Code § 25.1-305 et seq. (2014).

13 151 P.3d 1166 (Cal. 2007).

14 Agins v. City of Tiburon, 447 U.S. 255, 260 (1980).

15 Lingle v. Chevron U.S.A., 544 U.S. 528, 542 (2005).

16 For general discussion of other-regarding and reference-dependent preferences in the context of inequality, see Congdon, Kling, and Mullainathan 2011, 145–49.

17 For a third metaphor of property—as a tree with a trunk that represents the core entitlement to control the use of the asset and branches representing many resource-specific bundles of entitlements—see Di Robilant 2013. The tree concept may be viewed as a variant on the bundle-of-sticks conception of property.

18 But see Levine-Schnur and Parchomovsky (2016), who argue that empirical data on land expropriations in Israel do not support the internalization-of-costs ("fiscal illusion") rationale of takings compensation.

19 Some scholars, however, have raised efficiency arguments against full compensation, such as the concern that it would grant owners incentives to overinvest in land, disregarding the risk of a future taking. Therefore, so the argument goes, compensation should be either denied (forcing owners who desire protection to purchase insurance in the market) or reduced to the value of the land as it would have been developed had the government not paid compensation. Blume and Rubinfeld 1984; Kaplow 1986. For criticism of this position, see Lewinsohn-Zamir 1996, 62–69; Serkin 2005, 714–18.

20 See also Epstein (2017, 183–89) for criticism of the disparate treatment of physical and nonphysical injuries to property.

21 But see Wyman (2007), who criticizes the commonly accepted goal of making the landowner subjectively whole, due to the existence of problematic preferences (e.g., objectionable preferences or extremely expensive ones). As an alternative, she argues that we should aim to make the landowner objectively whole, according to an external standard of the socially valuable life. We believe that in most takings contexts, landowners' preferences would not be problematic enough to

justify their disregard, even under objective theories of welfare. Such theories accept that fulfilling people's wishes is an important—though not necessarily decisive—element of human welfare. On objective theories of well-being and their application to property law, see generally Lewinsohn-Zamir 2003.

22 Scholars have suggested various self-assessment techniques to overcome the incentive of property owners to exaggerate their reported valuation. It was advocated, for instance, that compensation be determined according to owners' self-valuations, declared either in advance, before any conflict had arisen, or after the government considers expropriation of the property. Truthfulness would be achieved by basing property taxes on self-assessments and requiring future sale prices to at least equal self-declared values. Alternatively, owners selling their property below their former evaluations would have to pay the difference to the government or to their favored charity. See, e.g., A. Bell and Parchomovsky 2007; Fennell 2004. A major problem with such proposals is that nonaffluent owners may be unable to pay higher taxes that reflect their true, above-market valuation of the property. Interestingly, an empirical study that Chang (2012) conducted in Taiwan found that during the years 1954–77, when takings compensation was tied to ex ante self-assessments that served also as the basis for taxation, landowners reported values that were below fair market value. Chang posits that this was due to the fact that the probabilities of expropriation were much lower than the property tax rates. A different problem with self-assessment techniques is that they are discriminatory, because owners whose land is considered for expropriation will be required to pay higher taxes than owners who do not face a threat of eminent domain (Lewinsohn-Zamir 2009, 1400–01, 1444–46).

23 Scholars have noted additional uncompensated costs that render the market-value compensation measure incomplete, such as lost goodwill and moving expenses (Krier and Serkin 2004, 866; Wyman 2007, 254–55). Other theorists countered that this undercompensation problem has been overstated because, for example, takers are often required by state laws to pay additional compensation to owners in the form of "relocation assistance" (Garnett 2006, 121–26). Be that as it may, loss of goodwill is relevant only to operating businesses, and relocation costs are borne only when the expropriated land had been occupied formerly. In contrast, the injury from the coercive nature of the transfer itself potentially is relevant to all takings cases, including those involving undeveloped and unoccupied land.

CHAPTER 4. REDISTRIBUTION THROUGH PROPERTY LAW

1 Arguably, above a certain quantity, the attainment of further property ceases to increase or only marginally increases its owner's well-being. Up to this point, however, raising the quantity of property beyond the minimum level significantly enhances a person's well-being. See Hurka 1993, 171–75.

2 In contrast, other writers argue that quality housing standards may successfully redistribute wealth to low-income tenants if certain market conditions exist. These conditions include the inability of landlords to exit the market, or public

provision of supplemental subsidized housing, and the existence of a group of tenants who do not attach much value to improved housing. The various conditions are discussed in Ackerman 1971, 1097–98, 1102–19, 1186–88; Kennedy 1987, 497–506. An empirical investigation into the effect of certain landlord and tenant reforms concluded that, in fact, tenants were not made financially worse-off, due to factors such as increased consumer preference for ownership (as opposed to tenancy) and increased housing subsidies for the poor. See Rabin 1984, 561–78.

3   Another basic assumption of the critique of redistributive legal rules is that people's well-being consists solely of satisfying their actual preferences. Therefore, the object of redistribution should be money, which will provide them with the means to fulfill their desires. However, according to an objective theory of human well-being—that strives to advance additional goals besides preference satisfaction—there are advantages to redistribution in kind. The latter form of redistribution directly provides for the goods that are deemed necessary for people's well-being. Thus, even if the implied warranty of habitability fails to redistribute income in favor of tenants (because the market responds by raising the rents or altering other terms in the lease), it may still succeed in redistributing the objective good of minimal-quality housing (for an elaboration of this point, see Lewinsohn-Zamir 2006, 337–53).

4   However, a few experimental studies have found an identifiability effect in scenarios involving groups: Ritov and Zamir 2014; Nordgren and Morris McDonnell 2011.

5   As already mentioned, earlier studies of the identifiability effect have demonstrated that identification is not always advantageous, but rather can be detrimental to the identified person when her behavior is perceived to be blameworthy (Kogut 2011; Small and Loewenstein 2005). Interestingly, although the scenarios in Lewinsohn-Zamir, Ritov, and Kogut (2017) involved sanctions against wrongdoers, identifiability always resulted in greater consideration of the wrongdoer's interests. One possible explanation is that the transgressions in the scenarios were comparatively mild and did not involve moral turpitude. Another explanation is that the vignettes focused respondents' attention on the burden that should be inflicted on the wrongdoer. This issue requires further research.

6   Only one study observed an identifiability effect in the latter case: Nordgren and Morris McDonnell 2011.

7   In reality, taxes are sometimes earmarked for specific expenditures, and this practice may increase public support for taxes. See Listokin and Schizer 2013, 198–99; Rivlin 1989, 116. However, such support does not appear to stem from any earmarking per se, but rather requires a close alignment between the source of the tax and the expected use of the revenue—for example, when revenues raised from taxing pollutants are used for environmental protection, or motor fuel taxes are employed for highways. See Hemel and Porter 2016. Therefore, it is unlikely that earmarking taxes for the benefit of *identified* individuals, on its own, would increase public support for redistributive taxes and transfer payments.

8 An extreme example of leveling down is to enhance equality between the blind and the sighted by putting out the eyes of the sighted (Temkin 1993, 247–48). While some writers support equality measures that only lower the level of those who are better-off, others argue that we should mitigate inequality by raising the level of the worse-off. The latter view focuses not on equality per se but on giving priority to those who are worse-off. See Temkin 1993, 245–82.

CHAPTER 5. TRANSACTING PROPERTY

1 213 Cal. App. 2d 729, 735 (Cal. Ct. App. 1963).

2 In practice, markets partially fill this gap, as lenders and insurers often require information about property inspection and condition prior to approving loans or issuing insurance policies.

3 The question of whether partial nondisclosure may "debias" excess risk aversion in residential real estate transactions is interesting and, to our knowledge, unexplored. One difficulty with answering this question is determining whether, or when, real estate buyers are irrationally risk-averse. As William Fischel (2005) has described, homes are a large, undiversified asset that expose homeowners to significant financial risk by virtue of their lack of diversification and percentage of household wealth. In this light, much of what appears to be risk aversion is in fact a rational response to the riskiness of residential real estate as an asset class.

4 See Fla. Stat. § 475.278(1)(b).

5 For an example of a state-prescribed dual agency disclosure, see Louisiana Real Estate Commission Agency Disclosure Form, www.vicksburgrealestate.com/Agency_Disclosure_Form-Dec02.pdf.

6 On November 12, 2010, the FDA proposed graphic visual warnings on cigarette boxes to discourage cigarette purchase. Proposed Rule, 75 Fed. Reg. 69,525 (November 12, 2010) (to be codified at 21 C.F.R. § 1141 (2011)). This proposed rule was eventually published as Final Rule, 76 Fed. Reg. 36,628 (June 22, 2011) (codified at 21 C.F.R. § 1141 (2011)).

7 Variable ratio reinforcement occurs when a reward follows after an average number of responses, with the actual number of responses required to elicit the reward varying unpredictably over time (Skinner 1974, 60–61). For example, a slot machine with a one-to-four win-lose ratio may offer the player a payoff after his second attempt and then another payoff on his eighth attempt, averaging to a one-to-four ratio. This schedule of reinforcement tends to "hook" people into continued responses, as they believe the next win or reward is imminent.

8 See Consumer Fin. Prot. Bureau, *Know before You Owe*, www.consumerfinance.gov/knowbeforeyouowe/ (accessed February 20, 2018).

CHAPTER 6. DISCRIMINATION AND EXCLUSION

1 See Fair Housing Act, 42 U.S.C. § 3601 et seq. Currently, seventeen states and the District of Columbia prohibit discrimination based on sexual orientation. The

federal FHA does not explicitly provide that sexual orientation is a protected class. See 42 U.S.C. § 3604.

2 See 42 U.S.C. § 3608 (requiring the secretary of the federal Housing and Urban Development Agency to affirmatively further the fair housing policies described in the subchapter); 80 Fed. Reg. 42,272 (2015) (the implementation of this rule has been delayed by a subsequent rule, 83 Fed. Reg. 683 (2018).

3 Inclusionary zoning typically requires that localities implement mandatory set-asides so that new residential units offer a percentage of housing units affordable to low-income individuals or families (Mandelker 2003, § 7.27). Typically, developers receive incentives as well to reduce the financial impact of the set-aside.

4 See County of Westchester v. HUD, 116 F. Supp. 3d 251 (S.D.N.Y. 2015).

5 See Fair Housing Act, 42 U.S.C. §§ 3612–14.

6 Texas Department of Housing and Community Affairs v. Inclusive Communities Project, Inc., 132 S. Ct. 2507 (2015).

7 Judicial interpretations of Title VII of the Civil Rights Act of 1964, section 703(a) (2), and the Age Discrimination in Employment Act of 1967 extend disparate action liability to employment discrimination.

8 132 S. Ct. 2507 (2015); Brief for the Petitioners at 42–46; 2014 WL 6466935. For a discussion of the amici briefs raising constitutional concerns, see Bagenstos 2016, at 1127.

9 See 24 C.F.R. § 100.500(c)(3).

10 132 S. Ct. at 2511–12.

11 It is theoretically possible that there is only conscious bias and people lie about their conscious prejudice to conform to social norms and cast themselves in a favorable light. Most experimental work on implicit bias uses the implicit association test (IAT). This test, which is completed on a computer or in a lab, uses images and rapid responses by participants to images (e.g., African American and white faces) to elicit and test automatic and unconscious associations. The experiment compares the automatic responses to questions that participants answer beforehand indicating their level of prejudice and bias, and, if prior reported prejudice is less, the conclusion is that implicit (unconscious) bias is present. Given the vast quantity of research on implicit bias, it seems likely that not all implicit bias is fabricated by participants in this manner and that the IAT captures some level of meaningful, nonconscious bias. For a balanced review and meta-analysis, see Greenwald et al. 2009.

12 See Fair Housing Act, 42 U.S.C. § 3601 et seq.; Shelley v. Kraemer, 334 U.S. 1 (1948) (restrictive covenants); Buchanan v. Warley, 245 U.S. 60 (1917) (racial zoning); Hills v. Gatreaux, 425 U.S. 284 (1976) (discrimination in public housing site selection to maintain segregation). Restrictive covenants typically require a party (the owner, a buyer, etc.) not to do something. This limitation "runs with the land" to bind not only the present buyer but also future buyers (Singer 2017, § 6.1). Racially restrictive covenants prohibited African Americans and in some cases Jewish people from buying homes bound by the covenant.

13 In her work on "cues for control," Margo Monteith has found evidence that thinking about the guilt and other negative emotions we experience after becoming
aware of stereotyping or discriminating against someone can be cues or "warning
signals" that prompt self-reflection and prejudice inhibition in subsequent situations (Monteith et al. 2002, 1046). However, Monteith cautions that her work does
not establish that people use cues for control outside the laboratory or that they
are able to automate these cues and use them repeatedly. Her experiments made
respondents' prejudice highly salient to them, which, as she observes, is unlikely
to happen in real life (1046–47).

14 These results are discouraging, though, as Lai et al. (2016, 1013) note, it could be
that there are effective interventions still unknown or that many sessions of the
intervention are necessary for participants to learn to override their biases.

15 See Texas Dep't of Community Affairs v. Inclusive Communities Project, Inc., 135
S. Ct. at 2523–24.

16 The federal agency responsible for housing discrimination, the US Department of
Housing and Urban Development (HUD), is required by law to seek conciliation,
meaning settlement, "to the extent feasible" on all housing discrimination complaints filed with HUD pursuant to the FHA; for cases brought by private parties
or nongovernmental agencies, settlement negotiation frequently occurs before
trial as well. Settlement offers an opportunity for housing providers to rectify
unintentional biases—albeit at a cost. However, conciliation can prevent the punishing effects of mounting legal fees in cases where an insurer is not paying for the
defendant's legal counsel. See 42 U.S.C. § 810(b)(1) and 24 C.F.R. § 103.300(a).

17 See 42 U.S.C. § 3604 (a) and (d) (refusal to sell or rent), § 3604(b) (discrimination
in terms, conditions, or services of sale or rental), and § 3605 (discrimination by
businesses engaged in selling, brokering, or appraising property).

18 The "Mrs. Murphy" exemption applies to buildings occupied or by law intended to be occupied by no more than four families living independently of
each other. See 42 U.S.C. §3603(b); United States v. Hunter, 459 F.2d 205 (4th
Cir. 1972) (an exempt owner is "free to indulge his discriminatory preferences
in renting or selling that dwelling" but does not have a "right to publicize his
intent to so discriminate").

19 Religious organizations and private clubs are exempt from liability for refusals to
rent, sell, or allow one to occupy or from granting preference to club or religious
group members. See 42 U.S.C. § 3607.

20 The underlying mechanism driving the effect on social norms is unclear and appears likely due to multiple variables. Psychologist Isidor Chein explained, "Much
prejudiced behavior does not stem from prejudiced attitudes or motives, nor
even faulty information, but rather from the need to conform to prevailing social
norms" (1946, 415). Other research supports the role of culture and social group
membership in stereotyping and bias (Pettigrew 1958, 38–40; Sherif and Sherif
1953). There is also evidence of a role for cognition: social norms increase the
cognitive accessibility of stereotypes (Sechrist and Stangor 2001, 650–51).

21 See 899 F.2d 24 (D.C. Cir. 1990).

22 47 U.S.C.A. § 230; Chicago Lawyers' Committee for Civil Rights v. Craigslist, 519 F.3d 666 (7th Cir. 2008).

23 See 114 Cong. Rec. 2276, 3422, 9559, and 9591 (1968). The Supreme Court has endorsed this interpretation. In Trafficante v. Metropolitan Life Insurance Co., the Court implicitly recognized residential integration as a major goal of the FHA when it upheld standing for white residents of an apartment complex to sue for their landlord's racial discrimination against African American applicants based on their injuries from segregation. See 409 U.S. 205 (1972).

24 Prior to reporting, there may also be breakdowns in whether people perceive that they have been discriminated against. The psychology evidence is mixed on whether people exhibit "minimization" or "vigilance" bias, meaning whether they perceive discrimination more or less often than is warranted (for a review, see Kaiser and Major 2006, 802–12). There appears to be variability in perceptions based on experience and demographics. People who are better educated, are older, have more job authority, have promotion experience, or are union members are more likely to state that negative outcomes are due to discrimination rather than their own abilities (Hirsh and Lyons 2010).

25 The mediating variables (e.g., anxiety, arousal, or effects on working memory) that lead from stereotype activation to impaired performance in stereotype threat are not clear; it appears likely that multiple mediators are in play (Quinn, Kallen, and Spencer 2010, 385).

26 336 A.2d 713 (N.J. 1975) (Mt. Laurel I); 456 A.2d 390 (N.J. 1983) (Mt. Laurel II). This has occurred at the local government level as well. For example, in the famous Mt. Laurel I and II cases, the New Jersey Supreme Court held that localities must provide a "fair share" of affordable housing. A state agency subsequently allowed localities to meet most of their obligation by paying other localities to create additional affordable housing, thereby concentrating low-income residents to their detriment.

CHAPTER 7. PROPERTY RULES VERSUS LIABILITY RULES

1 Since most entitlements are protected by either a property rule or a liability rule, we shall not discuss in this chapter the third type of rule addressed in Calabresi and Melamed's article—rules prohibiting alienation of entitlements. On inalienability rules, see Calabresi and Melamed 1972, 1111–15; Fennell 2009; Radin 1987; Rose-Ackerman 1985.

2 Boomer v. Atlantic Cement Co., Inc., 257 N.E.2d 870 (N.Y. 1970).

3 In a recent article, Calabresi (2014) somewhat modified his view with respect to the role of liability rules. The original article (Calabresi and Melamed 1972) implied that when liability rules are employed, they should necessarily mimic the outcome that would otherwise have been reached by the consensual market. Calabresi (2014) now claims that liability rules should—and do—have a broader role. For example, punitive damages—i.e., damages surpassing the entitlement holder's

losses—do not attempt to mirror the market, but rather represent the collectiv-
ity's judgment that the entitlement should not be transferred. This refinement of
the Calabresi-Melamed rule is immaterial for our purposes. In this chapter, we
focus on the main point of dispute in the literature, namely, whether liability rules
should be employed even when property rules are a feasible option.

4 Note that in many cases, bargaining under a property rule will be carried out in
advance—that is to say, before any breach of the entitlement owner's rights has
occurred. Therefore, we should not fear the same degree of animosity that can
obstruct successful bargaining conducted ex post (i.e., after such a breach), before
the filing of a lawsuit, or around an existing court order. On these problems see
Jolls, Sunstein, and Thaler 1998, 1497–98; Farnsworth 1999.

5 It is worthwhile to note that even in laboratory experiments proposers made less
generous offers if they were encouraged to feel that they had justifiably "won"
the role of proposer (for instance, by being the highest scorers in a preliminary
general knowledge quiz), rather than randomly assigned to this role. Responders,
however, often shared notions of the proposers' entitlement and so did not reject
these relatively low offers. See Hoffman et al. 1994, 350–52, 362–64.

6 For a persuasive critique of Bucaffusco and Sprigman's argument in the context of
intellectual property, see Tur-Sinai 2011.

7 Bar-Gill and Engel (2018) have also tested how an entitlement's degree of protection affects the likelihood of trade. Specifically, they examined how seven remedial
options (a property rule and six variants of liability rules, with damages ranging
from zero to above the potential taker's valuation of the entitlement) affected
owners' willingness to "bribe" takers not to take their entitlement, and the takers'
willingness to accept these payments. Although the findings indicate that a weaker
legal remedy is conducive to efficient bargaining, this study focused on the impact
of fairness norms on the parties' willingness to pay and willingness to accept and
deliberately avoided mentioning "property." Moreover, the experimental design
most probably prevented the emergence of an endowment effect at all because the
object of bargaining was a token representing an entitlement to a certain sum of
money. As explained in this chapter, such exchange goods do not produce an EE
because they are valued only for the trading possibilities they afford.

8 An EE exists, however, if the value of the financial instruments or bargaining
chips is uncertain. Samuelson and Zeckhouser 1988, 12–22; van Dijk and van
Knippenberg 1996.

9 The experimental findings, however, have also shown that the availability of
substitutes, although a significant factor, did not eliminate the EE. Adamowicz,
Bhardwaj, and Macnab 1993, 425. This latter result may be explained partially by
the fact that television and radio broadcasts are an imperfect substitute for a live
hockey game. It is possible that the EE would have been further reduced if a better
substitute were provided.

10 Bargaining can occur also under a liability rule, because reaching agreement
on the transfer of the asset can save both parties litigation costs. However, such

negotiations are much more prone to failure than negotiations under property rules. To see why this may be the case, recall the ultimatum game. As explained earlier, one of the reasons that a majority of proposers offer generous shares of the pie to responders (40 to 50 percent on average; such offers are then accepted by responders) is their knowledge that rejection of the offer by the latter would result in no profit for themselves. This risk does not exist when bargaining under a liability rule because both parties are aware that the transfer can ultimately be coerced. In this respect, negotiations in the shadow of liability rules resemble a "dictator game" in which one player proposes a division of some gains between herself and a second player. However—and contrary to an ultimatum game—the second player cannot reject the dictator's offer and thus affect the dictator's own payoff. Experiments with dictator games have found that offers are much lower than in ultimatum games (28 percent on average) and that a large percentage of dictators (36 percent) choose to keep all the gains for themselves (Engel 2011; see also Hoffman, McCabe, and Smith 2008). The power to coerce a transfer under a liability rule resembles the power of a dictator in the dictator game. Similarly, therefore, we should expect liability rules to discourage potential takers from offering fair divisions of the profits from the trade in the preliminary bargaining stage, as they can force a transfer on the owner in the subsequent compulsory stage. At this latter stage, compensation is usually based on the value of the taken asset, and owners are not entitled to any share of the gains. Consequently, unacceptable low offers in the negotiation stage are likely to be rejected, and coerced transfers—allowed by liability rules—would indeed become necessary (for further discussion of bargaining under liability rules, see Lewinsohn-Zamir 2001a, 239–50).

11 Lee (2013, 607–18) argues that the commonly applied compensation measure for expropriations of land—objective market value—is actually fairer than commonly acknowledged because market prices at least partially reflect owners' subjective valuation of their property. Even assuming that this is the case, Lee's argument does not take into account that the value of property to its owner is not necessarily fixed. Our discussion suggests that an owner's subjective valuation may be lower when she voluntarily parts with the asset and higher when such parting is coerced upon her. Consequently, calculating compensation for forced transfers of assets according to the value revealed in voluntary sales of comparable properties would still lead to systematic undercompensation of owners. For further discussion of takings compensation, see chapter 3.

CHAPTER 8. IN-KIND REMEDIES VERSUS MONETARY REMEDIES

1 Wilkinson-Ryan and Baron (2009) elicited laypersons' opinions regarding the morality of breach of contract. They found that participants viewed breach of contract motivated by the prospect of making greater profits as more immoral than breach aimed at cutting losses, and that participants therefore thought that promisees should receive overcompensatory damages in the former case.

2 One may claim that development rights and cash are not equivalent in terms of their long-term effect on the landowner's wealth, because additional development on the remainder of the land may further increase its value in the future. This claim is not persuasive. Even if participants took this long-term consideration into account, a cash award may also be invested in real estate stocks or used to purchase additional land.

3 Interestingly, the experiments indicated not only that businesspeople share laypersons' reluctance to accept monetary redress but also that the more years of experience the businesspeople have, the greater their inclination to insist on in-kind remedies (Lewinsohn-Zamir 2013, 173–74).

4 See also the experimental study by Uhlmann and Zhu (2013), which found that a particular piece of monetary currency is not always interchangeable with another, similar piece of currency. For example, participants thought that the actual piece of currency a person had originally lost should be returned to him, rather than another piece of currency of equivalent economic value, even when they did not believe that the owner would be able to tell the difference between the two.

5 See also Ellickson (2008, 102–06, 110–11) for the advantages of in-kind, reciprocal gift exchanges over money among participants in a household relationship.

6 Additional support for people's preference for receiving the thing itself rather than its monetary equivalent may be found in Engel and Freund's (2017) stylized laboratory experiment. The authors showed that when participants had strong preferences for the contract object, they were much more willing to enter into the contract when they were guaranteed its specific performance. Thus, the participants were considerably more inclined to donate money to a favored charity if they could purchase "insurance" that the money would indeed reach that charity, than when they could only receive damages for nonfulfillment of the donation.

7 In delineating the limits of the acceptable addition to the remainder, one may draw on the vast literature on transferable development rights (TDR). The technique of TDR allows the shift of nonutilized development rights from the original parcel of land to another parcel owned by the same person or by other people (in the latter case, the recipient purchases the development rights from their former owner) (Costonis 1973). To prevent overdevelopment, TDR programs commonly set ceilings on the quantity of development rights that may be transferred to a recipient parcel (say, 15 percent) (Stevenson 1998, 1339–43).

8 But see Shai Stern (2016, 743–47), who recommends that in-kind remedies be used sparingly in expropriation contexts. Among other considerations, Stern fears that an in-kind remedy might overincentivize takings of property because the government would believe that such a remedy indeed succeeds in placing landowners in their pretaking position. At the same time, Stern acknowledges that this fear is mitigated by the higher costs of implementing a relocation scheme for landowners.

9 See also Dickinson (2017), who advocates "inclusionary takings" legislation. Accordingly, municipalities and developers would be required to provide affordable

housing in economic development projects benefiting from expropriations, in order to prevent displacement of low-income families from the neighborhood.

10 Empirical studies of contract remedies suggest additional reasons why people may opt for monetary redress, and these may sometimes be relevant for the choice of remedy with respect to property. Anidjar, Zamir, and Katz (forthcoming) conducted a quantitative analysis of the judgments of the Israeli Supreme Court on remedies for breach of contract over sixty-nine years, from the establishment of Israel in 1948 to 2016. Interestingly, they found that although in 1970 the common law rule under which damages were the standard remedy for breach was replaced with a new law that entitles the injured party to request enforced performance of the contract (subject to certain exceptions), the tendency to sue for such performance and the willingness of courts to award this remedy have actually declined after 1970. Importantly, however, Anidjar, Zamir, and Katz have also found a significant correlation between the average length of legal proceedings—which have increased dramatically since the mid-1970s—and the inclination to sue for and award enforced performance. It stands to reason that the longer the legal proceeding, the less attractive an in-kind remedy is. Imagine, for instance, receiving a laptop computer or a car a few years after the date set in the contract. Thus, these empirical results should not be interpreted as a preference for monetary compensation in and of itself. Likewise, Arbel (2015) discovered in interviews with eighteen people (both lawyers and litigants) various reasons why enforced performance is not always requested or awarded. For example, attorneys (rather than clients) may prefer monetary relief because it eases their fee collection, and it can be difficult to ensure the quality of performance pursuant to a judicial order. These reasons, too, are practical and may prevail even if people generally prefer in-kind remedies to monetary ones.

11 The code of Indiana, for example, enables in-kind redress in the form of an alternative parcel when agricultural land is expropriated by the state. However, this remedy requires the consent of both the injured landowner and the expropriating authority. See Ind. Code Ann. §32-24-4.5-8.

12 A possible example is land readjustment. There are compelling reasons to allow readjustment processes to go forward even without the consent of all the affected landowners (which, if required, would grant each landowner a holdout position). As explained earlier in the text, land readjustment is a particularly useful tool for addressing the needs of the landowners, and the consideration that an injured party should not be forced to deal with the person who wronged her is inapplicable in this context. Therefore, the advantages of bypassing negotiations with multiple landowners may outweigh the possible costs to the minority of unwilling landowners.

REFERENCES

Abeler, Johannes, Armin Falk, Lorenz Goette, and David Huffman. 2011. Reference Points and Effort Provision. *American Economic Review* 101:470–92.

Ackerman, Bruce A. 1971. Regulating Slum Housing Markets on Behalf of the Poor: Of Housing Codes, Housing Subsidies and Income Redistribution Policy. *Yale Law Journal* 80:1093–197.

———. 1977. *Private Property and the Constitution*. New Haven, CT: Yale University Press.

Adamowicz, Wiktor L., Vinay Bhardwaj, and Bruce Macnab. 1993. Experiments on the Difference between Willingness to Pay and Willingness to Accept. *Land Economics* 69:416–27.

Ahuvia, Aaron C. 2005. Beyond the Extended Self: Loved Objects and Consumers' Identity Narratives. *Journal of Consumer Research* 32:171–84.

Akerlof, George A. 1970. The Market for "Lemons": Quality Uncertainty and the Market Mechanism. *Quarterly Journal of Economics* 84:488–500.

Alchian, Armen A., and Harold Demsetz. 1972. Production, Information Costs, and Economic Organization. *American Economic Review* 62:777–95.

Alcock, John. 2009. *Animal Behavior: An Evolutionary Approach*. 9th ed. Sunderland, MA: Sinauer Associates.

Alexander, Gregory S. 2009. The Social-Obligation Norm in American Property Law. *Cornell Law Review* 94:745–819.

Allport, Gordon W. 1954. *The Nature of Prejudice*. Oxford: Addison-Wesley.

Alterman, Rachelle. 1988. Exactions Law and Social Policy in Israel. In Rachelle Alterman, ed. *Private Supply of Public Services: Evaluation of Real Estate Exactions, Linkage, and Alternative Land Policies*. New York: NYU Press, 182–200.

———. 2007. Much More Than Land Assembly: Land Readjustment for the Supply of Urban Public Services. In Yu-Hung Hong and Barrie Needham, eds. *Analyzing Land Readjustment: Economics, Law, and Collective Action*. Cambridge, MA: Lincoln Institute of Land Policy, 57–85.

———. 2010. Comparative Analysis: A Platform for Cross-National Learning. In Rachelle Alterman, ed. *Takings International: A Comparative Perspective on Land Use Regulations and Compensation Rights*. Chicago: American Bar Association Publishing, 21–74.

Altman, Irwin, and Setha M. Low. 1992. Place Attachment: A Conceptual Inquiry. In Irwin Altman and Setha M. Low, eds. *Place Attachment*. Vol. 1. New York: Plenum Press, 1–12.

American Farm Bureau Federation Survey. 2005. October 29–November 2. Zogby International.

Anderson, Michelle Wilde, and Victoria C. Plaut. 2012. Property Law: Implicit Bias and the Resilience of Spatial Color Lines. In Justin D. Levinson and Robert J. Smith, eds. *Implicit Bias across the Law*. Cambridge: Cambridge University Press, 25–44.

Anidjar, Leon Y., Ori Katz, and Eyal Zamir. Forthcoming. Enforced Performance in Common-Law versus Civil Law Systems: An Empirical Study of a Legal Transformation. *American Journal of Comparative Law*. http://ssrn.com/abstract=3294452.

Arbel, Yonathan A. 2015. Contract Remedies in Action: Specific Performance. *West Virginia Law Review* 118:369–410.

Ariely, Dan, and Itamar Simonson. 2003. Buying, Bidding, Playing, or Competing? Value Assessment and Decision Dynamics in Online Auctions. *Journal of Consumer Psychology* 13:113–23.

Arkes, Hal R., and Catherine Blumer. 1985. The Psychology of Sunk Cost. *Organizational Behavior and Human Decision Processes* 35:124–40.

Arkes, Hal R., and Laura Hutzel. 2000. The Role of Probability of Success Estimates in the Sunk Cost Effect. *Journal of Behavioral Decision Making*. 13:295–306.

Armor, David A., and Shelley E. Taylor. 2002. When Predictions Fail: The Dilemma of Unrealistic Optimism. In Thomas Gilovich, Dale Griffin, and Daniel Kahneman, eds. *Heuristics and Biases: The Psychology of Intuitive Judgment*. New York: Cambridge University Press, 334–47.

Aronson, Elliot. 2012. *The Social Animal*. 11th ed. New York: Worth Publishers.

Aronson, Elliot, and Judson Mills. 1959. The Effect of Severity of Initiation on Liking for a Group. *Journal of Abnormal and Social Psychology* 59:177–81.

Aronson, Joshua, Michael J. Lustina, Catherine Good, and Kelli Keough. 1999. When White Men Can't Do Math: Necessary and Sufficient Factors in Stereotype Threat. *Journal of Experimental Social Psychology* 35:29–46.

Axelrod, Robert. 1973. An Information-Processing Model of Perception and Cognition. *American Political Science Review*, 67:1248–66.

Ayres, Ian. 1998. Protecting Property with Puts. *Valparaiso Law Review* 32:793–831.

Ayres, Ian, and Eric Talley. 1995. Solomonic Bargaining: Dividing a Legal Entitlement to Facilitate Coasean Trade. *Yale Law Journal* 104:1027–117.

Babcock, Linda, and George Loewenstein. 1997. Explaining Bargaining Impasse: The Role of Self-Serving Biases. *Journal of Economic Perspectives* 11:109–26.

Babcock, Linda, George Loewenstein, Samuel Issacharoff, and Colin Camerer. 1995. Biased Judgments of Fairness in Bargaining. *American Economic Review* 85:1337–43.

Babe, Katie. 2005. The Property Tax Relief for the Elderly: A Survey of the Nation. *Marquette Elder's Advisor* 6:325–60.

Bagchi, Aditi. 2008. Distributive Injustice and Private Law. *Hastings Law Journal* 60:105–48.

Bagenstos, Samuel R. 2016. Disparate Impact and the Role of Classification and Motivation in Equal Protection Law after Inclusive Communities. *Cornell Law Review* 101:1115–69.

Baggett, Travis P., James J. O'Connell, Daniel E. Singer, and Nancy A. Rigoti. 2010. The Unmet Health Care Needs of Homeless Adults: A National Study. *American Journal of Public Health* 100:1326–33.

Baker, Lynn A., and Robert E. Emery. 1993. When Every Relationship Is Above Average: Perceptions and Expectations of Divorce at the Time of Marriage. *Law and Human Behavior* 17:439–50.

Ball, Dwayne, and Lori H. Tasaki. 1992. The Role and Measurement of Attachment in Consumer Behavior. *Journal of Consumer Psychology* 1:155–72.

Banner, Stuart. 2011. *American Property: A History of How, Why, and What We Own.* Cambridge, MA: Harvard University Press.

Bar-Gill, Oren, and Christoph Engel. 2018. How to Protect Entitlements: An Experiment. *Journal of Law and Economics* 61:525–53.

Baron, Jonathan, and Ilana Ritov. 1994. Reference Points and Omission Bias. *Organizational Behavior and Human Decision Processes* 59:475–98.

Barrad, Catherine M. 1993. Genetic Information and Property Theory. *Northwestern University Law Review* 87:1037–86.

Barros, D. Benjamin. 2006. Home as a Legal Concept. *Santa Clara Law Review* 46:255–306.

———. 2009. Legal Questions for the Psychology of Home. *Tulane Law Review* 83:645–60.

Baumeister, Roy F. 1998. The Self. In Daniel T. Gilbert, Susan T. Fiske, and Gardner Linzey, eds. *The Handbook of Social Psychology*. Boston: McGraw-Hill, 680–81.

Baumeister, Roy F., and Mark R. Leary. 1995. The Need to Belong: Desire for Interpersonal Attachments as a Fundamental Human Motivation. *Psychological Bulletin* 117:497–529.

Bazerman, M. H., G. Loewenstein, and D. A. Moore. 2002. Why Good Accountants Do Bad Audits. *Harvard Business Review* 80:96–102.

Beaglehole, Ernest. 1932. *Property: A Study in Social Psychology.* New York: Macmillan.

Beaman, Arthur L., Bonnel Klentz, Edward Diener, and Soren Svanum. 1979. Self-Awareness and Transgression in Children: Two Field Studies. *Journal of Personality and Social Psychology* 37:1835–46.

Beattie, Jane, and Jonathan Baron. 1995. In-Kind and Out-of-Kind Penalties: Preferences and Valuation. *Journal of Experimental Psychology Applied* 1:136–51.

Beggan, James K. 1992. On the Social Nature of Nonsocial Perception: The Mere Ownership Effect. *Journal of Personality and Social Psychology* 62:229–37.

Beggan, James K., and Ellen M. Brown. 1994. Association as a Psychological Justification for Ownership. *Journal of Psychology* 128:365–80.

Belk, Russell W. 1987. Identity and the Relevance of Market, Personal, and Community Objects. In Jean Umiker-Sebeok, ed. *Marketing and Semiotics: New Directions in the Study of Signs for Sale*. Berlin: Mouton de Gruyter, 151–64.

———. 1988. Possessions and the Extended Self. *Journal of Consumer Research* 15:139–68.

———. 1991. The Ineluctable Mysteries of Possessions. In Floyd W. Rudmin, ed. *To Have Possessions: A Handbook on Ownership and Property*. Corte Madera, CA: Select Press. 17–56.

Bell, Abraham, and Gideon Parchomovsky. 2001. Givings. *Yale Law Journal* 111:547–618.

———. 2005. Of Property and Federalism. *Yale Law Journal* 115:72–115.

———. 2007. Taking Compensation Private. *Stanford Law Review* 59:871–906.

———. 2017. Partial Takings. *Columbia Law Review* 117:2043–93.

Bell, Jeannine. 2007. Hate Thy Neighbor. *Ohio State Journal of Criminal Law* 5:47–77.

Ben-Shahar, Omri, and Carl E. Schneider. 2014. *More Than You Wanted to Know: The Failure of Mandated Disclosure*. Princeton, NJ: Princeton University Press.

Bergh, Andreas. 2008. A Critical Note on the Theory of Inequity Aversion. *Journal of Socio-Economics* 37:1789–96.

Blackhall, J. Cameron. 2005. *Planning Law and Practice*. 3rd ed. London: Cavendish.

Blackstone, William. 1893. *Commentaries on the Laws of England in Four Books. Notes Selected from the Editions of Archibold, Christian, Coleridge, Chitty, Stewart, Kerr, and Others, Barron Field's Analysis, and Additional Notes, and a Life of the Author by George Sharswood. In Two Volumes*. Vol. 1, bk. 2. Philadelphia: J. B. Lippincott.

Blair, Irene V., Charles M. Judd, and Kristine M. Chapleau. 2004. The Influence of Afrocentric Facial Features in Criminal Sentencing. *Psychological Science* 15:674–79.

Blake, Peter R., and Paul L. Harris. 2011. Early Representations of Ownership. In Hildy Ross and Ori Friedman, eds. *Origins of Ownership of Property*. San Francisco: Wiley Periodicals, 39–52.

Blake, P. R., et al. 2015. The Ontogeny of Fairness in Seven Societies. *Nature* 528:258–61.

Blume, Lawrence, and Daniel L. Rubinfeld. 1984. Compensation for Takings: An Economic Analysis. *California Law Review* 72:569–628.

Blumenthal, Jeremy A. 2007. Emotional Paternalism. *Florida State University Law Review* 35:1–72.

———. 2009. "To Be Human": A Psychological Perspective on Property Law. *Tulane Law Review* 83:609–44.

Bodenhausen, Galen V. 1990. Stereotypes as Judgmental Heuristics: Evidence of Circadian Variations in Discrimination. *Psychological Science* 1:319–22.

Boehne, Donna M., and Paul W. Paese. 2000. Deciding Whether to Complete or Terminate an Unfinished Project: A Strong Test of the Project Completion Hypothesis. *Organizational Behavior and Human Decision Processes* 81:178–94.

Bolan, Marc. 1997. The Mobility Experience and Neighborhood Attachment. *Demography* 34:225–37.

Bolton, Gary E., and Axel Ockenfels. 2000. A Theory of Equity, Reciprocity, and Competition. *American Economic Review* 90:166–93.

Bonam, Courtney M., Hilary B. Bergsieker, and Jennifer L. Eberhardt. 2016. Polluting Black Space. *Journal of Experimental Psychology: General* 145:1561–82.

Bovens, Luc. 2009. The Ethics of *Nudge*. In Till Grune-Yanoff and Sven Ove Hansson, eds. *Preference Change: Approaches from Philosophy, Economics and Psychology*. Dordrecht: Springer, 207–19.

Bradbury, Jack W., and Sandra L. Vehrencamp. 1998. *Principles of Animal Communication*. Sunderland, MA: Sinauer Associates.

Brasel, Adam S., and James Gips. 2014. Tablets, Touchscreens, and Touchpads: How Varying Touch Interfaces Trigger Psychological Ownership and Endowment. *Journal of Consumer Psychology* 24:226–33.

Braver, Sanford L., and Ira Mark Ellman. 2013. Citizens' Views about Fault in Property Division. *Family Law Quarterly* 47:419–35.

Brenner, Lyle, Yuval Rottenstreich, Sanjay Sood, and Baler Bilgin. 2007. On the Psychology of Loss Aversion: Possession, Valence, and Reversals of the Endowment Effect. *Journal of Consumer Research* 34:369–76.

Brewer, Marilynn B., and Rupert Brown. 1998. Intergroup Relations. In Daniel T. Gilbert, Susan T. Fiske, and Gardner Linzey, eds., *The Handbook of Social Psychology*. Vol. 2. Boston: McGraw-Hill, 554–94.

Brinberg, David, and Pat Castell. 1982. A Resource Exchange Theory Approach to Interpersonal Interactions: A Test of Foa's Theory. *Journal of Personality and Social Psychology* 43:260–69.

Brinig, Margaret F., and F. H. Buckley. 1996. The Market for Deadbeats. *Journal of Legal Studies* 25:201–32.

Bronsteen, John, Christopher Buccafusco, and Jonathan S. Masur. 2014. *Happiness and the Law*. Chicago: University of Chicago Press.

Bruce, Jon W., and James W. Ely. 2007. *The Law of Easements and Licenses in Land*. St. Paul, MN: West Group.

Bruner, Jerome S. 1957. On Perceptual Readiness. *Psychological Review* 64:123–52.

Buccafusco, Christopher, and Christopher J. Sprigman. 2010. Valuing Intellectual Property: An Experiment. *Cornell Law Review* 96:1–45.

———. 2011. The Creativity Effect. *University of Chicago Law Review* 78:31–52.

Buchanan, James M. 1993. *Property as a Guarantor of Liberty*. Brookfield, VT: Edward Elgar Publishing.

Buckner, John C., Ellen L. Bassuk, Linda Weinreb, and Margaret G. Brooks. 1999. Homelessness and Its Relation to the Mental Health and Behavior of Low-Income School-Age Children. *Developmental Psychology* 35:246–57.

Bühren, Christoph, and Marco Plessner. 2014. The Trophy Effect. *Journal of Behavioral Decision Making* 27:363–77.

Burke, Barlow. 2003. *Personal Property*. 3rd ed. St. Paul, MN: West Group.

Burke, Barlow, and Joseph Snoe. 2016. *Property: Examples and Explanations*. 5th ed. New York: Wolters Kluwer.

Burnham, Terence C. 2003. Engineering Altruism: A Theoretical and Experimental Investigation of Anonymity and Gift-Giving. *Journal of Economic Behavior and Organization* 50:133–44.

Byun, Sang-Eun, and Brenda Sternquist. 2008. The Antecedents of In-Store Hoarding: Measurement and Application in the Fast Fashion Retail Environment. *International Review of Retail, Distribution and Consumer Research* 18:133–47.

———. 2012. Here Today, Gone Tomorrow: Consumer Reactions to Perceived Limited Availability. *Journal of Marketing Theory and Practice* 20:223–34.

Cacioppo, John T., Louise Hawkley, John M. Ernst, Mary Burleson, Gary G. Berntson, Bita Nouriani, and David Spiegel. 2006. Loneliness within a Nomological Net: An Evolutionary Perspective. *Journal of Research in Personality* 40:1054–85.

Cagney, Kathleen A., Christopher R. Browning, James Iveniuk, and Ned English. 2014. The Onset of Depression during the Great Recession: Foreclosure and Older Adult Mental Health. *American Journal of Public Health* 104:498–505.

Cain, Daylian, George Loewenstein, and Don A. Moore. 2005. The Dirt on Coming Clean: Perverse Effects of Disclosing Conflicts of Interest. *Journal of Legal Studies* 34:1–25.

Cain, Patricia A. 2009. Two Sisters vs. a Father and Two Sons. In Gerald Korngold and Andrew P. Morriss, eds. *Property Stories*. 2nd ed. New York: Thomson Reuters/Foundation Press, 99–122.

Calabresi, Guido. 2014. A Broader View of the Cathedral: The Significance of the Liability Rule, Correcting a Misapprehension. *Law and Contemporary Problems* 77:1–13.

Calabresi, Guido, and A. Douglas Melamed. 1972. Property Rules, Liability Rules, and Inalienability: One View of the Cathedral. *Harvard Law Review* 85:1089–128.

Camerer, Colin. 1995. Individual Decision Making. In John H. Kagel and Alvin E. Roth, eds. *The Handbook of Experimental Economics*. Princeton, NJ: Princeton University Press, 587–703.

Camerer, Colin, Linda Babcock, George Loewenstein, and Richard Thaler. 1997. Labor Supply of New York City Cabdrivers: One Day at a Time. *Quarterly Journal of Economics* 112:407–41.

Campbell, Karen E. 1990. Networks Past: A 1939 Bloomington Neighborhood. *Social Forces* 69:139–55.

Carlisle-Frank, Pamela L. 1992. The Relocation Experience: Analysis of Factors Thought to Influence Adjustment to Transition. *Psychological Reports* 70:835–38.

Carmon, Ziv, and Dan Ariely. 2000. Focusing on the Forgone: How Value Can Appear So Different to Buyers and Sellers. *Journal of Consumer Research* 27:360–70.

Carter, Matt, and Andrea V. Brambila. 2012. Buyer and Seller Beware: Your Agent May Not Represent Your Best Interests. *Inman*, February 24. www.inman.com/2012/02/24/buyer-and-seller-beware-your-agent-may-not-represent-your-best-interests/.

Carter, Travis J., and Thomas Gilovich. 2010. The Relative Relativity of Material and Experiential Purchases. *Journal of Personality and Social Psychology* 98:146–59.

———. 2012. I Am What I Do, Not What I Have: The Differential Centrality of Experiential and Material Purchases to the Self. *Journal of Personality and Social Psychology* 102:1304–17.

Chabris, Christopher, and Daniel Simons. 2009. *The Invisible Gorilla: How Our Intuitions Deceive Us.* New York: Crown.

Chang, Yun-chien. 2012. Self-Assessment of Takings Compensation: An Empirical Study. *Journal of Law, Economics and Organization* 28:265–85.

———. 2015. Optional Law in Property: Theoretical Critiques and a New View of the Cathedral. *New York University Journal of Law and Liberty* 9:459–506.

Chark, Robin, and A. V. Muthukrishnan. 2013. The Effect of Physical Possession on Preference for Product Warranty. *International Journal of Research in Marketing* 30:424–25.

Charness, Gary, and Uri Gneezy. 2008. What's in a Name? Anonymity and Social Distance in Dictator and Ultimatum Games. *Journal of Economic Behavior and Organization* 68:29–35.

Chein, Isidor. 1946. Some Considerations in Combating Intergroup Prejudice. *Journal of Educational Sociology* 19:412–19.

Christopherson, Robert C. 2005. Missing the Forest for the Trees: The Illusory Half-Policy of Senior Citizen Property Tax Relief. *Elder Law Journal* 13:195–226.

Cialdini, Robert B., John T. Cacioppo, Rodney Bassett, and John A. Miller. 1978. Low-Ball Procedure for Producing Compliance: Commitment Then Cost. *Journal of Personality and Social Psychology* 36:463–76.

City of Portland, Oregon. 2018. Standards for Neighborhood System. www.portland-oregon.gov/civic/40260.

Coase, R. H. 1960. The Problem of Social Cost. *Journal of Law and Economics* 3:1–44.

Cohen, David, and Jack L. Knetsch. 1992. Judicial Choice and Disparities between Measures of Economic Values. *Osgoode Hall Law Journal* 30:737–70.

Cohen, Glen I. 2015. Identified versus Statistical Lives in US Civil Litigation: Of Standing, Ripeness, and Class Actions. In I. Glen Cohen, Norman Daniels, and Nir Eyal, eds. *Identified versus Statistical Lives.* New York: Oxford University Press, 161–81.

Cohen, Glen I., Norman Daniels, and Nir Eyal. 2015. Statistical versus Identified Persons: An Introduction. In Glen I. Cohen, Norman Daniels, and Nir Eyal, eds. *Identified versus Statistical Lives: An Interdisciplinary Perspective.* New York: Oxford University Press, 1–10.

Collins, Stephen. 2008. Saving Fair Housing on the Internet: The Case for Amending the Communications Decency Act. *Northwestern University Law Review* 102:1471–99.

Collinson, Rob. 2011. Rental Housing Affordability Dynamics, 1990–2009. *Cityscape* 13:71–103.

Congdon, William J., Jeffrey R. Kling, and Sendhil Mullainathan. 2011. *Policy and Choice: Public Finance through the Lens of Behavioral Economics.* Washington, DC: Brookings Institution Press.

The Constitution of the Kingdom of Bhutan, Art. 9(2). 2008. www.nationalcouncil.bt/assets/uploads/docs/acts/2017/Constitution_of_Bhutan_2008.pdf.

Converse, John, Jr., and Uriel G. Foa. 1993. Some Principles of Equity in Interpersonal Exchanges. In Uriel G. Foa, John Converse Jr., Kjell Y. Törnblom, and Edna B.

Foa, eds. *Resource Theory: Explorations and Applications*. Bingley: Emerald Group Publishing. 31–40.

Cooper, David J., and John H. Kagel. 2015. Other-Regarding Preferences: A Selective Survey of Experimental Results. In John H. Kagel and Alvin E. Roth, eds. *The Handbook of Experimental Economics*. Vol. 2. Princeton, NJ: Princeton University Press. 217–89.

Cooper, Joel. 2007. *Cognitive Dissonance: Fifty Years of a Classic Theory*. London: Sage.

Cooter, Robert, and Thomas Ulen. 2012. *Law and Economics*. 6th ed. Boston: Pearson Addison Wesley.

Corbin, Arthur. 1922. Taxation of Seats on the Stock Exchange. *Yale Law Journal* 31:429–31.

Corfield, Frederick, and Richard R. J. A. Carnwath. 1978. *Compulsory Acquisition and Compensation*. London: Butterworths.

Correll, Joshua, Bernadette Park, Charles M. Judd, and Bernd Wittenbrink. 2002. The Police Officer's Dilemma: Using Ethnicity to Disambiguate Potentially Threatening Individuals. *Journal of Personality and Social Psychology* 83:1314–29.

Correll, Joshua, Bernd Wittenbrink, Bernadette Park, Charles M. Judd, and Arina Goyle. 2011. Dangerous Enough: Moderating Racial Bias with Contextual Threat Cues. *Journal of Experimental Social Psychology* 47:184–89.

Costonis, John J. 1973. Development Rights Transfer: An Exploratory Essay. *Yale Law Journal* 83:75–129.

Coulson, N. Edward. 1999. Why Are Hispanic- and Asian-American Homeownership Rates So Low? Immigration and Other Factors. *Journal of Urban Economics* 45:209–27.

Craswell, Richard. 1993. Property Rules and Liability Rules in Unconscionability and Related Doctrines. *University of Chicago Law Review* 60:1–66.

Csikszentmihalyi, Mihaly, and Eugene Rochberg-Halton. 1981. *The Meaning of Things: Domestic Symbols and the Self*. Cambridge: Cambridge University Press.

Cuba, Lee, and David M. Hummon. 1993. A Place to Call Home: Identification with Dwelling, Community, and Region. *Sociological Quarterly* 34:111–31.

Curran, Christopher, and Joel L. Schrag. 2000. Does It Matter Whom an Agent Serves? Evidence from Recent Changes in Real Estate Agency Law. *Journal of Law and Economics* 43:265–84.

Dagan, Hanoch. 1999. Takings and Distributive Justice. *Virginia Law Review* 85:741–804.

———. 2011. *Property: Values and Institutions*. New York: Oxford University Press.

Dana, David A., and Thomas W. Merrill. 2002. *Property: Takings*. New York: Foundation Press.

Davy, Benjamin. 2007. Mandatory Happiness? Land Readjustment and Property in Germany. In Yu-Hung Hong and Barrie Needham, eds. *Analyzing Land Readjustment: Economics, Law, and Collective Action*. Cambridge, MA: Lincoln Institute of Land Policy. 37–55.

De Dreu, Carsten K. W., and Daan van Knippenberg. 2005. The Possessive Self as a Barrier to Conflict Resolution: Effects of Mere Ownership, Process Accountability, and Self-Concept Clarity on Competitive Cognitions and Behavior. *Journal of Personality and Social Psychology* 89:345–57.

DeJoy, David M. 1989. The Optimism Bias and Traffic Accident Risk Perception. *Accident Analysis and Prevention* 21:333–40.

De Morris, Amalia Alarcon, and Paul Leistner. 2009. From Neighborhood Association System to Participatory Democracy—Broadening and Deepening Public Involvement in Portland, Oregon. *National Civic Review* 98:47–55.

Demsetz, Harold. 1967. Toward a Theory of Property Rights. *American Economic Review* 57:347–59.

DeScioli, Peter, Rachel Karpoff, and Julian De Freitas. 2017. Ownership Dilemmas: The Case of Finders versus Landowners. *Cognitive Science* 41:502–22.

Desmond, Matthew. 2012. Eviction and the Reproduction of Urban Poverty. *American Journal of Sociology* 118:88–133.

Desmond, Matthew, and Rachel Tolbert Kimbro. 2015. Eviction's Fallout: Housing, Hardship, and Health. *Social Forces* 94:295–324.

de Soto, Hernando. 2000. *The Mystery of Capital: Why Capitalism Triumphs in the West and Fails Everywhere Else*. New York: Basic Books.

Dickerson, Andrew, Arne Hole, and Luke Munford. 2014. The Relationship between Well-Being and Commuting Revisited: Does the Choice of Methodology Matter? *Regional Science and Urban Economics* 49:321–29.

Dickinson, Gerald S. 2017. Inclusionary Takings Legislation. *Villanova Law Review* 62:135–74.

Diener, Ed. 2000. Subjective Well-Being: The Science of Happiness and a Proposal for a National Index. *American Psychologist* 55:34–43.

DiPasquale, Denise, and Edward Glaeser. 1999. Incentives and Social Capital: Are Homeowners Better Citizens? *Journal of Urban Economics* 45:354–84.

Di Robilant, Anna. 2013. Property: A Bundle of Sticks or a Tree? *Vanderbilt Law Review* 66:869–903.

Dittmar, Helga. 1992. *The Social Psychology of Material Possessions: To Have Is to Be*. New York: St. Martin's Press.

Dobbin, Frank, and Alexandra Kalev. 2016. Why Diversity Programs Fail. *Harvard Business Review* 94(7):52–60.

Dobbs, Dan B., Paul T. Hayden, and Ellen M. Bublick. 2011. *The Law of Torts*. St. Paul, MN: Thomson West.

Doleac, Jennifer L., and Benjamin Hansen. 2017. The Unintended Consequences of "Ban the Box": Statistical Discrimination and Employment Outcomes When Criminal Histories Are Hidden. Working Paper, January 1. https://papers.ssrn.com/sol3/papers.cfm?abstract_id=2812811.

Dommer, Sara L., and Vanitha Swaminathan. 2013. Explaining the Endowment Effect through Ownership: The Role of Identity, Gender, and Self-Threat. *Journal of Consumer Research* 39:1034–50.

Donnenwerth, Gregory V., and Uriel G. Foa. 1974. Effects of Resource Class on Retaliation to Injustice in Interpersonal Exchange. *Journal of Personality and Social Psychology* 29:785–93.

Dovidio, John F. 2002. On the Nature of Contemporary Prejudice: The Third Wave. *Journal of Social Issues* 57:829–49.

Dovidio, John F., Miles Hewstone, Peter Glick, and Victoria M. Esses. 2010. Prejudice, Stereotyping and Discrimination: Theoretical and Empirical Overview. In John F. Dovidio, Miles Hewstone, Peter Glick, and Victoria M. Esses, eds. *The SAGE Handbook of Prejudice, Stereotyping, and Discrimination*. London: Sage, 3–28.

Dukeminier, Jesse, James E. Krier, Gregory S. Alexander, Michael H. Schill, and Lior Jacob Strahilevitz. 2017. *Property*. New York: Aspen.

Dunn, Elizabeth, Timothy D. Wilson, and Daniel T. Gilbert. 2003. Location, Location, Location: The Misprediction of Satisfaction in Housing Lotteries. *Personality and Social Psychology Bulletin* 29:1421–32.

Dunning, David, Joanna E. Anderson, Thomas Schlösser, Daniel Ehlebracht, and Detlef Fetchenhauer. 2014. Trust at Zero Acquaintance: More a Matter of Respect Than an Expectation of Reward. *Journal of Personality and Social Psychology* 107:122–41.

Dyal-Chand, Rashmi. 2015. Regulating Sharing: The Sharing Economy as an Alternative Capitalist System. *Tulane Law Review* 90:241–309.

Edin, Kathryn, and Laura Lein. 1997. *Making Ends Meet: How Single Mothers Survive Welfare and Low-Wage Work*. New York: Russell Sage Foundation.

Eisenberg, Melvin A. 2006. The Disgorgement Interest in Contract Law. *Michigan Law Review* 105:559–602.

Eisenberg, Theodore, John Goerdt, Brian Ostrom, David Rottman, and Martin T. Wells. 1997. The Predictability of Punitive Damages. *Journal of Legal Studies* 26:623–61.

Ellickson, Robert C. 1977. Suburban Growth Controls: An Economic and Legal Analysis. *Yale Law Journal* 86:385–512.

———. 1989. Bringing Culture and Human Frailty to Rational Actors: A Critique of Classical Law and Economics. *Chicago-Kent Law Review* 65:23–56.

———. 1994. *Order without Law: How Neighbors Settle Disputes*. Cambridge, MA: Harvard University Press.

———. 1998. New Institutions for Old Neighborhoods. *Duke Law Journal* 48:75–110.

———. 2008. *The Household: Informal Order around the Hearth*. Princeton, NJ: Princeton University Press.

Elster, Jon. 1990. Selfishness and Altruism. In Jane J. Mansbridge, ed. *Beyond Self Interest*. Chicago: University of Chicago Press, 44–52.

Ely, James W. 1992. *The Guardian of Every Other Right: A Constitutional History of Property Rights*. New York: Oxford University Press.

Engel, Christoph. 2011. Dictator Games: A Meta Study. *Experimental Economics* 14:583–610.

Engel, Christoph, and Lars Freund. 2017. Behaviorally Efficient Remedies: An Experiment. Working Paper, September 4. https://ssrn.com/abstract=2988653.

Epley, Nicholas, Adam Waytz, and John T. Cacioppo. 2007. On Seeing Human: A Three-Factor Theory of Anthropomorphism. *Psychological Review* 114:864–86.

Epstein, Richard A. 1979. Possession as the Root of Title. *Georgia Law Review* 13:1221–43.

———. 1982. Notice and Freedom of Contract in the Law of Servitudes. *Southern California Law Review* 55:1353–68.

———. 1985. *Takings: Private Property and the Power of Eminent Domain*. Cambridge, MA: Harvard University Press.

———. 1986. Past and Future: The Temporal Dimension in the Law of Property. *Washington University Law Quarterly* 64:667–722.

———. 1990. Property and Necessity. *Harvard Journal of Law and Public Policy* 13:2–9.

———. 1992. Rights and "Rights Talk." *Harvard Law Review* 105:1106–23.

———. 1998. Possession. In Peter Newman, ed. *The New Palgrave Dictionary of Economics and the Law*. New York: Stockton Press, 62–68.

———. 2017. Disappointed Expectations: How the Supreme Court Failed to Clean Up Takings Law in *Murr v. Wisconsin*. *New York University Journal of Law and Liberty* 11:151–217.

Equal Justice Society and Wilson Sonsini Goodrich & Rosati. 2014. Lessons from *Mt. Holly*: Leading Scholars Demonstrate Need for Disparate Impact Standard to Combat Implicit Bias. *Hastings Race and Poverty Law Journal* 11:241–68.

Etzioni, Amitai. 1988. *The Moral Dimension: Toward a New Economics*. New York: Free Press.

———. 1991. The Socio-economics of Property. *Journal of Social Behavior and Personality* 6:465–68.

Eyer, Katie R. 2012. That's Not Discrimination: American Beliefs and the Limits of Anti-Discrimination Law. *Minnesota Law Review* 96:1275–362.

Fagundes, David. 2017. Buying Happiness: Property, Acquisition, and Subjective Well-Being. *William and Mary Law Review* 58:1851–931.

———. 2018. Why Less Property Is More: Inclusion, Dispossession, and Subjective Well-Being. *Iowa Law Review* 103:1361–1418.

Failinger, Marie. 2001. Remembering Mrs. Murphy: A Remedies Approach to the Conflict Between Gay/Lesbian Renters and Religious Landlords. *Capital University Law Review* 29:383–431.

Farnsworth, Ward. 1999. Do Parties to Nuisance Cases Bargain after Judgment? A Glimpse inside the Cathedral. *University of Chicago Law Review* 66:373–436.

Fee, John. 2006. Eminent Domain and the Sanctity of the Home. *Notre Dame Law Review* 81:783–819.

Fehr, Ernst, and Urs Fischbacher. 2002. Why Social Preferences Matter: The Impact of Non-Selfish Motives on Competition, Cooperation and Incentives. *Economic Journal* 112:C1–C33.

Fehr, Ernst, and Klaus M. Schmidt. 1999. A Theory of Fairness, Competition, and Cooperation. *Quarterly Journal of Economics* 114:817–68.

Feldman, Yuval, Amos Schurr, and Doron Teichman. 2013. Reference Points and Contractual Choices: An Experimental Examination. *Journal of Empirical Legal Studies* 10:512–41.

Fennell, Lee Anne. 2003. Death, Taxes, and Cognition. *North Carolina Law Review* 81:567–652.

———. 2004. Taking Eminent Domain Apart. *Michigan State Law Review* 2004:957–1004.

———. 2005. Revealing Options. *Harvard Law Review* 118:1399–488.

———. 2006. Properties of Concentration. *University of Chicago Law Review* 73:1227–97.

———. 2009. Adjusting Alienability. *Harvard Law Review* 122:1403–65.

———. 2016. Fee Simple Obsolete. *New York University Law Review* 91:1457–516.

Fennell, Lee Anne, and Richard H. McAdams. 2016. The Distributive Deficit in Law and Economics. *Minnesota Law Review* 100:1051–130.

Festinger, Leon. 1957. *A Theory of Cognitive Dissonance*. Stanford, CA: Stanford University Press.

Fetchenhauer, Detlef, and David Dunning. 2009. Do People Trust Too Much or Too Little? *Journal of Economic Psychology* 30:263–76.

Fischel, William A. 1995. *Regulatory Takings: Law, Economics, and Politics*. Cambridge, MA: Harvard University Press.

———. 2005. *The Homevoter Hypothesis: How Home Values Influence Local Government Taxation, School Finance, and Land-Use Policies*. Cambridge, MA: Harvard University Press.

Fischer, Claude S. 2002. Ever-More Rooted Americans. *City and Community* 1:177–98.

Fishkin, Joseph. 2014. The Anti-Bottleneck Principle in Employment Discrimination Law. *Washington University Law Review* 91:1429–518.

Fiske, Alan P., and Nick Haslam. 1996. Social Cognition Is Thinking about Relationships. *Current Directions in Psychological Science* 5:143–48.

Fiske, Alan Page, Shinobu Kitayama, Hazel Rose Markus, and Richard E. Nisbett. 1998. The Cultural Matrix of Social Psychology. In Daniel T. Gilbert, Susan T. Fiske, and Gardner Lindzey, eds. *Handbook of Social Psychology*. Vol. 2. 4th ed. Boston: McGraw-Hill, 915–81.

Fiske, Susan T. 1998. Stereotyping, Prejudice, and Discrimination. In Daniel T. Gilbert, Susan T. Fiske, and Gardner Lindzey, eds. *Handbook of Social Psychology*. Vol. 2, 4th ed. Boston: McGraw-Hill, 357–411.

Fiske, Susan T., and Beth A. Morling. 1996. Salience. In Anthony S. R. Manstead and Miles Hewstone, eds. *The Blackwell Encyclopedia of Social Psychology*. Malden, MA: Blackwell, 489.

Fiske, Susan T., and Shelley E. Taylor. 2017. *Social Cognition: From Brains to Culture*. Los Angeles: Sage.

Foa, Edna B., and Uriel G. Foa. 1976. Resource Theory of Social Exchange. In John W. Thibaut, Janet T. Spence, and Robert C. Carson, eds. *Contemporary Topics in Social Psychology*. Morristown, NJ: General Learning Press. 99–131.

Foa, Edna B., Jim L. Turner, and Uriel G. Foa. 1972. Response Generalization in Aggression. *Human Relations* 25:337–50.

Foa, Uriel G. 1993. Interpersonal and Economic Resources. In Uriel G. Foa, John Converse Jr., Kjell Y. Törnblom, and Edna B. Foa, eds. *Resource Theory: Explorations and Applications*. San Diego: Academic Press, 13–30.

Fraser, Colin, Brendan Burchell, Dale F. Hay, and Gerard Duveen. 2001. *Introducing Social Psychology*. Cambridge: Blackwell.

Fredrickson, Barbara L., and Christine Branigan. 2005. Positive Emotions Broaden the Scope of Attention and Thought-Action Repertoires. *Cognition and Emotion* 19:313–32.

Fried, Marc. 1966. Grieving for a Lost Home: Psychological Costs of Relocation. In James Q. Wilson, ed. *Urban Renewal: The Record and the Controversy*. Cambridge, MA: MIT Press, 359–79.

Friedman, Lawrence M. 1975. *The Legal System: A Social Science Perspective*. New York: Russell Sage Foundation.

Friedman, Milton R. 1997. *Friedman on Leases*. 4th ed. New York: Practicing Law Institute.

Friedman, Ori. 2008. First Possession: An Assumption Guiding Inferences about Who Owns What. *Psychonomic Bulletin and Review* 15:290–95.

———. 2010. Necessary for Possession: How People Reason about the Acquisition of Ownership. *Personality and Social Psychology Bulletin* 36:1161–69.

Friedman, Ori, and Karen R. Neary. 2008. Determining Who Owns What: Do Children Infer Ownership from First Possession? *Cognition* 107:829–49.

Friedman, Ori, Karen R. Neary, Margaret A. Defeyter, and Sarah L. Malcolm. 2011. Ownership and Object History. In Hildy Ross and Ori Friedman, eds. *Origins of Ownership of Property*. San Francisco: Wiley Periodicals, 79–89.

Frost, Randy, and Tamara Hartl. 1996. A Cognitive-Behavioral Mode of Compulsive Hoarding. *Behaviour Research and Therapy* 34:341–50.

Gaertner, Samuel L., and John F. Dovidio. 1986. The Aversive Form of Racism. In John F. Dovidio and Samuel L. Gaertner, eds. *Prejudice, Discrimination, and Racism*. San Diego: Academic Press, 61–89.

———. 2005. Understanding and Addressing Contemporary Racism: From Aversive Racism to the Common Ingroup Identity Model. *Journal of Social Issues* 61:615–39.

Gal, David. 2006. A Psychological Law of Inertia and the Illusion of Loss Aversion. *Judgment and Decision Making* 1:23–32.

Galin, Amira, Miron Gross, Irit Kela-Egozi, and Sigal Sapir. 2006. The Endowment Effect on Academic Chores Trade-Off (ACTO). *Theory and Decision* 60:335–57.

Garcia, Donna M., April Horstman Reser, Rachel B. Amo, Sandrine Redesdorff, and Nyla R. Branscombe. 2005. Perceivers' Responses to In-Group and Out-Group Members Who Blame a Negative Outcome on Discrimination. *Personality and Social Psychology Bulletin* 31:769–80.

Gardiner, J'Noel, Jeffrey Heisler, Jarl G. Kallberg, and Crocker H. Liu. 2007. The Impact of Dual Agency. *Journal of Real Estate Finance and Economics* 35(1):39–55.

Garland, Howard. 1990. Throwing Good Money after Bad: The Effect of Sunk Costs on the Decision to Escalate Commitment to an Ongoing Project. *Journal of Applied Psychology* 75:728–31.

Garnett, Nicole Stelle. 2006. The Neglected Political Economy of Eminent Domain. *Michigan Law Review* 105:101–50.

Gawronski, Bertram, Galen V. Bodenhausen, and Andrew P. Becker. 2007. I Like it, Because I Like Myself: Associative Self-Anchoring and Post-Decisional Change of Implicit Evaluations. *Journal of Experimental Social Psychology* 43:221–32.

Ger, Güliz, and Russell W. Belk. 1996. Cross-Cultural Differences in Materialism. *Journal of Economic Psychology* 17:55–77.

Gilbert, Daniel. 2006. *Stumbling on Happiness*. New York: Random House.

Gilens, Martin. 1999. *Why Americans Hate Welfare: Race, Media, and the Politics of Antipoverty Policy*. Chicago: University of Chicago Press.

Gjersoe, Nathalia L., George E. Newman, Vladimir Chituc, and Bruce Hood. 2014. Individualism and the Extended Self: Cross-Cultural Differences in the Valuation of Authentic Objects. *PLoS One* 9:e90787. https://journals.plos.org/plosone/article?id=10.1371/journal.pone.0090787.

Glaser, Jack, Katherine Spencer, and Amanda Charbonneau. 2014. Racial Bias and Public Policy. *Policy Insights from the Behavioral and Brain Sciences* 1:88–94.

Glassman, Amy M., and Shannellah Verna. 2016. Disparate Impact One Year after *Inclusive Communities*. *Journal of Affordable Housing and Community Development Law* 25:11–24.

Glendon, Mary Ann. 1989. *The Transformation of Family Law: State, Law, and Family in the United States and Western Europe*. Chicago: University of Chicago Press.

Gneezy, Uri, and Aldo Rustichini. 2000. A Fine Is a Price. *Journal of Legal Studies* 29:1–18.

Godsil, Rachel D. 2004. Viewing the Cathedral from Behind the Color Line: Property Rules, Liability Rules, and Environmental Racism. *Emory Law Journal* 53:1807–85.

Goetz, Edward G., and Mara Sidney. 1994. Revenge of the Property Owners: Community Development and the Politics of Property. *Journal of Urban Affairs* 16:319–34.

Goodman, Laurie, and Christopher Mayer. 2018. Homeownership and the American Dream. *Journal of Economic Perspectives* 32:31–58.

Goodman, Lisa A., Leonard Saxe, and Mary Harvey. 1991. Homelessness as Psychological Trauma: Broadening Perspectives. *American Psychologist* 46:1219–25.

Gordon, Deborah S. 2017. Mor[t]ality and Identity: Wills, Narratives, and Cherished Possessions. *Yale Journal of Law and the Humanities* 28:265–317.

Grand, William D. 1986. Implied and Statutory Warranties in the Sale of Real Estate: The Demise of Caveat Emptor. *Real Estate Law Journal* 15:44–56.

Greenberg, Deena, Carl Gershenson, and Matthew Desmond. 2016. Discrimination in Evictions: Empirical Evidence and Legal Challenges. *Harvard Civil Rights–Civil Liberties Law Review* 53:601–45.

Greenberg, Jeff L., and Tom Pyszczynski. 1985. The Effect of an Overheard Ethnic Slur on Evaluations of the Target: How to Spread a Social Disease. *Journal of Experimental Social Psychology* 21:61–72.

Greenwald, Anthony G., and Linda Hamilton Krieger. 2006. Implicit Bias: Scientific Foundations. *California Law Review* 94:945–67.

Greenwald, Anthony G., Andrew T. Poehlman, Eric Luis Uhlmann, and Mahzarin R. Banaji. 2009. Understanding and Using the Implicit Association Test: III. Meta-analysis of Predictive Validity. *Journal of Personality and Social Psychology* 97:17–41.

Gropp, Reint, John K. Scholz, and Michelle J. White. 1997. Personal Bankruptcy and Credit Supply and Demand. *Quarterly Journal of Economics* 112:217–51.

Gruenfeld, Deborah H., and Larissa Z. Tiedens. 2010. Organizational Preferences and Their Consequences. In Susan T. Fiske, Daniel T. Gilbert, and Gardner Lindzey, eds. *Handbook of Social Psychology*. New York: Wiley, 1252–87.

Güth, Werner. 1995. On Ultimatum Bargaining Games: A Personal Review. *Journal of Economic Behavior and Organization* 27:329–44.

Hahm, Pyong C. 1963. The Korean People and Their Property Rights. *American Journal of Comparative Law* 12:61–69.

Haidt, Jonathan. 2001. The Emotional Dog and Its Rational Tail: A Social Intuitionist Approach to Moral Judgment. *Psychological Review* 108:814–34.

Hamilton, Walter H. 1931. The Ancient Maxim Caveat Emptor. *Yale Law Journal* 40:1133–87.

Hammack, Judd, and Gardner M. Brown Jr. 1974. *Waterfowl and Wetlands: Toward Bioeconomic Analysis*. Washington, DC: RFF Press.

Hampton, Keith, and Barry Wellman. 2003. Neighboring in Netville: How the Internet Supports Community and Social Capital in a Wired Suburb. *City and Community* 2:277–311.

Hanemann, Michael W. 1991. Willingness to Pay and Willingness to Accept: How Much Can They Differ? *American Economic Review* 81:635–47.

Hans, Valerie P., and Valerie F. Reyna. 2011. To Dollars from Sense: Qualitative to Quantitative Translation in Jury Damage Awards. *Journal of Empirical Legal Studies* 8:120–47.

Hansmann, Henry, and Reinier Kraakman. 2002. Property, Contract, and Verification: The *Numerus Clausus* Problem and the Divisibility of Rights. *Journal of Legal Studies* 31:S373–S420.

Harpaz-Rotem, Ilan, Robert A. Rosenheck, and Rani Desai. 2006. The Mental Health of Children Exposed to Maternal Mental Illness and Homelessness. *Community Mental Health Journal* 42:437–48.

Harris, Jim W. 1996. *Property and Justice*. Oxford: Oxford University Press.

Haslam, Alexander S., Penelope J. Oakes, Craig McGarty, John C. Turner, Katherine J. Reynolds, and Rachael A. Eggins. 1996. Stereotyping and Social Influence: The Mediation of Stereotype Applicability and Sharedness by the Views of In-Group and Out-Group Members. *British Journal of Social Psychology* 35:369–97.

Hausman, Daniel M., and Brynn Welch. 2010. Debate: To Nudge or Not to Nudge? *Journal of Political Philosophy* 18:123–36.

Hegel, Georg Wilhelm Friedrich. 1967. *Hegel's Philosophy of Right*. Ed. T. M. Knox. London: Oxford University Press.

Heller, Michal, and Rick Hills. 2008. Land Assembly Districts. *Harvard Law Review* 1465–527.

Helliwell, John F., Richard Layard, and Jeffrey D. Sachs. 2018. *World Happiness Report.* http://worldhappiness.report/ed/2018/.

Helmholz, Richard H. 1983. Adverse Possession and Subjective Intent. *Washington University Law Quarterly* 61:331–58.

Hemel, Daniel Jacob, and Ethan Porter. 2016. Aligning Taxes and Spending: Theory and Experimental Evidence. Working Paper, July 12. http://ssrn.com/abstract=2807969.

Henderson-King, Eaaron I., and Richard E. Nisbett. 1996. Anti-black Prejudice as a Function of Exposure to the Negative Behavior of a Single Black Person. *Journal of Personality and Social Psychology* 71:654–64.

Herman, Daniel B., Ezra S. Susser, and Elmer L. Struening. 1998. Homelessness, Stress, and Psychopathology. In Bruce P. Dohrenwend, ed. *Adversity, Stress, and Psychopathology.* New York: Oxford University Press. 132–41.

Heyman, James E., Yesim Orhun, and Dan Ariely. 2004. Auction Fever: The Effect of Opponents and Quasi-endowment on Product Valuations. *Journal of Interactive Marketing* 18:7–21.

Hinds, Pamela J., Kathleen M. Carley, and David Krackhardt. 2000. Choosing Work Group Members: Balancing Similarity, Competence, and Familiarity. *Organizational Behavior and Human Decision Processes* 81:226–51.

Hirschman, Albert O. 1970. *Exit, Voice and Loyalty: Responses to Decline in Firms, Organizations, and States.* Cambridge, MA: Harvard University Press.

Hirsh, Elizabeth, and Christopher J. Lyons. 2010. Perceiving Discrimination on the Job: Legal Consciousness, Workplace Context, and the Construction of Racial Discrimination. *Law and Society Review* 44:269–98.

Hoffman, Elizabeth, Kevin McCabe, Keith Shachat, and Vernon Smith. 1994. Preferences, Property Rights, and Anonymity in Bargaining Games. *Games and Economic Behavior* 7:346–80.

Hoffman, Elizabeth, Kevin McCabe, and Vernon Smith. 2008. Reciprocity in Ultimatum and Dictator Games: An Introduction. In Charles R. Plott and Vernon L. Smith, eds. *Handbook of Experimental Economics Results.* Vol. 1. Amsterdam: North-Holland. 411–53.

Hoffman, Elizabeth, and Matthew Spitzer. 1993. Willingness to Pay vs. Willingness to Accept: Legal and Economic Implications. *Washington University Law Review* 71:59–114.

Hohfeld, Wesley. 1913. Some Fundamental Legal Conceptions as Applied in Judicial Reasoning. *Yale Law Journal* 23:16–59.

Holmes, Oliver Wendell. 1881. *The Common Law.* Cambridge, MA: Harvard University Press.

———. (1897) 1997. The Path of the Law. *Harvard Law Review* 110:991–1009.

Hong, Yu-Hung. 2007. Assembling Land for Urban Development: Issues and Opportunities. In Yu-Hung Hong and Barrie Needham, eds. *Analyzing Land Readjustment:*

Economics, Law, and Collective Action. Cambridge, MA: Lincoln Institute of Land Policy, 3–34.

Honoré, A. M. 1961. Ownership. In A. G. Guest, ed. *Oxford Essays in Jurisprudence*. Oxford: Clarendon Press, 107–47.

Hood, Bruce, Sandra Weltzien, Lauren Marsh, and Patricia Kanngiesser. 2016. Picture Yourself: Self-Focus and the Endowment Effect in Preschool Children. *Cognition* 152:70–77.

House, James S., Debra Umberson, and Karl R. Landis. 1988. Structures and Processes of Social Support. *Annual Review of Sociology* 14:293–318.

Huang, Yunhui, and Yin Wu. 2016. Ownership Effect Can Be a Result of Other-Derogation: Evidence from Behavioral and Electrophysiological Studies. *PloS One* 11:e0166054. doi:10.1371/journal.pone.0166054.

Hurka, Thomas. 1993. *Perfectionism*. Oxford: Oxford University Press.

Hynes, Richard M. 2006. Credit Markets, Exemptions, and Households with Nothing to Exempt. *Theoretical Inquiries in Law* 7:493–522.

Isoni, Andrea, Graham Loomes, and Robert Sugden. 2011. The Willingness to Pay–Willingness to Accept Gap, the "Endowment Effect," Subject Misconceptions, and Experimental Procedures for Eliciting Valuations: Comment. *American Economic Review* 101:991–1011.

Jacoby, Melissa B. 2007. Bankruptcy Reform and Homeownership Risk. *University of Illinois Law Review* 2007:323–46.

Janis, Irving L. 1971. Groupthink. *Psychology Today* 5:432–443.

———. 1972. *Groupthink: Psychological Studies of Policy Decisions and Fiascoes*. Boston: Houghton Mifflin.

Jefferson, Therese, and Ross Taplin. 2012. Relational Aspects of Decisions to See. *Journal of Socio-Economics* 41:697–704.

Johnson, Noel D., and Alexandra A. Mislin. 2011. Trust Games: A Meta-analysis. *Journal of Economic Psychology* 32:865–89.

Joint Center for Housing Studies of Harvard University. 2017. America's Rental Housing. www.jchs.harvard.edu/sites/default/files/harvard_jchs_americas_rental_housing_2017_0.pdf.

Jolls, Christine. 1998. Behavioral Economics Analysis of Redistributive Legal Rules. *Vanderbilt Law Review* 51:1653–78.

Jolls, Christine, and Cass R. Sunstein. 2006. Debiasing through Law. *Journal of Legal Studies* 35:199–241.

Jolls, Christine, Cass R. Sunstein, and Richard H. Thaler. 1998. A Behavioral Approach to Law and Economics. *Stanford Law Review* 50:1471–550.

Jones, Jeffrey Douglas. 2011a. Property and Personhood Revisited. *Wake Forest Journal of Law and Policy* 1(1):93–136.

———. 2011b. Property Rights, Property Wrongs, and Chattel Dispossession Under Self-Storage Leases. *Tennessee Law Review* 78:1015–50.

Kahneman, Daniel. 1992. Reference Points, Anchors, Norms, and Mixed Feelings. *Organizational Behavior and Human Decision Processes* 51:296–312.

Kahneman, Daniel, Jack L. Knetsch, and Richard H. Thaler. 1986. Fairness and the Assumptions of Economics. In Robin M. Reder and Melvin R. Hogarth, eds. *Rational Choice: The Contrast between Economics and Psychology*. Chicago: University of Chicago Press, 101–16.

———. 1990. Experimental Tests of the Endowment Effect and the Coase Theorem. *Journal of Political Economy* 98:1325–48.

———. 1991. The Endowment Effect, Loss Aversion, and Status Quo Bias. *Journal of Economic Perspectives* 5:193–206.

———. 2008. The Endowment Effect: Evidence of Losses Valued More Than Gains. In Charles R. Plott, and Vernon L. Smith, eds. *Handbook of Experimental Economics Results*. Vol. 1. Amsterdam: North-Holland. 939–55.

Kahneman, Daniel, Paul Slovic, and Amos Tversky. 1982. *Judgment under Uncertainty: Heuristics and Biases*. Cambridge: Cambridge University Press.

Kahneman, Daniel, and Amos Tversky. 1979. Prospect Theory: An Analysis of Decision under Risk. *Econometrica* 47:263–92.

———. 1982. The Psychology of Preferences. *Scientific American* 246:160–73.

———. 1984. Choices, Values, and Frames. *American Psychologist* 39:341–50.

Kaiser, Cheryl R., and Brenda Major. 2006. A Social Psychological Perspective on Perceiving and Reporting Discrimination. *Law and Social Inquiry* 31:801–30.

Kaiser, Cheryl R., and Carol T. Miller. 2001. Stop Complaining! The Social Costs of Making Attributions to Discrimination. *Personality and Social Psychology Bulletin* 27:254–63.

———. 2003. Derogating the Victim: The Interpersonal Consequences of Blaming Events on Discrimination. *Group Processes and Intergroup Relations* 6:227–37.

Kanngiesser, Patricia, Nathalia Gjersoe, and Bruce M. Hood. 2010. The Effect of Creative Labor on Property-Ownership Transfer by Preschool Children and Adults. *Psychological Science* 21:1236–41.

Kanngiesser, Patricia, and Bruce Hood. 2014. Not by Labor Alone: Considerations for Value Influence Use of the Labor Rule in Ownership Transfers. *Cognitive Science* 38:353–66.

Kaplow, Louis. 1986. An Economic Analysis of Legal Transitions. *Harvard Law Review* 99:509–617.

Kaplow, Louis, and Steven Shavell. 1994. Why the Legal System Is Less Efficient Than the Tax in Redistributing Income. *Journal of Legal Studies* 23:667–82.

———. 1996. Property Rules versus Liability Rules: An Economic Analysis. *Harvard Law Review* 109:713–90.

———. 2000. Should Legal Rules Favor the Poor? Clarifying the Role of Legal Rules and the Income Tax in Redistributing Income. *Journal of Legal Studies* 29:821–36.

———. 2001. Fairness versus Welfare. *Harvard Law Review* 114:961–1389.

Karlins, Marvin, Thomas L. Coffman, and Gary Walters. 1969. On the Fading of Social Stereotypes: Studies in Three Generations of College Students. *Journal of Personality and Social Psychology* 13:1–16.

Kassin, Saul, Steven Fein, and Hazel Rose Markus. 2008. *Social Psychology*. 7th ed. Boston: Houghton Mifflin.

Keeton, W. Page, Dan B. Dobbs, Robert E. Keeton, and David G. Owen. 1984. *Prosser and Keeton on the Law of Torts*. 5th ed. St. Paul, MN: West.

Kelly, James J., Jr. 2006. "We Shall Not Be Moved": Urban Communities, Eminent Domain and the Socioeconomics of Just Compensation. *St. John's Law Review* 80:923–90.

Kennedy, Duncan. 1987. The Effect of the Warranty of Habitability on Low Income Housing: "Milking" and Class Violence. *Florida State University Law Review* 15:485–520.

Kerner, Deborah A., Erin Driver-Linn, Timothy D. Wilson, and Daniel T. Gilbert. 2006. Loss Aversion Is an Affective Forecasting Error. *Psychological Science* 17:649–53.

Kets, Willemien, and Alvaro Sandroni. 2015. Challenging Conformity: A Case for Diversity. Working Paper, November 16. www.brown.edu/conference/nsf-decentralization/sites/brown.edu.conference.nsf-decentralization/files/uploads/13%20Diversity_2015-1115%20(1).pdf.

Klick, Jonathan, and Gregory Mitchell. 2006. Government Regulation of Irrationality: Moral and Cognitive Hazards. *Minnesota Law Review* 90:1620–63.

Kluegel, James R., and Eliot R. Smith. 1986. *Beliefs about Inequality: Americans' Views of What Is and What Ought to Be*. New York: A. de Gruyter.

Knetsch, Jack L., and J. A. Sinden. 1984. Willingness to Pay and Compensation Demanded: Experimental Evidence of an Unexpected Disparity in Measures of Value. *Quarterly Journal of Economics* 99:507–21.

Knetsch, Jack L., and Wei-Kang Wong. 2009. The Endowment Effect and the Reference State: Evidence and Manipulations. *Journal of Economic Behavior and Organization* 71:407–13.

Kogut, Tehila. 2009. Public Decisions or Private Decisions? When the Specific Case Guides Public Decisions. *Journal of Behavioral Decision Making* 22:91–100.

———. 2011. Someone to Blame: When Identifying a Victim Decreases Helping. *Journal of Experimental Social Psychology* 47:748–55.

Kogut, Tehila, and Ilana Ritov. 2005a. The "Identified Victim" Effect: An Identified Group, or Just a Single Individual? *Journal of Behavioral Decision Making* 18:157–67.

———. 2005b. The Singularity Effect of Identified Victims in Separate and Joint Evaluations. *Organizational Behavior and Human Decision Processes*. 97:106–16.

———. 2007. "One of Us": Outstanding Willingness to Help Save a Single Identified Compatriot. *Organizational Behavior and Human Decision Processes* 104:150–57.

———. 2010. The Identifiable Victim Effect: Causes and Boundary Conditions. In Daniel M. Oppenheimer and Christopher Y. Olivola, eds. *The Science of Giving: Experimental Approaches to the Study of Charity*. New York: Routledge.

Komesar, Neil K. 1973. Return to Slumville: A Critique of the Ackerman Analysis of Housing Code Enforcement and the Poor. *Yale Law Journal* 82:1175–93.

Korobkin, Russell B. 1998. The Status Quo Bias and Contract Default Rules. *Cornell Law Review* 83:608–87.

———. 2003. The Endowment Effect and Legal Analysis. *Northwestern University Law Review* 97:1227–93.

———. 2014. Wrestling with the Endowment Effect, or How to Do Law and Economics without the Coase Theorem. In Eyal Zamir and Doron Teichman, eds. *The Oxford Handbook of Behavioral Economics and the Law.* New York: Oxford University Press. 300–34.

Korobkin, Russell B., and Thomas S. Ulen. 2000. Law and Behavioral Science: Removing the Rationality Assumption from Law and Economics. *California Law Review* 88:1051–144.

Kőszegi, Botond, and Matthew Rabin. 2005. A Model of Reference-Dependent Preferences. *Quarterly Journal of Economics* 121:1133–65.

Kreiczer-Levy, Shelly. 2016. Consumption Property in the Sharing Economy. *Pepperdine Law Review* 43:61–124.

Krieger, Linda Hamilton. 1994–1995. The Content of Our Categories: A Cognitive Bias Approach to Discrimination and Equal Employment Opportunity. *Stanford Law Review* 47:1161–1248.

Krier, James E., and Stewart J. Schwab. 1995. Property Rules and Liability Rules: The Cathedral in Another Light. *New York University Law Review* 70:440–84.

Krier, James E., and Christopher Serkin. 2004. Public Ruses. *Michigan State Law Review* 2004:859–75.

Krivo, Lauren J., and Robert L. Kaufman. 2004. Housing and Wealth Inequality: Racial-Ethnic Differences in Home Equity in the United States. *Demography* 41:585–605.

Krysan, Maria. 2008. Does Race Matter in the Search for Housing? An Exploratory Study of Search Strategies, Experiences, and Locations. *Social Science Research* 37:581–603.

Krysan, Maria, Mick P. Couper, Reynolds Farley, and Tyrone Forman. 2009. Does Race Matter in Neighborhood Preferences? Results from a Video Experiment. *American Journal of Sociology* 115:527–59.

Kunda, Ziva. 1990. The Case for Motivated Reasoning. *Psychological Bulletin* 108:480–98.

Lai, Calvin K., et al. 2014. Reducing Implicit Racial Preferences: I. A Comparative Investigation of 17 Interventions. *Journal of Experimental Psychology: General* 143:1765–85.

Lai, Calvin K., et al. 2016. Reducing Implicit Racial Preferences: II. Intervention Effectiveness across Time. *Journal of Experimental Psychology: General* 145:1001–16.

Lastovicka, John L., and Nancy J. Sirianni. 2011. Truly, Madly, Deeply: Consumers in the Throes of Material Possession Love. *Journal of Consumer Research* 38:323–42.

Lawson, F. H., and Bernard Rudden. 1982. *The Law of Property.* 2nd ed. Oxford: Clarendon Press.

LeBarr, A. Nicole, and Judith M. Shedden. 2017. Psychological Ownership: The Implicit Association between Self and Already-Owned versus Newly-Owned Objects. *Consciousness and Cognition* 48:190–97.

Lee, Brian Angelo. 2013. Just Undercompensation: The Idiosyncratic Premium in Eminent Domain. *Columbia Law Review* 113:593–655.

Lefcoe, George. 2016. *Real Estate Law and Business: Brokering, Buying, Selling, and Financing Realty*. Durham, NC: Carolina Academic Press.

Leighninger, Matt. 2008. The Promise and Challenge of Neighborhood Democracy: Lessons from the Intersection of Government and Community. www.grassrootsgrantmakers.org/wp-content/uploads/2011/07/Neighborhood_Democracy_6-30-09.pdf.

Lemley, Mark A. 2012. Contracting around Liability Rules. *California Law Review* 100:463–86.

Levene, Merrick, Christina Starmans, and Ori Friedman. 2015. Creation in Judgments about the Establishment of Ownership. *Journal of Experimental Social Psychology* 60:103–09.

Levine-Schnur, Ronit, and Gideon Parchomovsky. 2016. Is the Government Fiscally Blind? An Empirical Examination of the Effect of the Compensation Requirement on Eminent Domain Exercises. *Journal of Legal Studies* 45:437–70.

Lewin-Epstein, Noah, Amit Kaplan, and Asaf Levanon. 2003. Distributive Justice and Attitudes toward the Welfare State. *Social Justice Research* 16:1–27.

Lewinsohn-Zamir, Daphna. 1996. Compensation for Injuries to Land Caused by Planning Authorities: Towards a Comprehensive Theory. *University of Toronto Law Journal* 46:47–127.

———. 1998. Consumer Preferences, Citizen Preferences and the Provision of Public Goods. *Yale Law Journal* 108:377–406.

———. 2001a. The Choice between Property Rules and Liability Rules Revisited: Critical Observations from Behavioral Studies. *Texas Law Review* 80:219–60.

———. 2001b. Contemporary Property Law Scholarship: A Comment. *Theoretical Inquiries in Law* 2:97–105.

———. 2003. The Objectivity of Well-Being and the Objectives of Property Law. *New York University Law Review* 78:1669–1754.

———. 2006. In Defense of Redistribution in Private Law. *Minnesota Law Review* 91:326–97.

———. 2008. More Is Not Better Than Less: An Exploration in Property Law. *Minnesota Law Review* 92:634–713.

———. 2009. Identifying Intense Preferences. *Cornell Law Review* 94:1391–458.

———. 2012. Taking Outcomes Seriously. *Utah Law Review* 2012:861–902.

———. 2013. Can't Buy Me Love: Monetary versus In-Kind Remedies. *University of Illinois Law Review* 2013:151–94.

———. 2014. Do the Right Thing: Indirect Remedies in Private Law. *Boston University Law Review* 94:55–103.

———. 2015. The Importance of Being Earnest: Two Notions of Internalization *University of Toronto Law Journal* 65:37–84.

Lewinsohn-Zamir, Daphna, Ilana Ritov, and Tehila Kogut. 2017. Law and Identifiability. *Indiana Law Journal* 92:505–55.

Liberman, Nira, Lorraine C. Idson, Christopher J. Camacho, and E. Tory Higgins. 1999. Promotion and Prevention Choices between Stability and Change. *Journal of Personality and Social Psychology* 77:1135–45.

Listokin, Lior, and David M. Schizer. 2013. I Like To Pay Taxes: Taxpayer Support for Government Spending and the Efficiency of the Tax System. *Tax Law Review* 66:179–216.

Locke, John. (1690) 1967. *Locke: Two Treatises of Government*. Cambridge: Cambridge University Press.

Loewenstein, George, Daylian M. Cain, and Sunita Sah. 2011. The Limits of Transparency: Pitfalls and Potential of Disclosing Conflicts of Interest. *American Economic Review: Papers and Proceedings* 101:423–28.

Loewenstein, George, and Samuel Issacharoff. 1994. Source Dependence in the Valuation of Objects. *Journal of Behavioral Decision Making* 7:157–68.

Loewenstein, George, Samuel Issacharoff, Colin Camerer, and Linda Babcock. 1993. Self-Serving Assessments of Fairness and Pretrial Bargaining. *Journal of Legal Studies* 22:135–59.

Loewenstein, George, Leigh Thompson, and Max H. Bazerman. 1989. Social Utility and Decision Making in Interpersonal Contexts. *Journal of Personality and Social Psychology* 57:426–41.

Lord, Charles G., Lee Ross, and Mark R. Lepper. 1979. Biased Assimilation and Attitude Polarization: The Effects of Prior Theories on Subsequently Considered Evidence. *Journal of Personality and Social Psychology* 37:2098–109.

Maciá, Maria M. 2016. Pinning Down Subjective Valuations: A Well-Being Analysis Approach to Eminent Domain. *University of Chicago Law Review* 83:945–99.

Macrae, Neil C., Alan B. Milne, and Gaden V. Bodenhausen. 1994. Stereotypes as Energy-Saving Devices: A Peek Inside the Cognitive Toolbox. *Journal of Personality and Social Psychology* 66:37–47.

Maddux, William M., Haiyang Yong, Carl Falk, Hajo Adam, Wendi Adair, Yumi Endo, Ziv Carmon, and Steven J. Heine. 2010. For Whom Is Parting with Possessions More Painful? Cultural Differences in the Endowment Effect. *Psychological Science* 21:1910–17.

Maio, Gregory M., Victoria M. Esses, and David W. Bell. 1994. The Formation of Attitudes toward New Immigrant Groups. *Journal of Applied Social Psychology* 24:1762–76.

Major, Brenda, and Sara S. M. Townsend. 2010. Coping with Bias. In John F. Dovidio, Miles Hewstone, Peter Glick, and Victoria M. Esses, eds. *The SAGE Handbook of Prejudice, Stereotyping, and Discrimination*. London: Sage, 410–25.

Malhotra, Naresh K. 1982. Information Load and Consumer Decision Making. *Journal of Consumer Research* 8:419–30.

Mandel, David R. 2002. Beyond Mere Ownership: Transaction Demand as a Moderator of the Endowment Effect. *Organizational Behavior and Human Decision Processes* 88:737–47.

Mandelker, Daniel R. 2003. *Land Use Law.* 5th ed. Newark, NJ: Matthew Bender.

Mannix, Elizabeth, and Margaret A. Neale. 2005. What Differences Makes a Difference? The Promise and Reality of Diverse Teams in Organizations. *Psychological Science in the Public Interest* 6(2):31–55.

Mansbridge, Jane J. 1990. *Beyond Self-Interest.* Chicago: University of Chicago Press.

Manzo, Lynne C., Rachel G. Kleit, and Dawn Couch. 2008. "Moving Three Times Is Like Having Your House on Fire Once": The Experience of Place and Impending Displacement among Public Housing Residents. *Urban Studies* 45:1855–78.

Margolis, Howard. 1982. *Selfishness, Altruism and Rationality: A Theory of Social Choice.* Cambridge: Cambridge University Press.

Markell, David, Tom Tyler, and Sarah F. Brosnan. 2012. What Has Love Got to Do with It? Sentimental Attachments and Legal Decision-Making. *Villanova Law Review* 57:209–60.

Markovits, Daniel, and Alan Schwartz. 2011. The Myth of Efficient Breach: New Defenses of the Expectation Interest. *Virginia Law Review* 97:1939–2008.

Markowitz, Ezra M., Paul Slovic, Daniel Västfjäll, and Sara D. Hodges. 2013. Compassion Fade and the Challenge of Environmental Conservation. *Judgment and Decision Making* 8:397–406.

Markus, Hazel Rose, and Shinobu Kitayama. 1991. Culture and the Self: Implications for Cognition, Emotion, and Motivation. *Psychological Review* 98:224–53.

Marzilli-Ericson, Keith M., and Andreas Fuster. 2011. Expectations as Endowments: Evidence on Reference-Dependent Preferences from Exchange and Valuation Experiments. *Quarterly Journal of Economics* 126:1879–907.

———. 2014. The Endowment Effect. *Annual Review of Economics* 6:555–79.

Maslow, Abraham H. 1970. *Motivation and Personality.* 2nd ed. New York: Harper and Row.

Massey, Douglas S., Gretchen A. Condran, and Nancy A. Denton. 1987. The Effect of Racial Segregation on Black Social and Economic Well-Being. *Social Forces* 66:29–56.

Mazar, Nina, On Amir, and Dan Ariely. 2008. The Dishonesty of Honest People: A Theory of Self-Concept Maintenance. *Journal of Marketing Research* 45:633–44.

Mazar, Nina, and Dan Ariely. 2006. Dishonesty in Everyday Life and Its Policy Implications. *Journal of Public Policy and Marketing* 25:117–26.

Mazzella, Ronald, and Alan Feingold. 1994. The Effects of Physical Attractiveness, Race, Socioeconomic Status, and Gender of Defendants and Victims on Judgments of Mock Jurors: A Meta-analysis. *Journal of Applied Social Psychology* 24:1314–38.

McAdams, Richard H. 1997. The Origin, Development, and Regulations of Norms. *Michigan Law Review* 96:338–433.

———. 2015. *The Expressive Powers of Law: Theories and Limits.* Cambridge, MA: Harvard University Press.

McCaffery, Edward J. 1994. Cognitive Theory and Tax. *UCLA Law Review* 41:1861–947.

McCaffery, Edward J., and Jonathan Baron. 2005. The Political Psychology of Redistribution. *UCLA Law Review* 52:1745–92.

McGraw, A. Peter, Philip E. Tetlock, and Orie V. Kristel. 2003. The Limits of Fungibility: Relational Schemata and the Value of Things. *Journal of Consumer Research* 30:219–29.

McPherson, Miller, Lynn Smith-Lovin, and James M. Cook. 2001. Birds of a Feather: Homophily in Social Networks. *Annual Review of Sociology* 47:414–44.

Merges, Robert P. 1994. Of Property Rules, Coase, and Intellectual Property. *Columbia Law Review* 94:2655–73.

Merrill, Thomas W. 1985. Property Rules, Liability Rules, and Adverse Possession. *Northwestern University Law Review* 79:1122–54.

———. 1998. Property and the Right to Exclude. *Nebraska Law Review* 77:730–55.

———. 2005. The Kelo Decision: Investigating Takings of Homes and Other Private Property: Hearing before the Senate Committee on the Judiciary. 109th Cong. 14–16 (statement of Thomas W. Merrill, Professor, Columbia University Law School).

Merrill, Thomas W., and Henry E. Smith. 2000. Optimal Standardization in the Law of Property: The Numerus Clausus Principle. *Yale Law Journal* 110:1–70.

———. 2007. The Morality of Property. *William and Mary Law Review* 48:1849– 96.

———. 2011. Making Coasean Property More Coasean. *Journal of Law and Economics* 54:S77–S104.

Messick, David M., and Keith P. Sentis. 1979. Fairness and Preference. *Journal of Experimental Social Psychology* 15:418–34.

Metcalf, Cherie. 2014. Property Law Culture: Public Law, Private Preferences and the Psychology of Expropriation. *Queen's Law Journal* 39:685–731.

Michelman, Frank I. 1967. Property, Utility and Fairness: Comments on the Ethical Foundations of "Just Compensation" Law. *Harvard Law Review* 80:1165–258.

———. 1988. Takings, 1987. *Columbia Law Review* 88:1600–29.

Miller, David. 1992. Distributive Justice: What the People Think. *Ethics* 102:555–93.

Molnar, Janice M., William R. Rath, and Tovah P. Klein. 1990. Constantly Compromised: The Impact of Homelessness on Children. *Journal of Social Issues* 46:109–24.

Monteith, Margo J., Leslie Ashburn-Nardo, Corrine I. Voils, and Alexander M. Czopp. 2002. Putting the Brakes on Prejudice: On the Development and Operation of Cues for Control. *Journal of Personality and Social Psychology* 83:1029–50.

Moran, Simone, and Ilana Ritov. 2002. Initial Perceptions in Negotiations: Evaluation and Response in "Logrolling" Offers. *Journal of Behavioral Decision Making* 15:101–24.

Morewedge, Carey K., and Colleen E. Giblin. 2015. Explanations of the Endowment Effect: An Integrative Review. *Trends in Cognitive Sciences* 19:339–48.

Morewedge, Carey K., Linda L. Shu, Daniel T. Gilbert, and Timothy D. Wilson. 2009. Bad Riddance or Good Rubbish? Ownership and Not Loss Aversion Causes the Endowment Effect. *Journal of Experimental Social Psychology* 45:947–51.

Morris, Madeline. 1993. The Structure of Entitlements. *Cornell Law Review* 78:822–98.

Moscovici, Serge, and Marisa Zavalloni. 1969. The Group as a Polarizer of Attitudes. *Journal of Personality and Social Psychology* 12:125–35.

Muir, William K. 1967. *Prayer in the Public Schools: Law and Attitude Change.* Chicago: University of Chicago Press.

Mukhija, Vinit, Lara Regus, Sara Slovin, and Ashok Das. 2010. Can Inclusionary Zoning Be an Effective and Efficient Housing Policy? Evidence from Los Angeles and Orange Counties. *Journal of Urban Affairs* 32:229–52.

Mullainathan, Sendhil, and Eldar Shafir. 2013. *Scarcity: Why Having Too Little Means So Much.* London: Allen Lane.

Mulvaney, Timothy M., and Joseph W. Singer. 2018. Move Along to Where? Property in Service of Democracy. In G. Muller, R. Brits, B. V. Slade, J. Van Wyk, and G. J. Pienaar, eds. *Transformative Property Law: A Tribute to André van der Walt.* Cape Town, South Africa: Juta and Co.

Murphy, Liam, and Thomas Nagel. 2002. *The Myth of Ownership: Taxes and Justice.* New York: Oxford University Press.

Myers, David G. 2000. The Funds, Friends, and Faith of Happy People. *American Psychologist* 55:61–62.

Nadler, Janice, and Shari Seidman Diamond. 2008. Eminent Domain and the Psychology of Property Rights: Proposed Use, Subjective Attachment, and Taker Identity. *Journal of Empirical Legal Studies* 5:713–49.

Nadler, Janice, Shari Seidman Diamond, and Matthew M. Patton. 2008. Government Takings of Private Property. In Nathaniel Persily, Jack Citrin, and Patrick Egan, eds. *Public Opinion and Constitutional Controversy.* New York: Oxford University Press, 286–309.

Nagin, Daniel S., and Greg Pogarsky. 2003. An Experimental Investigation of Deterrence: Cheating, Self-Serving Bias, and Impulsivity. *Criminology* 41:167–94.

Nancekivell, Shaylene E., Julia W. Van de Vondervoort, and Ori Friedman. 2013. Young Children's Understanding of Ownership. *Child Development Perspectives* 7:243–47.

Nash, Jane Gradwohl, and Robert A. Rosenthal. 2014. An Investigation of the Endowment Effect in the Context of a College Housing Lottery. *Journal of Economic Psychology* 42:74–82.

Nash, Jonathan R. 2009. Packaging Property: The Effects of Paradigmatic Framing of Property Rights. *Tulane Law Review* 83:691–734.

Nash, Jonathan R., and Stephanie M. Stern. 2010. Property Frames. *Washington University Law Review* 87:449–504.

National Association of Realtors. 2012. Social Benefits of Homeownership and Housing Stability. www.nar.realtor/sites/default/files/migration_files/social-benefits-of-stable-housing-2012-04.pdf.

———. 2018. Quick Real Estate Statistics. www.nar.realtor/research-and-statistics/quick-real-estate-statistics.

National Center for Education Statistics. 2003. National Assessment of Adult Literacy (Key Findings). https://nces.ed.gov/naal/kf_demographics.asp.

National Center for State Courts. 2015. Civil Justice Initiative: The Landscape of Civil Litigation in State Courts. www.ncsc.org/~/media/Files/PDF/Research/CivilJustice-Report-2015.ashx.

National Fair Housing Alliance. 2018. Making Every Neighborhood a Place of Opportunity: 2018 Fair Housing Trends Report. https://nationalfairhousing.org/wp-content/uploads/2018/04/NFHA-2018-Fair-Housing-Trends-Report.pdf.

National Institute of Mental Health. 2018. Major Depression. www.nimh.nih.gov/health/statistics/major-depression.shtml.

Neale, Margaret, and Max Bazerman. 1991. *Cognition and Rationality in Negotiation*. New York: Free Press.

Neale, Margaret A., Vandra L. Huber, and Gregory B. Northcraft. 1987. The Framing of Negotiations: Contextual versus Task Frames. *Organizational Behavior and Human Decision Processes* 39:228–41.

Nedelsky, Jennifer. 1990. *Private Property and the Limits of American Constitutionalism: The Madisonian Framework*. Chicago: University of Chicago Press.

———. 2011. *Law's Relations: A Relational Theory of Self, Autonomy, and Law*. Oxford: Oxford University Press.

Nelson, Robert H. 2006. New Community Associations for Established Neighborhoods. *Review of Policy Research* 23:1123–41.

Nesselroade, K. Paul, Jr., James K. Beggan, and Scott T. Allison. 1999. Possession Enhancement in an Interpersonal Context: An Extension of the Mere Ownership Effect. *Psychology and Marketing* 16:21–34.

Nickerson, Raymond S. 1998. Confirmation Bias: A Ubiquitous Phenomenon in Many Guises. *Review of General Psychology* 2:175–220.

Nimmer, Melville B., and David Nimmer. 2017. *Nimmer on Copyright: A Treatise on the Law of Literary, Musical and Artistic Property, and the Protection of Ideas*. New York: Bender.

Nordgren, Loran F., and Mary-Hunter Morris McDonnell. 2011. The Scope-Severity Paradox: Why Doing More Harm Is Judged to Be Less Harmful. *Social Psychological and Personality Science* 2:97–102.

Norton, Michael I., Daniel Mochon, and Dan Ariely. 2012. The IKEA Effect: When Labor Leads to Love. *Journal of Consumer Psychology* 22:453–60.

Novemsky, Nathan, and Daniel Kahneman. 2005a. The Boundaries of Loss Aversion. *Journal of Marketing Research* 42:119–28.

———. 2005b. How Do Intentions Affect Loss Aversion? *Journal of Marketing Research* 42:139–40.

Nussbaum, Martha. 2011. *Creating Capabilities: The Human Development Approach*. Cambridge, MA: Harvard University Press.

Nussbaum, Martha, and Amartya Sen. 1993. *The Quality of Life*. Oxford: Clarendon Press.

O'Bryant, Shirley. 1982. The Value of Home to Older Persons: Relationship to Housing Satisfaction. *Research on Aging* 4:349–63.

Oishi, Shigehiro. 2010. The Psychology of Residential Mobility: Implications for the Self, Social Relationships, and Well-Being. *Perspectives on Psychological Science* 5:5–21.

Oliveri, Rigel C. 2010. Discriminatory Housing Advertisements On-Line: Lessons from Craigslist. *Indiana Law Review* 43:1125–83.

———. 2015. Beyond Disparate Impact: How the Fair Housing Movement Can Move On. *Washburn Law Journal* 54:625–47.

Orth, John V. 1997. Tenancy by the Entirety: The Strange Career of the Common-Law Marital Estate. *BYU Law Review* 1997:35–49.

Ortona, Guido, and Francesco Scacciati. 1992. New Experiments on the Endowment Effect. *Journal of Economic Psychology* 13:277–96.

Ostrom, Elinor. 2010. Beyond Markets and States: Polycentric Governance of Complex Economic Systems. *American Economic Review* 100:641–72.

Palamar, Max, Doan T. Le, and Ori Friedman. 2012. Acquiring Ownership and Attribution of Responsibility. *Cognition* 124:201–08.

Pappas, Michael. 2016. Singled Out. *Maryland Law Review* 76:122–68.

Parchomovsky, Gideon, and Peter Siegelman. 2004. Selling Mayberry: Communities and Individuals in Law and Economics. *California Law Review* 92:75–146.

Parchomovsky, Gideon, Peter Siegelman, and Steve Thel. 2007. Of Equal Wrongs and Half Rights. *New York University Law Review* 82:738–89.

Peck, Joann, Victor A. Barger, and Andrea Webb. 2013. In Search of a Surrogate for Touch: The Effect of Haptic Imagery on Perceived Ownership. *Journal of Consumer Psychology* 23:189–96.

Peck, Joann, and Suzanne B. Shu. 2009. The Effect of Mere Touch on Perceived Ownership. *Journal of Consumer Research* 36:434–47.

Peñalver, Eduardo M., and Sonia K. Katyal. 2007. Property Outlaws. *University of Pennsylvania Law Review* 155:1095–186.

Penner, James E. 1996. The Bundle of Rights Picture of Property. *UCLA Law Review* 43:711–820.

Pettigrew, Thomas F. 1958. Personality and Sociocultural Factors in Intergroup Attitudes: A Cross-National Comparison. *Journal of Conflict Resolution* 2:29–42.

Pettigrew, Thomas F., and Linda R. Tropp. 2006. A Meta-Analytic Test of Intergroup Contact Theory. *Journal of Personality and Social Psychology* 90:751–83.

Pevalin, D.J. 2009. Housing Repossessions, Evictions and Common Mental Illness in the UK: Results from a Household Panel Study. *Journal of Epidemiology and Community Health* 63:949–51.

Pew Research Center. 2011. Wealth Gaps Rise to Record Highs between Whites, Blacks and Hispanics. www.pewresearch.org/wp-content/uploads/sites/3/2011/07/SDT-Wealth-Report_7-26-11_FINAL.pdf.

Pi, Daniel, Francesco Parisi, and Barbara Luppi. 2014. Biasing, Debiasing, and the Law. In Eyal Zamir and Doron Teichman, eds. *The Oxford Handbook of Behavioral Economics and the Law*. Oxford: Oxford University Press, 143–66.

Piaget, Jean. 2002. *The Language and Thought of the Child*. 3rd ed. New York: Routledge Classics.

Pierce, Jon L., Tatiana Kostova, and Kurt T. Dirks. 2001. Toward a Theory of Psychological Ownership in Organizations. *Academy of Management Review* 26:298–310.

———. 2003. The State of Psychological Ownership: Integrating and Extending a Century of Research. *Review of General Psychology* 7:84–107.

Pizzi, William T., Irene V. Blair, and Charles M. Judd. 2005. Discrimination in Sentencing on the Basis of Afrocentric Features. *Michigan Journal of Race and Law* 10:327–53.

Plott, Charles R., and Kathryn Zeiler. 2005. The Willingness to Pay–Willingness to Accept Gap, the "Endowment Effect," Subject Misconceptions, and Experimental Procedures for Eliciting Valuations. *American Economic Review* 95:530–45.

———. 2007. Exchange Asymmetries Incorrectly Interpreted as Evidence of Endowment Effect Theory and Prospect Theory? *American Economic Review* 97:1449–66.

Polinsky, A. Mitchell. 2011. *An Introduction to Law and Economics*. 4th ed. New York: Wolters Kluwer Law and Business.

Polites, Greta L., and Elena Karahanna. 2012. Shackled to the Status Quo: The Inhibiting Effects of Incumbent System Habit, Switching Costs, and Inertia on New System Acceptance. *MIS Quarterly* 36:21–42.

Pollack, Craig Evan, and Julia Lynch. 2009. Health Status of People Undergoing Foreclosure in the Philadelphia Region. *American Journal of Public Health* 99:1833–39.

Posner, Eric A., and E. Glen Weyl. 2017. Property Is Only Another Name for Monopoly. *Journal of Legal Analysis* 9:51–123.

Posner, Richard A. 2009. Let Us Never Blame a Contract Breaker. *Michigan Law Review* 107:1349–64.

———. 2014. *Economic Analysis of Law*. 9th ed. New York: Wolters Kluwer Law and Business.

Powell, Benjamin, and Edward Stringman. 2005. "The Economies of Inclusionary Zoning Reclaimed": How Effective Are Price Controls? *Florida State University Law Review* 33:471–99.

Prentice, Deborah A. 1987. Psychological Correspondence of Possessions, Attitudes, and Values. *Journal of Personality and Social Psychology* 53:993–1003.

Primus, Richard A. 2003. Equal Protection and Disparate Impact: Round Three. *Harvard Law Review* 117:494–587.

Proshansky, Harold M., Abbe K. Fabian, and Robert Kaminoff. 1983. Place-Identity: Physical World Socialization of the Self. *Journal of Environmental Psychology* 3:57–83.

Putnam, Robert D. 2000. *Bowling Alone: The Collapse and Revival of American Community*. New York: Simon and Schuster.

Quinn, Diane M., Rachel W. Kallen, and Steven J. Spencer. 2010. Stereotype Threat. In John F. Dovidio, Miles Hewstone, Peter Glick, and Victoria M. Esses, eds. *The SAGE Handbook of Prejudice, Stereotyping, and Discrimination*. London: Sage, 379–95.

Rabin, Edward H. 1984. The Revolution in Residential Landlord-Tenant Law: Causes and Consequences. *Cornell Law Review* 69:517–84.

Rachlinski, Jeffrey J., and Forest Jourden. 1998. Remedies and the Psychology of Ownership. *Vanderbilt Law Review* 51:1541–82.

Radin, Margaret J. 1982. Property and Personhood. *Stanford Law Review* 34:957–1016.

———. 1986. Residential Rent Control. *Philosophy and Public Affairs* 15:350–80.

———. 1987. Market-Inalienability. *Harvard Law Review* 100:1849–937.

———. 1988. The Liberal Conception of Property: Cross Currents in the Jurisprudence of Takings. *Columbia Law Review* 88:1667–96.

———. 1991. Diagnosing the Takings Problem. In John W. Chapman, ed. *Nomos XXXIII: Compensatory Justice*. New York: NYU Press, 248–78.

Rawls, John. 1993. *Political Liberalism*. New York: Columbia University Press.

Reb, Jochen, and Terry Connolly. 2007. Possession, Feelings of Ownership and the Endowment Effect. *Judgment and Decision Making* 2:107–14.

Reich, Charles. 1964. The New Property. *Yale Law Journal* 73:733–87.

Richins, Marsha L. 1994. Valuing Things: The Public and Private Meanings of Possessions. *Journal of Consumer Research* 21:504–21.

Ricketson, Sam, and Jane C. Ginsburg. 2006. *International Copyright and Neighbouring Rights: The Berne Convention and Beyond*. 2nd ed. New York: Oxford University Press.

Rigamonti, Cyrill P. 2006. Deconstructing Moral Rights. *Harvard International Law Journal* 7:353–412.

Rinne, Ulf. 2014. Anonymous Job Applications and Hiring Discrimination. https://wol.iza.org/uploads/articles/48/pdfs/anonymous-job-applications-and-hiring-discrimination.pdf.

Ritov, Ilana, and Jonathan Baron. 1990. Reluctance to Vaccinate: Omission Bias and Ambiguity. *Journal of Behavioral Decision Making* 3:263–77.

———. 1992. Status-Quo and Omission Biases. *Journal of Risk and Uncertainty* 5:49–61.

Ritov, Ilana, and Tehila Kogut. 2011. Ally or Adversary: The Effect of Identifiability in Inter-group Conflict Situations. *Organizational Behavior and Human Decision Processes* 116:96–103.

Ritov, Ilana, and Eyal Zamir. 2014. Affirmative Action and Other Group Tradeoff Policies: Identifiability of Those Adversely Affected. *Organizational Behavior and Human Decision Processes* 125:50–60.

Rivera, Ryan P. 2004. State Homestead Exemptions and Their Effect on Federal Bankruptcy Laws. *Real Property, Probate and Trust Journal* 39:71–106.

Rivlin, Alice M. 1989. The Continuing Search for a Popular Tax. *American Economic Review* 79:113–17.

Robbennolt, Jennifer K. 2006. Apologies and Settlement Levers. *Journal of Empirical Legal Studies* 3:333–73.

Roberts, Jennifer, Robert Hodgson, and Paul Dolan. 2011. It's Driving Her Mad: Gender Differences in the Effects of Commuting on Psychological Well-Being. *Journal of Health Economics* 30:1064–76.

Rohan, Patrick J., Bernard H. Goldstein, and Charles S. Bobis. 2018. *Real Estate Broker-age Law and Practice*. Vol. 10. New York: Matthew Bender.

Root, William C. 2002. Man's Best Friend: Property or Family Member—An Examination of the Legal Classification of Companion Animals and Its Impact on Damages Recoverable for Their Wrongful Death or Injury. *Villanova Law Review* 47:423–50.

Roschk, Holger, and Katja Gelbrich. 2014. Identifying Appropriate Compensation Types for Service Failures: A Meta-analytic and Experimental Analysis. *Journal of Service Research* 17:195–211.

Rose, Carol M. 1985. Possession as the Origin of Property. *University of Chicago Law Review* 52:73–88.

———. 2000. Left Brain, Right Brain and History in the New Law and Economics of Property. *Oregon Law Review* 79:417–92.

———. 2015. The Law Is Nine-Tenths of Possession: An Adage Turned on Its Head. In Yun-chien Chang, ed. *Law and Economics of Possession*. Cambridge: Cambridge University Press, 40–64.

Rose-Ackerman, Susan. 1985. Inalienability and the Theory of Property Rights. *Columbia Law Review* 85:931–69.

Rossano, Federico, Hannes Rakoczy, and Michael Tomasello. 2011. Young Children's Understanding of Violations of Property Rights. *Cognition* 121:219–27.

Roster, Catherine A., Joseph R. Ferrari, and M. Peter Jurkat. 2016. The Dark Side of Home: Assessing Possession "Clutter" on Subjective Well-Being. *Journal of Environmental Psychology* 46:32–41.

Roth, Alvin E. 1995. Bargaining Experiments. In *The Handbook of Experimental Economics*, John H. Kagel and Alvin E. Roth, eds. Princeton, NJ: Princeton University Press. 253–348.

Rudmin, Floyd W., and J. W. Berry. 1987. Semantics of Ownership: A Free-Recall Study of Property. *Psychological Record* 37:257–68.

Rutherglen, George. 1987. Disparate Impact under Title VII: An Objective Theory of Discrimination. *Virginia Law Review* 73:1297–345.

Sabin, Janice A., and Anthony G. Greenwald. 2012. The Influence of Implicit Bias on Treatment Recommendations for 4 Common Pediatric Conditions: Pain, Urinary Tract Infections, Attention Deficit Hyperactivity Disorder, and Asthma. *American Journal of Public Health* 102:988–95.

Sah, Sunita. 2017. Policy Solutions to Conflicts of Interest: The Value of Professional Norms. *Behavioral Public Policy* 1:177–89.

Sah, Sunita, and George Loewenstein. 2010. Effect of Reminders of Personal Sacrifice and Suggested Rationalizations on Residents' Self-Reported Willingness to Accept Gifts. *Journal of the American Medical Association* 304:1204–11.

———. 2012. More Affected = More Neglected: Amplification of Bias in Advice to the Unidentified and Many. *Social Psychological and Personality Science* 3:365–72.

———. 2014. Nothing to Declare: Mandatory and Voluntary Disclosure Leads Advisors to Avoid Conflicts of Interest. *Psychological Science* 25:575–84.

Sah, Sunita, George Loewenstein, and Daylian M. Cain. 2013. The Burden of Disclosure: Increased Compliance with Distrusted Advice. *Journal of Personality and Social Psychology* 104:289–304.

The Saint Index Poll, Oct.–Nov. 2005. Center for Economic and Civic Opinion at the University of Massachusetts/Lowell.

Salcioglu, Ebru, Metin Başoğlu, and Maria Livanou. 2008. Psychosocial Determinants of Relocation in Survivors of the 1999 Earthquake in Turkey. *The Journal of Nervous and Mental Disease*. 196:55–61.

Sampson, Robert J. 1988. Local Friendship Ties and Community Attachment in Mass Society: A Multi-level Systemic Model. *American Sociological Review* 53:766–79.

Sampson, Robert J., and Stephen W. Raudenbush. 2004. Seeing Disorder: Neighborhood Stigma and the Social Construction of "Broken Windows." *Social Psychology Quarterly* 67:319–42.

Samuelson, William, and Richard Zeckhauser. 1988. Status Quo Bias in Decision Making. *Journal of Risk and Uncertainty* 1:7–59.

Sanchirico, Chris William. 2017. Optimal Redistributional Instruments in Law and Economics. In Francesco Parisi, ed. *The Oxford Handbook of Law and Economics*. Vol. 1, *Methodology and Concepts*. Oxford: Oxford University Press, 321–54.

Sarstedt, Marko, Doreen Neubert, and Kati Barth. 2016. The IKEA Effect. A Conceptual Replication. *Journal of Marketing Behavior* 2:307–12.

Sax, Joseph L. 1964. Takings and the Police Power. *Yale Law Journal* 74:36–76.

Schlenker, Barry R., David W. Dlugolecki, and Kevin Doherty. 1994. The Impact of Self-Presentations on Self-Appraisals and Behavior: The Power of Public Commitment. *Personality and Social Psychology Bulletin* 20:20–33.

Schmidt-Eichstaedt, Gerd. 2010. The Federal Republic of Germany. In Rachelle Alterman, ed. *Takings International: A Comparative Perspective on Land Use Regulations and Compensation Rights*. Chicago: American Bar Association Publishing, 271–92.

Schnably, Stephen J. 1993. A Critique of Radin's Theory of Property and Personhood. *Stanford Law Review* 45:347–407.

Schnidman, Frank. 1988. Land Readjustment: An Alternative to Development Exactions. In Rachelle Alterman, ed., *Private Supply of Public Services: Evaluation of Real Estate Exactions, Linkage, and Alternative Land Policies*. New York: NYU Press, 250–63.

Schoshinski, Robert S. 1980. *American Law of Landlord and Tenant*. Rochester, NY: Lawyers Cooperative Publishing.

Schwartz, Bryan P., and Melanie R. Bueckert. 2010. Canada. In Rachelle Alterman, ed. *Takings International: A Comparative Perspective on Land Use Regulations and Compensation Rights*. Chicago: American Bar Association Publishing, 93–106.

Schwemm, Robert G. 2001. Discriminatory Housing Statements and Section 3604(c): A New Look at the Fair Housing Act's Most Intriguing Provision. *Fordham Urban Law Journal* 29:187–316.

———. 2018. *Housing Discrimination: Law and Litigation*. Eagan, MN: Thomson Reuters.

Sechrist, Gretchen B., and Charles Stangor. 2001. Perceived Consensus Influences Intergroup Behavior and Stereotype Accessibility. *Journal of Personality and Social Psychology* 80:645–54.

Sen, Amartya. 1984. *Resources, Values and Development*. Cambridge, MA: Harvard University Press.

———. 1992. *Inequality Reexamined*. Cambridge, MA: Harvard University Press.

———. 2005. Human Rights and Capabilities. *Journal of Human Development* 6:151–66.

Sen, Sankar, and Eric J. Johnson. 1997. Mere-Possession Effects without Possession in Consumer Choice. *Journal of Consumer Research* 24:105–17.

Serkin, Christopher. 2005. The Meaning of Value: Assessing Just Compensation for Regulatory Takings. *Northwestern University Law Review* 99:677–742.

———. 2006. Big Differences for Small Governments: Local Governments and the Takings Clause. *New York University Law Review* 81:1624–98.

———. 2009. Existing Uses and the Limits of Land Use Regulations. *New York University Law Review* 84:1222–91.

———. 2016. *The Law of Property*. 2nd ed. St. Paul, MN: Foundation Press.

Shapiro, Scott, and Edward F. McClennen. 1998. Law-and-Economics from a Philosophical Perspective. In Peter Newman, ed. *The New Palgrave Dictionary of Economics and the Law*. Vol. 2. New York: Macmillan Reference. 460–65.

Shapiro, Thomas M. 2006. Race, Homeownership and Wealth. *Washington University Journal of Law and Policy* 20:53–74.

Sharot, Tali. 2011. The Optimism Bias. *Current Biology* 21:R941–45.

Shavell, Steven. 2004. *Foundations of Economic Analysis of Law*. Cambridge, MA: Harvard University Press.

———. 2006. Specific Performance versus Damages for Breach of Contract: An Economic Analysis. *Texas Law Review* 84:831–76.

Shaw, Alex, Vivian Li, and Kristina R. Olson. 2012. Children Apply Principles of Physical Ownership to Ideas. *Cognitive Science* 36:1383–403.

Sheehan, John. 2010. Australia. In Rachelle Alterman, ed. *Takings International: A Comparative Perspective on Land Use Regulations and Compensation Rights*. Chicago: American Bar Association Publishing, 107–18.

Sherif, Muzafer, O. J. Harvey, Jack White, William R. Hood, and Carolyn W. Sherif. 1961. *Intergroup Conflict and Cooperation: The Robbers Cave Experiment*. Norman, OK: University Book Exchange.

Sherif, Muzafer, and Carolyn Sherif. 1953. *Groups in Harmony and Tension*. New York: Harper Brothers.

Sherman, Robert J. 1995. The Visual Artists Rights Act 1990: American Artists Burned Again. *Cardozo Law Review* 17:373–430.

Shiffrin, Richard M., and Robert M. Nosofsky. 1994. Seven Plus or Minus Two: A Commentary on Capacity Limitations. *Psychological Review* 101:357–61.

Shih, Margaret, Todd L. Pittinsky, and Nalini Ambady. 1999. Stereotype Susceptibility: Identity Salience and Shifts in Quantitative Performance. *Psychological Science* 10:80–83.

Shu, Lisa S., Nina Mazar, Francesco Gino, Dan Ariely, and Max H. Bazerman. 2012. Signing at the Beginning Makes Ethics Salient and Decreases Dishonest Self-Reports in Comparison to Signing at the End. *Proceedings of the National Academy of Sciences* 109:15197–200.

Shu, Suzanne B., and Joann Peck. 2011. Psychological Ownership and Affective Reaction: Emotional Attachment Process Variables and the Endowment Effect. *Journal of Consumer Psychology* 21:439–52.

Simon, Herbert A. 1955. A Behavioral Model of Rational Choice. *Quarterly Journal of Economics* 69:99–118.

———. 1957. *Models of Man: Social and Rational*. New York: Wiley.

———. 1978. Rationality as Process and as Product of Thought. *American Economic Review* 68:1–16.

Simon, Ruth. 2008. Consumer Groups Push Tax Relief for Homeowners in Bailout. *Wall Street Journal*, September 27.

Simons, Daniel J., and Christopher M. Chabris. 1999. Gorillas in Our Midst: Sustained Inattentional Blindness for Dynamic Events. *Perception* 28:1059–74.

Simonson, Itamar, and Aimee Drolet. 2004. Anchoring Effects on Consumers' Willingness-to-Pay and Willingness-to-Accept. *Journal of Consumer Research* 31:681–90.

Singer, Joseph W. 2000. *Entitlement: The Paradoxes of Property*. New Haven, CT: Yale University Press.

———. 2017. *Property*. 5th ed. New York: Wolters Kluwer.

Skinner, B. F. 1974. *About Behaviorism*. New York: Alfred A. Knopf.

Slovic, Paul. 1995. The Construction of Preference. *American Psychologist* 50:364–71.

———. 2000. *The Perception of Risk*. New York: Taylor and Francis.

Small, Deborah A., and George Loewenstein. 2003. Helping *a* Victim or Helping *the* Victim: Altruism and Identifiability. *Journal of Risk and Uncertainty* 26:5–16.

———. 2005. The Devil You Know: The Effects of Identifiability on Punishment. *Journal of Behavioral Decision Making* 18:311–18.

Small, Deborah A., George Loewenstein, and Paul Slovic. 2007. Sympathy and Callousness: The Impact of Deliberative Thought on Donations to Identifiable and Statistical Victims. *Organizational Behavior and Human Decision Processes* 102:143–53.

Smith, Eliot R., and Diane M. Mackie. 2000. *Social Psychology*. 2nd ed. New York: Psychology Press.

Smith, Henry E. 2002. Exclusion versus Governance: Two Strategies for Delineating Property Rights. *Journal of Legal Studies* 31:453–87.

———. 2004. Property and Property Rules. *New York University Law Review* 79:1719–98.

———. 2012. Property as the Law of Things. *Harvard Law Review* 125:1691–726.

Smith, Stanley K., Stefan Rayer, and Eleanor A. Smith. 2008. Aging and Disability: Implications for the Housing Industry and Housing Policy in the United States. *Journal of the American Planning Association* 74:289–306.

Snyder, Mark, and Nancy Cantor. 1998. Understanding Personality and Social Behavior: A Functionalist Strategy. In Daniel T. Gilbert, Susan T. Fiske, and Gardner Linzey, eds. *The Handbook of Social Psychology*. Boston: McGraw-Hill, 635–79.

Somin, Ilya. 2009. The Limits of Backlash: Assessing the Political Response to *Kelo*. *Minnesota Law Review* 93:2100–78.

Sommers, Samuel R. 2006. On Racial Diversity and Group Decision Making: Identifying Multiple Effects of Racial Composition on Jury Deliberations. *Journal of Personality and Social Psychology* 90:597–612.

Spader, Jonathan, and Shannon Rieger. 2017. Patterns and Trends of Residential Integration in the United States since 2000. *Harvard Joint Center for Housing Studies Research Brief*. www.jchs.harvard.edu/sites/default/files/09192017_spader-rieger_integration_brief.pdf.

Spencer, Steven J., Claude M. Steele, and Diane M. Quinn. 1999. Stereotype Threat and Women's Math Performance. *Journal of Experimental Social Psychology* 35:4–28.

Stake, Jeffrey E. 2001. The Uneasy Case for Adverse Possession. *Georgetown Law Journal* 89:2419–74.

Stangor, Charles, Gretchen B. Sechrist, and John T. Jost. 2001. Changing Racial Beliefs by Providing Consensus Information. *Personality and Social Psychology Bulletin* 27:486–96.

Stangor, Charles, Janet K. Swim, Gretchen B. Sechrist, Jamie DeCoster, Katherine L. Van Allen, and Alison Ottenbreit. 2003. Ask, Answer, and Announce: Three Stages in Perceiving and Responding to Discrimination. *European Review of Social Psychology* 14:277–311.

Stangor, Charles, Janet K. Swim, Katherine L. Van Allen, and Gretchen B. Sechrist. 2002. Reporting Discrimination in Public and Private Contexts. *Journal of Personality and Social Psychology* 82:69–74.

Statista. 2018. Volume of Commercial Real Estate Transactions Completed in the United States from 2001 to 2016. www.statista.com/statistics/797653/volume-of-commercial-real-estate-transactions-completed-usa/.

Steele, Claude M., and Joshua Aronson. 1995. Stereotype Threat and the Intellectual Test Performance of African Americans. *Journal of Personality and Social Psychology* 69:797–811.

Steinbeck, John. (1939) 1992. *The Grapes of Wrath*. New York: Penguin Classics.

Steinglass, Peter, and Ellen Gerrity. 1990. Forced Displacement to a New Environment. In Joseph D. Noshpitz and R. Dean Coddington, eds. *Stressors and the Adjustment Disorders*. New York: Wiley.

Sterk, Stewart E. 1987. Neighbors in American Land Law. *Columbia Law Review* 87:55–104.

———. 2004. The Federalist Dimension of Regulatory Takings Jurisprudence. *Yale Law Journal* 114:203–71.

Stern, Shai. 2016. Just Remedies. *Rutgers University Law Review* 68:719–61.

Stern, Stephanie M. 2005. Temporal Dynamics of Disclosure: The Example of Residential Real Estate Conveyancing. *Utah Law Review* 2005:57–95.

———. 2006. Encouraging Conservation of Private Lands: A Behavioral Analysis of Financial Incentives. *Arizona Law Review* 48:541–84.

———. 2009. Residential Protectionism and the Legal Mythology of Home. *Michigan Law Review* 107:1093–144.

———. 2010. The Inviolate Home: Housing Exceptionalism in the Fourth Amendment. *Cornell Law Review* 95:905–56.

———. 2011. Reassessing the Citizen Virtues of Homeownership. *Columbia Law Review* 111:890–938.

———. 2013. The Dark Side of Town: The Social Capital Revolution in Residential Property. *Virginia Law Review* 99:811–77.

———. 2016. Outpsyched: The Battle of Expertise in Psychology-Informed Law. *Jurimetrics* 57:45–80.

———. 2017. Behavioral Leasing: Renter Equity as an Intermediate Housing Form. In Lee Anne Fennell and Benjamin J. Keys, eds. *Evidence and Innovation in Housing Law and Policy*. Cambridge: Cambridge University Press, 177–202.

———. 2019. A Social Norm Theory of Regulating Housing Speech under the Fair Housing Act. *Missouri Law Review* 84:435–79.

———. Forthcoming. Rent Control Sharing. *Law and Ethics of Human Rights*. Vol. 13.

Stevenson, Sarah J. 1998. Banking on TDRs: The Government's Role as Banker of Transferable Development Rights. *New York University Law Review* 73:1329–76.

Stoebuck, William B., and Dale A. Whitman. 2000. *The Law of Property*. 3rd ed. St. Paul, MN: West.

Strahilevitz, Lior J. 2005. The Right to Destroy. *Yale Law Journal* 114:781–854.

Strahilevitz, Michal A., and George Loewenstein. 1998. The Effect of Ownership History on the Valuation of Objects. *Journal of Consumer Research* 25:276–89.

Strother, Logan. 2016. Beyond *Kelo*: An Experimental Study of Public Opposition to Eminent Domain. *Journal of Law and Courts* 4:339–75.

Stutzer, Alois, and Bruno S. Frey. 2008. Stress That Doesn't Pay: The Commuting Paradox. *Scandinavian Journal of Economics* 110:339–66.

———. 2012. Recent Developments in the Economics of Happiness: A Selective Overview. IZA Discussion Paper No. 7078. http://ftp.iza.org/dp7078.pdf.

Sunstein, Cass R. 1986. Legal Interference with Private Preferences. *University of Chicago Law Review* 53:1129–74.

———. 2000a. Deliberative Trouble? Why Groups Go to Extremes. *Yale Law Journal* 110:71–119.

———. 2000b. Introduction. In Cass R. Sunstein, ed. *Behavioral Law and Economics*. New York: Cambridge University Press. 1–10.

———. 2002. Switching the Default Rule. *New York University Law Review* 77:106–34.

———. 2003. Hazardous Heuristics. *University of Chicago Law Review* 70:751–82.

Sunstein, Cass R., David Schkade, Daniel Kahneman, and Ilana Ritov. 2002. Predictably Incoherent Judgments. *Stanford Law Review* 54:1153–215.

Tajfel, Henri, and John Turner. 1986. The Social Identity of Intergroup Behavior. In Stephen Worchel and William G. Austin, eds. *Psychology of Intergroup Relations.* Chicago: Nelson Hall. 7–24.

Tarlock, Dan A. 2017. *Law of Water Rights and Resources.* Eagan, MN: Thomson Reuters.

Taylor, Garth D., Paul B. Sheatsley, and Andrew M. Greeley. 1978. Attitudes toward Racial Integration. *Scientific American* 238:42–49.

Taylor, Shelly E. 1989. *Positive Illusions: Creative Self-Deception and the Healthy Mind.* New York: Basic Books.

Teichman, Meir, and Uriel G. Foa. 1975. Effect of Resources Similarity on Satisfaction with Exchange. *Social Behavior and Personality* 3:213–24.

Temkin, Larry S. 1993. *Inequality.* New York: Oxford University Press.

Tenbrunsel, Ann E., and David M. Messick. 1999. Sanctioning Systems, Decision Frames, and Cooperation. *Administrative Science Quarterly* 44:684–707.

———. 2004. Ethical Fading: The Role of Self-Deception in Unethical Behavior. *Social Justice Research* 17:223–36.

Terry, Deborah J., and Michael Hogg. 1996. Group Norms and the Attitude-Behavior Relationship: A Role for Group Identification. *Personality and Social Psychology Bulletin* 22:776–93.

Thaler, Richard H. 1992. *The Winner's Curse: Paradoxes and Anomalies of Economic Life.* Princeton, NJ: Princeton University Press.

———. 2000. Mental Accounting Matters. In *Choices, Values, and Frames.* Daniel Kahneman and Amos Tversky, eds. New York: Cambridge University Press. 241–68.

Thaler, Richard H., and Cass R. Sunstein. 2008. *Nudge: Improving Decisions about Health, Wealth, and Happiness.* New Haven, CT: Yale University Press.

Thibaut, John, and Laurens Walker. 1975. *Procedural Justice: A Psychological Analysis.* Hillsdale, NJ: Erlbaum.

Thomas, David A. 2018. *Thompson on Real Property.* Vol. 4. New York: Michie.

Thompson, Barton, and Paul Goldstein. 2014. *Thompson and Goldstein's Property Law: Ownership, Use, and Conservation.* 2nd ed. New York: Foundation Press.

Tian, Kelly, and Russell W. Belk. 2005. Extended Self and Possessions in the Workplace. *Journal of Consumer Research* 32:297–310.

Tom, Gail, Stephanie Lopez, and Kivilcim Demir. 2006. A Comparison of the Effect of Retail Purchase and Direct Marketing on the Endowment Effect. *Psychology and Marketing* 23:1–10.

Tor, Avishalom, and Dotan Oliar. 2002. Incentives to Create under a "Lifetime-Plus-Years" Copyright Duration: Lessons from a Behavioral Economic Analysis of Eldred V. Ashcroft. *Loyola of Los Angeles Law Review* 36:437–92.

Tullock, Gordon. 1967. The Welfare Costs of Tariffs, Monopolies, and Theft. *Western Economic Journal* 5:224–32.

Turner, John C. 1987. *Rediscovering the Social Group: A Self-Categorization Theory.* Cambridge, MA: Blackwell.

Tur-Sinai, Ofer. 2011. The Endowment Effect in IP Transactions: The Case against Debiasing. *Michigan Telecommunications and Technology Law Review* 18:117–69.

Tversky, Amos, and Daniel Kahneman. 1974. Judgment under Uncertainty: Heuristics and Biases. *Science* 185 (4157): 1125–31.

———. 1979. Prospect Theory: An Analysis of Decision under Risk. *Econometrica* 47:263–92.

———. 1982. The Psychology of Preferences. *Scientific American* 246:160–73.

———. 1984. Choice, Values, and Frames. *American Psychologist* 39:341–50.

———. 1986. Rational Choice and the Framing of Decisions. *Journal of Business* 59:S251–78.

Tyler, Tom R. 1988. What Is Procedural Justice? Criteria Used by Citizens to Assess the Fairness of Legal Procedures. *Law and Society Review* 22:103–36.

———. 1989. The Psychology of Procedural Justice: A Test for the Group-Value Model. *Journal of Personality and Social Psychology* 57:830–38.

———. 2000. Social Justice: Outcome and Procedure. *International Journal of Psychology* 35:117–25.

———. 2006. *Why Do People Obey the Law*. Princeton, NJ: Princeton University Press.

Tyler, Tom R., and Jonathan Jackson. 2013. Popular Legitimacy and the Exercise of Legal Authority: Motivating Compliance, Cooperation and Engagement. *Psychology, Public Policy, and Law* 20:78–95.

Tyler, Tom R., and E. Allan Lind. 1988. *The Social Psychology of Procedural Justice*. New York: Plenum Press.

Uhlmann, Eric Luis, and Luke (Lei) Zhu. 2013. Money Is Essential: Ownership Intuitions Are Linked to Physical Currency. *Cognition* 127:220–29.

Ulen, Thomas S. 1984. The Efficiency of Specific Performance: Toward a Unified Theory of Contract Remedies. *Michigan Law Review* 83:341–403.

US Census Bureau. 2018. Quarterly Residential Vacancies and Homeownership, Second Quarter 2018. www.census.gov/housing/hvs/files/currenthvspress.pdf.

US Courts. 2016. Federal Judicial Caseload Statistics 2016. www.uscourts.gov/statistics-reports/federal-judicial-caseload-statistics-2016.

Van Boven, Leaf, and Thomas Gilovich. 2003. To Do or to Have? That Is the Question. *Journal of Personality and Social Psychology* 85:1193–1202.

Vanderbilt, Tom. 2005. Self-Storage Nation. *Slate*, July 18. https://slate.com/culture/2005/07/self-storage-in-america.html.

van Dijk, Eric, and Daan van Knippenberg. 1996. Buying and Selling Exchange Goods: Loss Aversion and the Endowment Effect. *Journal of Economic Psychology* 17:517–24.

———. 1998. Trading Wine: On the Endowment Effect, Loss Aversion, and the Comparability of Consumer Goods. *Journal of Economic Psychology* 19:485–95.

Vanlessen, Naomi, Rudi De Raedt, Ernst H. W. Koster, and Gilles Pourtois. 2016. Happy Heart, Smiling Eyes: A Systematic Review of Positive Mood Effects on Broadening of Visuospatial Attention. *Neuroscience and Biobehavioral Reviews* 68:816–37.

Vásquez-Vera, Hugo, Laia Palència, Ingrid Magna, Carlos Mena, Jaime Neira, and Carme Borrell. 2017. The Threat of Home Eviction and Its Effects on Health

Through the Equity Lens: A Systematic Review. *Social Science and Medicine* 175:199–208.

Vinokur, Amiram, and Eugene Burstein. 1974. Effects of Partially Shared Persuasive Arguments on Group-Induced Shifts: A Group-Problem-Solving Approach. *Journal of Personality and Social Psychology* 29:305–15.

Viscusi, W. Kip. 1992. *Fatal Tradeoffs: Public and Private Responsibilities for Risk*. New York: Oxford University Press.

Wadsworth, Barry J. 2004. *Piaget's Theory of Cognitive and Affective Development: Foundations of Constructivism*. 5th ed. New York: Pearson.

Waldron, Jeremy. 1988. *The Right to Private Property*. New York: Oxford University Press.

Walsh, James D. 1999. Reaching Mrs. Murphy: A Call for the Repeal of the Mrs. Murphy Exemption to the Fair Housing Act. *Harvard Civil Rights-Civil Liberties Law Review* 34:605–34.

Wang, Liang, Emiliano A. Valdez, and John Piggott. 2008. Securitization of Longevity Risk in Reverse Mortgages. *North American Actuarial Journal* 12:345–71.

Ward, Catherine, and Irene Styles. 2003. Lost and Found: Reinvention of the Self Following Migration. *International Journal of Applied Psychoanalytic Studies* 5:349–67.

Warren, Caleb, Peter McGraw, and Leaf Van Boven. 2011. Values and Preferences: Defining Preference Construction. *Cognitive Science* 2:193–205.

Watson, Jeanne. 1950. Some Social and Psychological Situations Related to Change in Attitude. *Human Relations* 1:15–56.

Weinstein, Neil D. 1980. Unrealistic Optimism about Future Life Events. *Journal of Personality and Social Psychology* 39:806–20.

———. 1987. Unrealistic Optimism about Susceptibility to Health Problems: Conclusions from a Community-Wide Sample. *Journal of Behavioral Medicine* 10:481–500.

Weisbach, David A. 2003. Should Legal Rules Be Used to Redistribute Income? *University of Chicago Law Review* 70:439–54.

Weisman, Joshua. 1995. Property Law. In Itzhak Zamir and Sylviane Colombo, eds. *The Law of Israel: General Surveys*. Jerusalem: The Harry and Michael Sacher Institute for Legislative Research and Comparative Law, The Hebrew University of Jerusalem. 231–73.

———. 1997. Long-Term Leases as an Alternative to Ownership. In J. W. Harris, ed. *Property Problems from Genes to Pension Funds*. London: Kluwer Law International, 105–17.

Wicklund, Robert, and Peter Gollwitzer. 1981. Symbolic Self-Completion, Attempted Influence, and Self-Deprecation. *Basic and Applied Social Psychology* 2:89–114.

Wilkinson-Ryan, Tess, and Jonathan Baron. 2009. Moral Judgement and Moral Heuristics in Breach of Contract. *Journal of Empirical Legal Studies* 6:405–23.

Willis, Lauren E. 2013. When Nudges Fail: Slippery Defaults. *University of Chicago Law Review* 80:1155–229.

Wilson, Timothy D., and Daniel T. Gilbert. 2005. Affective Forecasting: Knowing What to Want. *Current Directions in Psychological Science* 14:131–34.

Wittenbrink, Bernd, and Julia R. Henly. 1996. Creating Social Reality: Informational Social Influence and the Content of Stereotypic Beliefs. *Personality and Social Psychology Bulletin* 22:598–610.

Wolf, James R., Hal R. Arkes, and Waleed A. Muhanna. 2008. The Power of Touch: An Examination of the Effect of Duration of Physical Contact on the Valuation of Objects. *Judgment and Decision Making* 3:476–82.

Wright, Joshua D., and Douglas H. Ginsburg. 2012. Behavioral Law and Economics: Its Origins, Fatal Flaws, and Implications for Liberty. *Northwestern University Law Review* 106:1033–88.

Wyly, Elvin K., and Daniel J. Hammel. 2004. Gentrification, Segregation, and Discrimination in the American Urban System. *Environment and Planning* 36:1215–41.

Wyman, Katrina Miriam. 2007. The Measure of Just Compensation. *University of California Davis Law Review* 41:239–87.

Ye, Yang, and Bertram Gawronski. 2016. When Possessions Become Part of the Self: Ownership and Implicit Self-Object Linking. *Journal of Experimental Social Psychology* 64:72–87.

Yiannopoulos, A. N. 1982. Extinction of Predial Servitudes. *Tulane Law Review* 56:1285–316.

Zamir, Eyal. 2012. Loss Aversion and the Law. *Vanderbilt Law Review* 65:829–94.

———. 2015. *Law, Psychology, and Morality: The Role of Loss Aversion*. New York: Oxford University Press.

Zamir, Eyal, and Doron Teichman. 2018. *Behavioral Law and Economics*. New York: Oxford University Press.

Zelizer, Viviana A. 1997. *The Social Meaning of Money*. New York: Basic Books.

Zhao, Weihua, Tingyong Feng, and Rebecca Kazinka. 2014. The Extensibility of the Endowment Effect to Others Is Mediated by Degree of Intimacy. *Asian Journal of Social Psychology* 17:296–301.

Zywicki, Todd J. 2005. Institutions, Incentives, and Consumer Bankruptcy Reform. *Washington and Lee Law Review* 62:1071–138.

INDEX

adaptation, 60–61, 66

adverse possession: doctrine, 31–32; and endowment effect, 32–36; and psychological ownership, 35–36; role of touch, 34; statute of limitations, 33

affective forecasting, 61–62

anchoring, 113, 148

Ariely, Dan, 9, 26, 51, 149–50, 152

auctions: experimental, 26, 34; in self-storage facilities, 74–76

availability heuristic, 144

bailment, 78–82; created and curated possessions, 80; damages, 78–81; possessions linked to memories, 79–80; psychological evidence, 79–81; repairing identity with damages, 80–81

Beggan, James K., 9, 23, 35, 50–51, 107–202

Belk, Russell W., 9, 24, 49–51, 58, 67, 75–77, 79–81, 107, 202, 222

Blackstone, William, 1

bundle of rights, 3, 99–102

chattel. *See* personal property

child development of property perceptions, 25, 29–30

Coase theorem, 7

co-ownership of property: marital property, 128–29; joint tenancy, 53; tenancy by the entirety, 53–55, 59, 64–65; tenancy in common, 53, 65

cultural differences, 222–23

debiasing, 11–12, 44, 47, 153–54, 162–70, 218, 220, 224, 238n3

Ellickson, Robert C., 18, 28, 32, 104–5, 181, 207, 220

eminent domain. *See* takings

endowment effect, 22–23; and adverse possession, 32–33; in intangible resources, 26–27; loss aversion, 12, 22–23, 32, 61, 89, 104–5, 118–19, 144, 156, 198–200; ownership versus possession effects, 34–36; shortcomings of current research, 32–33; and takings, 89, 104–5, 111–12

Etzioni, Amitai, 9, 193

eviction. *See* landlord and tenant law

extended self, possessions and, 24, 107

Fair Housing Act, disparate impact claims, 161–70; debiasing, 165–70; and implicit bias, 163–70; *Texas Department of Housing and Community Affairs v. Inclusive Communities Project, Inc.*, 161–63

Fair Housing Act, prohibition on discriminatory speech, 170–80; Communications Decency Act, 175–76; discriminatory oral statements, 178–80; discriminatory publications, 174–78; and psychology of social norms, 178–80; remedies, 180; and social networks, 176; and stereotype threat, 178–79

Fifth Amendment. *See* takings

law, 40–41, 46; psychological explanations, 41–46; and regret aversion,
44–46; rights to destroy versus rights
to modification or non-use, 41, 44–46;
rights to use versus non–use, 40–41,
44–46; servitudes, 40, 44–46
ownership versus possession, psychology
of, 31–39; adverse possession, 31–36;
and endowment effect, 32–36; and
eviction, 38; psychological ownership,
9, 35–36; relative strength of possession effects, 34–39; rights of long–term
tenants, 38–39; role of touch, 34; and
self–help doctrine, 36–38

personal property, inconsistent legal
protection of, 73–78; bailments,78–81;
and bankruptcy exemptions, 74–77;
psychological attachment to, 58, 75–76;
role in identity, 24, 75–76, 80–81; in
self–storage laws, 74, 76
personal and fungible property: distinction between, 105–6; and takings
compensation 106–7
personhood theory, 6, 55–56, 105–7
Pierson v. Post, 25, 29–30
possession, physical versus nonphysical,
24–31; endowment effect for intangible
resources, 26–27; expanding the legal
concept of possession, 27–31; legal possession versus psychological possession, 25–31; and "new property," 27–28;
perceptions in children, 25–26; role of
touch, 27, 34; and rule of capture, 25,
29–30; and takings compensation, 24–
25, 28–29. *See also* ownership versus
possession, psychology of
procedural justice, 16, 96–97, 121
property forms: in rem, 2; numerus
clausus, 136–30; property forms as
schemas, 136–39
property, theories of private, 5–7; capabilities, 6; Coase theorem, 7; efficiency,

6–7; individual rights, 5–6; John
Locke, 5–6, 9; personhood theory, 6,
55–56, 105–7
property law, introduction to, 2–5
property rules versus liability rules:
definition and debate, 191–93; and
the endowment effect, 196–201; and
ultimatum games, 194–96; and undercompensation, 201–3
prospect theory, 43. *See also* framing
psychological ownership, 9, 35–36

Radin, Margaret J., 6, 55–56, 87, 100, 105–7
real estate defect disclosure: and anchoring,
148; and the availability heuristic, 144;
caveat emptor, 139–42; and cognitive
consistency, 147; and confirmation bias,
140–41; and illusion of attention, 140,
142–43; latent/patent defect common
law rule, 142–45; moral cuing, 150–51;
nudges and psychological contestation,
155–57; and over–optimism bias, 143–44;
seller deception, psychology of, 148–51;
statutory disclosure, 145–48; and sunk
cost effect, 146–47; Truth–in–Lending
Act/Real Estate Settlement Procedures
Act disclosure rule, 156–57
real estate transactions, dual agency brokerage: conflicts of interest, psychology of, 152–54; disclosure, 153–54; and
ethical fading, 153; statutes, 151–52;
transaction brokerage, 152, 154–55
redistribution: charitable giving and
humiliation, 121–22, 126; double
distortion argument, 117; and identifiability effect, 122–27; justifications
for, 115–16; and loss aversion, 118–19;
marital property, 128–29; singularity
effect, 125, 127; and source dependence,
16; and theories of well-being, 237n3,
119–21; through takings rules, 129–30;
and ultimatum and dictator games,
194–96, 243n10

Stephanie M. Stern is Professor of Law at the Chicago-Kent College of Law, where she teaches courses on property, land use, environmental, and remedies law. She conducts research that integrates behavioral science and property law, with a focus on housing law. Professor Stern lectures nationally and internationally on the implications of behavioral science for the design of property and land use law. Her research has been published in journals such as the *Columbia Law Review*, *Michigan Law Review*, *Cornell Law Review*, *Virginia Law Review*, and *Jurimetrics*.

Daphna Lewinsohn-Zamir is Dean of the Faculty of Law and Louis Marshall Professor of Environmental Law at the Hebrew University of Jerusalem. Her fields of interest are property law and theory, behavioral law and economics, and experimental legal studies. Lewinsohn-Zamir was a Visiting Professor at Chicago, New York University, and Georgetown Law Schools. Her articles have been published in venues such as the *Yale Law Journal*, *NYU Law Review*, *Cornell Law Review*, *Texas Law Review*, *University of Toronto Law Journal*, and *Law and Social Inquiry*.

www.ingramcontent.com/pod-product-compliance
Lightning Source LLC
Chambersburg PA
CBHW020247030426
42336CB00010B/651